6

1002
HuMOROuS
ILLuSTRATiONS

FOR PUBLIC SPEAKING

Other Books by Michael Hodgin

1001 Humorous Illustrations for Public Speaking
1001 More Humorous Illustrations for Public Speaking

1002 HuMoRouS ILLuStRaTiOnS

FOR PUBLIC SPEAKING

MICHAEL E. HODGIN

ZONDERVAN™

GRAND RAPIDS, MICHIGAN 49530 USA

ZONDERVAN™

1002 Humorous Illustrations for Public Speaking
Copyright © 2004 by Michael E. Hodgin

RequestsRequests for information should be addressed to:

Zondervan, *Grand Rapids, Michigan 49530*

LibraryLibrary of Congress Cataloging-in-Publication Data**

Hodgin, Michael, 1953–.
    1002 humorous illustrations for public speaking / Michael E. Hodgin.—1st ed.
      p. cm.
    Includes bibliographical references and index.
    ISBN 0-310-25602-X
    1. Public speaking.   2. American wit and humor. I. Title: One thousand two
humorous illustrations for public speaking.   II. Title.
PN4129.15.H63 2004
808.5'1'0207—dc22   2003024444

All Scripture quotations, unless otherwise indicated, are taken from the *Holy Bible: New International Version®*. NIV®. Copyright © 1973, 1978, 1984 by International Bible Society. Used by permission of Zondervan. All rights reserved.

The website addresses recommended throughout this book are offered as a resource to you. These websites are not intended in any way to be or imply an endorsement on the part of Zondervan, nor do we vouch for their content for the life of this book.

All rights reserved. No part of this publication may be reproduced, stored in a retrieval system, or transmitted in any form or by any means—electronic, mechanical, photocopy, recording, or any other—except for brief quotations in printed reviews, without the prior permission of the publisher.

Interior design by Tracey Moran

Printed in the United States of America

07 08 09 10 /❖ DC/ 10 9 8 7

Zondervan keeps telling me to dedicate these humor books. I dedicated the first book to eight people–all family –who helped me put the book together. I dedicated the second book to those who send us illustrations for *Parables, Etc.* and *The Pastor's Story File* and to all our subscribers. With this third book I think I'll take the approach that actors take when they win "best whatever" awards. I'll just start naming names. So here I go:

To Everett and Rose–for getting me started and keeping me going–they're my parents; to my brother Steve and my three sisters, Teresa, Debbie, and Jan–for long-term toleration and affection; to Renae–for marrying me and loving me; to my four children, Ryan, Michelle, Marie, and Reanna–for adding more value to life than any other human experience; to Stephanie–for marrying my son; to the three guys I may not know yet–for marrying my daughters; to my four closest male friends, Ron, Don, John, and John–who constantly encourage me and who would never do anything to hurt me; to the leaders of my church, Leon, Roy, Fred, Penni, Brett, Ken, Jayne, Garry, Kevin, Keith, Gary, Curtis, Marleen, Kelly, Jan, and Jan– who grant me the freedom to pastor and pursue other callings at the same time; to my fellow-pastors in the Eaton, Colorado, area who genuinely love me–Buddy, Craig, Jason, David, Gibb, Nathan, Jeff, Jerry, Jim, Curtis, Rex, and Phil; to those who have enjoyed studying with me over the past several years–Tom, Noah, Mike, Jeremiah, Gerald, Brody, John, Audra, Alan, Mic, Justin, and Lance; and to those who provide so many illustrations for Saratoga Press–Don, Billy, Dicky, Len, C. Richard, Steve, Debby, Frank, Gene, Mary, Babs, Michael, Jim, Deb, Dick, Jeff, Randall, Calvin, Nick, Bruce, Jay, John, Charles, Mike, Tish, David, Dan, and Barb.

Contents

Preface

Last week I officiated a memorial service for my friend Don Houchen. Don was a guy who loved the Lord and loved people. Don was a great salesman who sold all kinds of things since he was a boy. He just loved to connect people with things they could use. I first met him about twenty-two years ago when he began attending the church I was pastoring. Since then, we both went our different ways, but we maintained our friendship over the years.

Don was funny. I have gone on sales calls with Don and watched him work his magic. Most of his magic was performed with humor. He liked to see people laugh and smile. He made people feel good—about him and about themselves. After one particular sales call, he turned to me and said, "Anyone can sell this stuff to them, but I'll tell you why they buy from me: It's because they love me." I believed him. He was just that way. He loved to tell jokes and tease, but he was always careful not to hurt people or belittle them. Hurting people was not Don's style; uplifting them with a little happiness was more to his liking.

Don taught me more than just a few jokes and funny stories. He taught me how to love people and make them feel better. He taught me to use humor, not as a hostile weapon, but as a tool that makes people feel better and enjoy the message. Humor opens windows: It opens windows to the message we want to share with our listeners, and it opens windows to the hearts and minds of our listeners. Humor is a powerful window-opener for the effective public speaker.

1

How She Looks

After the doctor completed his examination of a woman, he took her husband to the side. "I don't like the looks of your wife at all," the doctor confided.

"She may not be much to look at, Doc," agreed the husband. "But listen, she's an excellent cook and the kids seem to like her."

Dates & Places Used:

2

TOPIC: Ability

Dogs and Bikes

An animal shelter attendant checked the identification tag of a dog that was brought in by the police. He then called the owner and explained that she would need to come to the animal shelter and pay the fines and charges, and then she could get her dog.

The woman asked, "What are these fines and charges?"

The attendant answered, "You have to pay the animal shelter's standard charges and the police department's fine because your dog was chasing a man on his bicycle."

The woman hesitated and said, "That must not be my dog! My dog doesn't know how to ride a bicycle!"

Dates & Places Used:

3

TOPIC: Ability

What I Can Do

There is an old joke about a man who, when he was asked if he could play a violin, answered, "I don't know. I've never tried."

This is psychologically a very wise reply. Those who have never tried to play a violin really do not know whether or not they can. Those who say too early in life and too firmly, "No, I'm not at all musical," shut themselves off prematurely from whole areas of life that may have proved rewarding.

Each of us has unknown possibilities, undiscovered potential-ities. One big advantage of having an open self-concept rather than a rigid one is that we will continue to expose ourselves to new experiences and therefore continue to discover more and more about ourselves as we grow older.

Dates & Places Used:

4

TOPIC: Ability

Seen the Dog Bowl

A mother asked her son, "Have you seen the dog bowl?" "No," the boy replied, "but he's pretty good at skating!"

Dates & Places Used:

5

TOPIC: Ability

One Could Get Hurt

A man decided to commit suicide. Saturating his body with gasoline, he put a rope around his neck and tied it to a tree limb that jutted out over a river. He put a pistol to his temple. He then set a match to his body, jumped from the tree, and pulled the trigger on the pistol. Missing his temple, the bullet hit the rope and cut it, and he fell into the water below, which immediately put out the flames. As he climbed back up the riverbank gasp-ing, he said, "Wow! If I wasn't such a good swimmer, I would have drowned!"

Dates & Places Used:

6

TOPIC: Ability

Milsap on Blindness

"People are always asking me if being blind heightened my sense of hearing. The answer is no. I can't hear the grass grow

or anything like that. The thing being blind did do for me was get me into a school where they taught me how to play the piano."
Dates & Places Used:

7

TOPIC: Abuse

Getting Off in Buffalo

An important executive boarded a New York to Chicago train. He explained to the porter, "I'm a heavy sleeper, and I want you to be sure to wake me at 3:00 A.M. to get off at Buffalo. Regardless of what I say, get me up and get me off the train. I may resist you, but I have to get off at Buffalo."

But the next morning the executive awakened just as the train pulled into Chicago. He was infuriated, and with abusive language he poured out his anger on the porter.

As the executive stomped down the platform toward the station, another passenger asked the porter, "How could you stand there and take that kind of talk from that fellow?"

The porter replied, "That was nothing. You should have heard what the man I put off in Buffalo said!"
Dates & Places Used:

8

TOPIC: Abuse

Completely Ignored

A man walked into a psychiatrist's office and said, "My problem is that people seem to ignore me."

The psychiatrist walked to the door and called out, "Next!"
Dates & Places Used:

9

Wanting to Kiss a Mule

A little prospector wearing clean shoes walked into a saloon. A big cowboy said to his friend, "Watch me make this dude dance." He walked over to the prospector and said, "You're a foreigner, aren't you?"

"You might say that," said the little prospector. "I'm from the city, and I'm prospecting for gold."

The cowboy said, "Tell me dude, can you dance?"

The little dude said, "No sir, I never did learn."

"Well I'm going to teach you. You'll be surprised how fast you can learn." With that the cowboy pulled out his gun and started shooting at the prospector's feet.

Hopping, jumping, and shaking, the prospector "danced" out the door.

About an hour later the cowboy left the saloon. As soon as he stepped out the door, he heard a click. He looked around, and there, next to his head, was the biggest shotgun he'd ever seen. The little prospector said, "Cowboy, have you ever kissed a mule?"

"No," said the cowboy, "but I always wanted to."

Dates & Places Used:

10

Careless Cruise Control

A man was standing in a motor home dealership when a motor home was towed in for repairs. The front of the home was badly damaged. The man was curious as to how the motor home had gotten so mangled, so he walked over to the service department to ask. The manager explained that the owner of the motor home had been driving on the interstate and had set the cruise control and gone back to the kitchen to make himself a sandwich.

There are just so many things to remember.

Dates & Places Used:

TOPIC: Accidents

The Golf Ball Missile

I read about Mathieu Boya, who was practicing his golf swing in a pasture adjacent to the Benin Air Base in Africa. The story goes that back in 1987 he accidentally destroyed his country's entire air force!

With one swing of the golf club, Boya set off an unbelievable series of events. The shot–"a glorious slice" it was called–hit a bird, which in turn dropped onto the windshield of a trainer jet, whose pilot was taxiing into position for takeoff. The pilot lost control of his plane and plowed into four shiny Albatross jets, totally demolishing the entire air force of Benin.

Boya was jailed immediately for "hooliganism," and his attorney said he had no chance of winning a trial. Meanwhile, the country had no money in its treasury and wanted Boya to pay $40 million to replace the jets. Boya made $275 per year and figured it would take 145,000 years to pay off his debt to society.

Few golfers could match that story, although I have heard of some complaining of their "wayward shots." The point is that we have seen what a chain reaction can do. Like falling dominoes, one event leads to a chain of events larger than could have been created by a single event.

But a positive chain of events can happen too. This Sunday our church will kick off our financial campaign. One good pledge can lead to a whole series of exciting things to come. It's time for many of our members to get out their pocketbooks and start some better things rolling at this church.

Dates & Places Used:

TOPIC: Accidents

Just the Good News

A woman called her husband at work to talk. He explained that he was very busy and asked her if she could wait until he came home.

His wife said she just wanted to share some good news and bad news. The husband really was busy and needed to get off the phone. He told his wife just to tell him the good news.

She answered, "The air bags work fine."

Dates & Places Used:

13

TOPIC: Accidents

Elderly Parking

Two elderly women talking: "The thing I hate about parking is the noisy crash."

Dates & Places Used:

14

TOPIC: Accomplishments

Motion or Action

Never mistake motion for action. *(Ernest Hemingway)*

Dates & Places Used:

15

TOPIC: Accomplishments

Speed of Death

Author and drama critic Alexander Woolcott liked to sit at the window of his New York apartment overlooking the East River and watch the boats go by. A visitor once asked him, "How can you sit here by the hour watching one battered old tugboat after another chugging by at ten knots? It sounds pretty dull."

Woolcott explained, "It's not always tugboats. Every now and then a dead body floats by."

His guest was taken up short and exclaimed, "A dead body? What's a dead body doing in the river?"

The reviewer shrugged and replied, "I can't say for sure, but my guess would be about five knots."

Dates & Places Used:

16

TOPIC: Accomplishments

Laying or Lying

A gal from the city asked an old farmer, "Which is grammatically correct: to say a hen is 'setting' or 'sitting'?"

The farmer replied, "I guess I don't know that one, miss, and it really don't interest me none. What does interest me when I hear a hen cackle is if she's 'laying' or 'lying.'"

Dates & Places Used:

17

TOPIC: Action

Prayer Gets Some Help

Many marvelous stories can be used to illustrate the various facets of prayer. In particular I like the story that English statesman William Gladstone told that illustrates prayer coupled with a sort of persistent (if also perverse) action. It seems Gladstone knew of a little girl in his neighborhood who believed strongly in the efficacy of prayer. Her current concern was a trap that her brother had made to catch birds. Being a bird lover, she prayed that God would frustrate her brother's designs and that he would be unsuccessful in his plan. She had shared this resolution with Gladstone and told him how hard she was praying.

One day, upon encountering her, Gladstone observed a particular radiance to her countenance. He said to her, "Julia, you look so pleased. Are you still confident your prayers will be answered?"

Julia smiled a knowing smile and retorted, "I know for sure that my prayers will be answered. Yesterday I kicked my brother's trap to pieces."

Dates & Places Used:

18

TOPIC: Action

Hit Home Runs—Then Talk

The former chaplain of the Boston Red Sox talked with a young player who was constantly quoting Scripture. He told the young man, "Son, don't quote Scripture until you hit home runs."

Sometimes we talk too much and produce too little.

Dates & Places Used:

19   TOPIC: Adversity

Wrong Drink

There's this guy in a restaurant just looking at his drink. He stays like that for a half hour. Then this big troublemaking truck driver walks into the restaurant as if he owns the place, steps over to the man, grabs his glass, and immediately drinks it all down.

The poor man starts crying. The truck driver is mean, but he never intended to make a grown man cry. He says, "Come on man, I was just funnin' with ya. Tell ya what: I'll buy ya another drink. But ya gotta stop that cryin'."

"No, it's not the drink," the man replied. "This is the worst day of my life. Nothing has gone right. First, I sleep in and get to work late, so my boss fires me. I leave the building, and someone has just stolen my car. The police say they can do nothing. I get a cab to return home, and when I leave it, I remember I left my wallet with my credit cards on the seat. When I get home my wife is driving away in our other car with all of her luggage on top. So I walk down here to this restaurant to end all this suffering. And then you show up and gulp down my entire drink. And all the poison I had was in that one glass!"

Dates & Places Used:

20   TOPIC: Adversity

Adversity Follows

Stopped by a policeman for driving without a taillight, a driver became quite distressed.

"Don't take it so hard," consoled the officer, "it's a minor offense."

"That's not the point," replied the troubled driver. "What worries me is, what's happened to my wife and my trailer?"

Dates & Places Used:

21

TOPIC: Advice

Sharing Is Part of Community

A certain fellow was about to make his first parachute jump. The plane carried him up to the proper altitude and he was told, "This is it, friend–jump!" So he leaped from the plane, counted to ten, and pulled the rip cord, but nothing happened. He was falling rapidly toward the earth and his life was flashing before his eyes. He pulled his second emergency cord. Nothing happened. Just then he looked down toward the earth and was surprised to see another man hurtling up toward him from the earth. He couldn't believe his eyes. As the two men passed each other, the falling parachutist yelled, "Do you know anything about parachutes?"

The ascending man cried out, "No. Do you know anything about gas stoves?"

Dates & Places Used:

22

TOPIC: Advice

Spectators versus Active Participants

Just remember: Every baseball team could use a man who plays every position perfectly, never strikes out, and never makes an error. The trouble is, there is no way to make him lay down his hot dog and come down out of the stands.

Dates & Places Used:

23

TOPIC: Advice

Wise Requests

We all admire the wisdom of those who come to us for advice.
Dates & Places Used:

24

TOPIC: Advice

Shark Pictures

While fishing off the Florida coast, a tourist capsized his boat. The man was not sure if it was safe to swim to shore, so when he saw a man with a camera standing on the shore, he called out to him, "Are there any alligators in these parts?"

"Nope," the man answered. "There used to be some, but they are long gone."

Feeling assured of his safety, the man began to swim toward shore. While swimming, he began to wonder what happened to the alligators. He stopped swimming for a moment and shouted to the man with the camera on shore, "What happened to the alligators?"

The man with the camera who stood on shore replied, "These waters are too shark-infested for alligators to last long."

The man with the camera who stood on shore got some great pictures.
Dates & Places Used:

25

TOPIC: Advice

Finding Valuable Plants

When weeding, the best way to make sure you are removing a weed and not a valuable plant is to pull on it. If it comes out of the ground easily, it was a valuable plant.
Dates & Places Used:

26

Removing Flies

Do not use a hatchet to remove a fly from your friend's forehead.

Dates & Places Used:

27

Can't Sit on Its Lap

The four-year-old daughter of a busy father had acquired a fixation for the story "The Three Little Pigs" and demanded that he read it to her night after night. The man, pleased with himself, tape-recorded the story. When the child next asked for it, he simply switched on the playback.

This worked for a couple of nights, but then one evening the little girl pushed the storybook at her father. "Now, honey," he said, "you know how to turn on the recorder by yourself."

"Yes," she said, "but I can't sit on its lap!"

Nothing can substitute for a parent–not a recorder, not a computer, nothing!

Dates & Places Used:

28

Kissing Her Back

Child: "Mommy, Grandma kissed me today!"
Mother: "Did you kiss her back?"
Child: "No, I didn't! I kissed her on her cheek."

Dates & Places Used:

29

It's All Relative

When Oliver Wendell Holmes was still on the U.S. Supreme Court, he and Justice Louis Brandeis took walks every afternoon. On one of these occasions Holmes, then ninety-two, paused to gaze in frank admiration at a beautiful young girl who passed them. He even turned to look at her as she continued down the street. Then, turning to Brandeis, he sighed, "Oh! What I wouldn't give to be seventy again!"

Dates & Places Used:

30

Too Much Sand

Regarding my age ... it's just that I have too much sand in the bottom of my hourglass.

Dates & Places Used:

31

In a Nursing Home

A minister went to visit an elderly couple who had just entered a nursing home. The wife had been losing touch with reality to a point that it really wasn't safe for them to remain in their house. But her concern was with her husband, who she thought was losing touch with reality. Very early in the visit the wife told the minister how her husband was going down fast. "If it continues," she said with a sigh, "I guess we'll just have to put him in a nursing home."

In a compassionate tone the husband said, "But, honey, we are in a nursing home."

She then looked at the minister, winked, and said, "You see what I mean."

Dates & Places Used:

32

Too Old to Fly?

This story is of my father in the years immediately following my mother's death. My dad, alone in a small town he had never liked, had made the usual mistakes: sold the house, changed locations, projected his loneliness outward into anger with the world. And then, at seventy, he did something he had been wanting to do since he was a boy–he signed up for flying lessons.

The aircraft pushed his reflexes, his endurance, and his patience. The ground school pushed the edges of his mind. But he wanted to fly, so he stuck with it. And at last there was only a physical between him and the solo flight. He went to the doctor and passed the medical exam only to have his hopes dashed when the doctor said, "Sorry, I can't let you solo. You're seventy years old."

As it turns out, there were no regulations about maximum age, so my father pushed ahead. He went to higher and higher authorities, submitted to more and more stringent physical examinations. Everybody agreed that he was physically fit, but still they said, "We can't let you solo. You're seventy years old."

Finally, my dad found a bureaucrat of high enough rank to admit there were no laws about maximum age. "Pass one more test and you're in." So my father took yet another round on the treadmill, and at the end the physician handed him a piece of paper that read: "Harry Killoran, Qualified for Solo Flight."

My dad shook the doctor's hand, put the paper in his wallet, and started to leave the office. "Wait a minute," said the doctor. "When are you going to fly?"

My dad looked at him, and I expect he grinned as he said, "Do you think I'm crazy? I'm not going up in any airplane alone. I'm seventy years old."

Dates & Places Used:

33

Agreeable Person

My idea of an agreeable person is a person who agrees with me. *(Benjamin Disraeli)*
Dates & Places Used:

34

Equal Opportunity Politics

A young couple were unable to resolve a heated argument. The husband finally proposed a truce by saying, "I'll tell you what: I'll admit that I'm wrong, if you'll admit that I'm right."

His wife agreed to his proposed terms, so the husband said, "I'm wrong."

The wife victoriously exclaimed, "You're right!"
Dates & Places Used:

35

A Hard Ride

A father and daughter were riding in a crowded elevator. Suddenly a woman in front of them turned around and slapped the father's face.

The elevator stopped, and the woman immediately stormed off as she looked back with a venomous look.

The father was obviously shaken and confused. He looked down at his daughter and asked, "What's her problem?"

The little girl answered, "She's just a mean lady who likes to hurt people, Daddy. I didn't like her either. She kept stepping on my toes until I pinched her bottom as hard as I could. That's when she started picking on you."
Dates & Places Used:

36

TOPIC: Anger

Deaf–Not Blind

On a visit to the library I happened to notice a man and a woman, both deaf, signing with intense gestures, apparently in a heated debate. The man said something, and the woman seemed upset. She started signing her reply very fast, to the point where the man couldn't understand a word. She also signed in big, wide gestures, which is the equivalent of volume. Finally, looking strained, her companion took her hands, "silencing" her. Then he signed, very small and slowly, "You don't have to shout; I'm not blind."

Dates & Places Used:

37

TOPIC: Anger

Old Hockey Injury

A man came to work one day with a bad limp. One of his coworkers noticed and asked him what had happened.

The man answered, "Oh, nothing. It's just an old hockey injury that acts up every once in a while."

The coworker was surprised at his answer. "I never knew you played hockey."

The man explained, "Oh, I never did play hockey; I hurt it last year during the Stanley Cup play-offs. When I lost five hundred dollars on the final game, I put my foot through the TV set!"

Dates & Places Used:

38

TOPIC: Anger

Germs and Jesus

A pastor's small son was told by his mother that he should wash his hands because there were germs living in all that dirt. He refused and complained, "Germs and Jesus! Germs and

Jesus! That's all I ever hear around this house, and I've never seen either one."
Dates & Places Used:

39 TOPIC: Anger

Slam the Cat

Deacons Arnold and Lee were going door-to-door inviting people to church. When they knocked on the door of a woman who was not happy to see them, she told them in no uncertain terms that she did not want to hear their message and slammed the door in their faces.

To her surprise, however, the door did not close and in fact bounced back open. This time she really put her back into it and slammed the door again with the same result.

Convinced that one of these rude young deacons was sticking his foot in the door, she reared back to give it a slam that would teach them a lesson, when Arnold said, "Ma'am, before you do that again you need to move your cat."
Dates & Places Used:

40 TOPIC: Anger

Piece of Your Mind

Before you begin to give someone a piece of your mind, consider carefully whether you can spare any.
Dates & Places Used:

41 TOPIC: Anger

Standing as One

An immigrant who recently arrived in the United States and knew very little English visited a North Carolina church so he could worship with fellow Christians during their Sunday morning service. The church was full, and the usher found the immigrant a seat in the front row next to a tall man and his family.

The immigrant decided to do whatever the tall man did. When the tall man stood up, the immigrant stood up. When the tall man sat down, the immigrant sat down. When the tall man bowed his head, the immigrant bowed his head. When the tall man knelt down, the immigrant knelt down. While he did not understand much of what was happening, the immigrant was enjoying the spirit of the service.

Suddenly the church became quiet. After the pastor spoke for several minutes, the tall man next to the immigrant rose to his feet. The immigrant stood to his feet alongside the tall man. The tall man immediately became upset and pushed the immigrant back down. The immigrant was hurt and did not understand the rude action of this tall man beside him.

After the service had concluded, the tall man tried to apologize to the immigrant for his sudden rudeness. He was finally able to explain in simple English that the pastor had dedicated his baby and had asked, "Will the father of this baby please stand up?"

Dates & Places Used:

42

TOPIC: Appearances

Sideways Gravity

A boy had just moved with his family into a new home. The kitchen door had self-closing hinges. When the boy saw the door close all by itself, he turned to his father and asked, "You mean there's *sideways gravity* too?"

Dates & Places Used:

43

TOPIC: Appearances

Exhausting Child

A little boy was playing outside on a cold, damp winter morning. As he played he watched the vapor of his breath. After a few

minutes he ran into the house and announced to his parents, "I'm exhausting."
Dates & Places Used:

TOPIC: Appearances

44

Jumping to Conclusions

A Hell's Angels type of guy—dirty jeans, leather, huge bare arms with lots of tattoos—attempted to enter a ritzy night club. The attendant at the door, trying to figure out some way to prevent him from entering without a fuss, told him that no one was allowed in without a tie. The burly bike rider went back out to his van and got a set of jumper cables, tied them around his neck, and went back to the club. The attendant took another look and said, "Okay, but don't start anything."
Dates & Places Used:

TOPIC: Appearances

45

Magic Factory Whistle

An American manufacturer was showing his machine factory to a potential customer from Albania. At noon, when the lunch whistle blew, two thousand men and women immediately stopped work and left the building.

"Your workers—they're escaping!" cried the visitor. "You've got to stop them."

"Don't worry; they'll be back," said the American. And indeed, at exactly one o'clock the whistle blew again and all the workers returned from their break.

When the tour was over, the manufacturer turned to his guest and said, "Well, now, which of these machines would you like to order?"

"Forget the machines," said the visitor. "How much do you want for that whistle?"
Dates & Places Used:

46

Predisposed to Panic

Three timid women from Nashville ventured to New York City in spite of the risk of mugging they so greatly feared. Sure enough, in their hotel elevator, a huge black man entered, and when the doors closed, he said, "Sit down!" The three women immediately squatted on the floor, but nothing else happened until the elevator stopped at the lobby and the man got out.

That night a dozen red roses awaited them in their room. The card read, "Please accept these flowers and my apology. You must not have seen my dog when I told it to 'Sit.' I was embarrassed and did not know what to do, so I just got off. I'm sorry." The card was signed, "Reggie Jackson."

I used this story to illustrate our predisposition to expect the worst to happen. I was speaking on the book of Job and was trying to contrast real tragedy–when the roof really falls in–with those imaginary tragedies we are sure are coming our way.

Dates & Places Used:

47

Hearing Different Messages

Two old women were sitting on the front porch one evening. One was listening to the crickets chirping. The other was listening to a choir rehearsing in the church across the street. The latter said to the former, "Isn't that heavenly music?"

"Yes," said the first woman. "And I understand they do it by rubbing their legs together."

Dates & Places Used:

48

Mixed Message

A man came up to another man and said to him, "Sir, I don't know you, but I must ask you a question. It's kind of personal, but I'm dying to ask you. Would you be offended at a personal question?"

The man was a bit taken aback but said, "Well, I guess not. What is it?"

He said, "I'm curious. Would you mind telling me if you're wearing a toupee?" The response came back immediately, "No, of course I'm not!"

But the man persisted. "Sir, you can be candid with me. I won't think less of you. Tell me honestly; are you wearing a toupee?"

By now the man was getting a bit ticked off and said, "Absolutely not," and started to leave.

But his questioner would not be dismissed and held on to the other man's arm. "Please, sir, be patient with me. Honest, you are wearing a toupee, aren't you?"

By now the man was really uncomfortable and just wanted to get away from the pest, so to get rid of him, he said, "Well, if you insist, okay, yes, I'm wearing a toupee."

"Really?" came the reply. "You'd never know it."

Dates & Places Used:

49

How Committed Are You?

Two New Yorkers who had never been out of the city decided they had just about had enough of city living, so they bought a ranch down in Texas. They determined they were going to live off the land like their ancestors.

The first thing they decided they needed in order to ranch was a mule. So they went to a neighboring rancher and asked him if he had a mule to sell. The rancher answered, "No, I'm afraid not."

They were disappointed but stayed to visit with the rancher for a few moments. One of them saw some honeydew melons stacked against the barn and asked the rancher, "What are those?"

The rancher, seeing that they were clueless city slickers, decided to have some fun. "Oh," he answered, "those are mule eggs. You take one of those eggs home and wait for it to hatch and you'll have a mule."

The city slickers were overjoyed at this and bought one of those mule eggs, put it in the back of their pickup truck, and headed down the bumpy country road toward their ranch. Suddenly they hit an especially treacherous bump and the honeydew melon bounced out the back of the truck, hit the road, and burst open. Seeing in his rearview mirror what had happened, the driver turned his truck around and drove back to see if he could retrieve his mule egg.

Meanwhile a big Texas jackrabbit hopping by saw the melon in the road and hopped over to it because he was thirsty. Standing in the middle of the mess, he began to eat. When the city slickers saw that their mule egg had burst open and a long-eared creature was in the middle of it, they shouted, "Our mule egg has hatched! Let's get our mule."

But seeing those two men coming toward it, the jackrabbit took off hopping with the two city fellows in hot pursuit. They gave everything they had to catch the rabbit, but finally they could go no further. Both men fell wearily onto the ground gasping for air while the jackrabbit hopped off into the distance. Raising himself up on his elbow, one of the men said to the other, "Well, I guess we lost our mule."

The other man nodded grimly. "Yes, but you know," he said, "I'm not sure I wanted to plow that fast anyway."

Dates & Places Used:

50

TOPIC: Application

Gonna Have a Wife

At Sunday school the teacher was teaching about how God created everything, including human beings. Little Tommy, a kindergartner, seemed especially intent when he heard how Eve had been created out of one of Adam's ribs.

Later in the week his mother noticed that he was lying down as though he were ill. She asked, "Tommy, what's the matter?"

Tommy responded, "I have a pain in my side. I think I'm gonna have a wife."

Dates & Places Used:

TOPIC: Appreciation

51

Office Essentials

An office worker went around telling everybody about the new office policy. To save energy, lighting in nonessential areas was to be cut down. When he returned, he noticed that the light over his desk had been turned off.

Dates & Places Used:

TOPIC: Appreciation

52

Simple Kindness

While my wife, Penny, and I were walking in the park the other day, a ten-year-old boy came racing around a tree, almost running into us, and said, "Dad, where's Amy?"

Instantly he realized his mistake and said, "Sir, I'm sorry, I thought you were my dad. I made a mistake."

I replied, "That's okay; everyone makes mistakes!"

As he began to walk away, I noticed he had a limp as well as the features of a child with Down's syndrome. After having walked about ten yards, as an afterthought, he turned around and started retracing his steps toward us.

"My name is Billy," he said. "You both were very nice to me. Can I give you a hug?"

After giving each of us a tight hug, he said, "I just wanted you to know that you're my friends and I'm going to be praying for you. I have to go now and find my sister, Amy. Good-bye and God bless you!"

Penny and I both had tears in our eyes as we watched Billy limp to the playground to play with his little sister. After Billy went down the slide, his mother came over to him and gave him a big hug. It was obvious that he was special to her.

Sometimes God uses the Billys of the world to break down our walls of sophistication to show us what genuine kindness is all about. We must never underestimate the impact that a hug, smile, or encouraging word may have on a person's life.

Dates & Places Used:

53

TOPIC: Arguments

Waste of Energy

One of the greatest wastes of energy known to humankind is arguing with someone whose opinion you don't give a hoot about anyhow.

Dates & Places Used:

54

TOPIC: Arguments

Argumentative Theories

There are two major theories as to how men can win arguments with their wives and maintain their respect. Neither theory, however, has yet worked.

Dates & Places Used:

55

TOPIC: Arguments

Tact and Enemies

Tact is the art of making a point without making an enemy.

Dates & Places Used:

56

TOPIC: Assistance

Hung Up to Dry

After hearing that one of the patients in a mental hospital had saved another from a suicide attempt by pulling him out of a bathtub, the director reviewed the rescuer's file and called him into his office.

"Mr. Phillips, your records and your heroic behavior indicate that you're ready to go home. I'm only sorry that the man you saved later killed himself with a rope around the neck."

"Oh, he didn't kill himself," Mr. Phillips replied. "I hung him up to dry."

Dates & Places Used:

57

TOPIC: Assistance

Long-Term Assistance

Give a man a fish and you will feed him for a day.
Teach him how to fish and you can sell him a rod.
Dates & Places Used:

58

TOPIC: Assistance

Move the Rock

A woman told the following parable at the end of what one suspects was a long day of meetings.

Now all of you nice ladies just imagine that you live in a house by a road on the top of a mountain. There was a big rock slide, and a large boulder came down right around the corner on this mountain road. And every car that came around the corner hit the boulder and smashed up.

Now I understand what you would do. You would run right out and take those people out of the smashed cars. You would bandage them up and bring them into your house, and you would feed them and pray with them. And when they got well, you would send them home.

Well, sisters, what I think you ought to do is send somebody out to move the rock!
Dates & Places Used:

59

TOPIC: Assistance

Throwing to Africa

A woman was sitting on a park bench feeding a loaf of fresh-baked bread to the pigeons. A man who was sitting nearby observed that she was feeding the pigeons a new loaf of bread. He watched her in disgust for a few minutes and then spoke harshly to her. "You should not waste that food on pigeons when there are dying children in Africa who could use that food!"

The woman glanced in the man's direction and then spoke softly. "Oh, I don't think I can throw this bread as far as Africa. Would you like to try?"
Dates & Places Used:

60

TOPIC: Assumptions

Dating Dinosaur Bones

Some tourists in the Chicago Museum of Natural History were marveling at the dinosaur bones. One of them asked the guard, "Can you tell me how old the dinosaur bones are?"

The guard replied, "They are three million four years and six months old."

"That's an awfully exact number," said the tourist. "How do you know their age so precisely?"

The guard answered, "Well, the dinosaur bones were three million years old when I started working here, and that was four and a half years ago."
Dates & Places Used:

61

Frogs or God

A pastor invited the children to come forward for the children's sermon. After they had seated themselves on the platform steps, he announced he was going to talk about frogs. He asked the group, "When I say 'frog' what's the first thing that comes to your mind?"

Promptly a child answered, "God."

Surprised, the pastor asked with obvious puzzlement, "Why do you think about God when I say 'frog'?"

The child replied, "Because I know you didn't bring us down here to talk about frogs."

Dates & Places Used:

62

Blind Police Officer

An elderly woman came home to find that her house had been broken into. She immediately called the police and frantically reported how her house had been burglarized.

The nearest unit to her house was a canine unit, which responded to the call. The police officer drove up to the house and proceeded to let the dog out of the car. The woman came running out of the house at the sight of the police car only to see the dog getting out.

She threw her hands up in the air and screamed, "Not only have I been robbed, but now they've sent me a blind police officer!"

Dates & Places Used:

63

Look Again

A man showed up at a talent agent's office in New York City—right in the middle of the Great White Way—back during the halcyon days of vaudeville. The jaded agent looked up with a jaundiced eye and said, "Yeah, whadda ya want?"

The man replied, "I'm looking for work in vaudeville."

"Who isn't? So whadda ya do?"

The man replied politely, "I do bird imitations!"

At this the agent sighed to himself and said, "Big deal. Bird imitations are a dime a dozen. Forget it, kid."

So the young man went to the window, opened it, stood there for a moment, started flapping his arms vigorously, and flew away.

Dates & Places Used:

64

TOPIC: Assumptions

Stop While You're Ahead

A burglar broke into an opulent home and was filling his sacks with stolen goods when he heard a deep growl. He looked down to see the biggest Doberman pinscher he had ever seen. But before he had a chance to do anything, he heard a small voice ask, "Who are you? Who are you?" He looked around but couldn't find anyone or anything that was saying it, and the dog just sat there. So he continued to rob the house until his bags were full. Then as he was ready to leave the house he noticed a parrot in a cage.

As he walked over to the cage the parrot said, "Who are you? Who are you?"

The crook looked at the bird and said, "Is that all you can say? 'Who are you? Who are you?'"

And the parrot replied, "Sic 'em!"

Dates & Places Used:

65

TOPIC: Attendance

Members Are like Cars

Church members are like automobiles—they start missing before they quit.

Dates & Places Used:

66

TOPIC: Attendance

Church on Fire!

Some years ago in the Midwest, a fire broke out one evening in a small church building. Nearly everyone from the little town came to watch the firemen battle the flames. The pastor noticed an inactive member standing nearby watching the smoke and flames. Walking over to this indifferent member, he said, "Well, I don't remember seeing you here before."

"Well," said the man, "I don't remember our church ever being on fire before."

Dates & Places Used:

67

TOPIC: Attendance

The Parable of the Rattlesnake

Once upon a time a family that had been very active lost all interest in the church. The preacher, the elders, and all their fellow church members pleaded with them to get involved again, but nothing they said or did seemed to work. One day the father and his sons were out in the fields working. A big rattlesnake bit one of the boys, and he became very sick, nigh unto death. The doctor did all he could for the boy and then told the family, "All we can do now is pray." Immediately the father sent for the minister of the church.

This is the prayer the preacher is reported to have prayed: "O wise and righteous Father in heaven, we pray for this boy's full recovery. But we also thank you for this rattlesnake. This family hasn't been in church for years, and we pray that this serpent will be the means to bring them all to a spirit of genuine repentance. Already this snake has done more to turn them around than all the pleas of their fellow Christians. Dear Lord, it may be that what the whole church needs is bigger and better rattlesnakes."

Dates & Places Used:

68

TOPIC: Attendance

Unwanted Sabbatical

One congregation decided to show their appreciation for their pastor by giving him a six-month sabbatical. He declined, saying, "On the one hand, I am afraid that such a long absence might affect the attendance in worship. On the other hand, I am afraid that my absence might *not* affect the attendance in worship."

Dates & Places Used:

69

TOPIC: Attendance

The Boy God Made

A minister promised to visit the kindergarten Sunday school class the following Sunday, so the teacher anxiously prepared. When the minister asked the children who created them, Jimmy was to say, "God made me." The rest of the class was to sit quietly.

The big day came, and the minister paid his visit. He said, "Can anyone tell me who made us?"

Silence. He repeated the question. Still there was silence.

Finally, a little girl raised her hand and said, "The boy that God made is sick today."

Dates & Places Used:

70

TOPIC: Attitude

Optimist in the Desert

An American touring in the Sahara was dressed in a bathing suit. A Bedouin gazed at him in amazement.

"I'm going swimming," the tourist explained.

"But the ocean is eight hundred miles away," the Arab informed him.

"Eight hundred miles!" the American exclaimed with a huge smile. "Boy, what a beach!"

Dates & Places Used:

71

TOPIC: Attitude

Optimistic Attitude

I'm always fascinated by stories of people who have managed to develop a different mental attitude than that commonly held by those around them: the poor man who refuses to think poor, the sick woman who focuses on what she can do rather than on her handicap. Such people display the kind of attitude suggested by the old story of the boy who was given a roomful of manure and deduced that there must be a gift of a pony nearby.

Dates & Places Used:

72

TOPIC: Attitude

Open or Vacant Mind

An open mind is not the same as a vacant mind.

Dates & Places Used:

73

TOPIC: Authority

Referee Aroma

The football game was grueling, and tempers were flaring. The referee called a penalty and marked off fifteen yards against the home team. One of the home team players was infuriated. He ran to the referee and screamed, "You stink!"

The referee picked up the football and marked off another fifteen-yard penalty. He then turned to the irate player who was still fifteen yards behind him and yelled to him, "How is my aroma from here?"

Dates & Places Used:

TOPIC: Authority

Driving through Texas

Two men driving through Texas were pulled over by a state trooper. The trooper walked up and tapped on the window with his nightstick. The driver rolled down the window, and *whack*, the trooper smacked him in the head with the stick.

The driver said, "What did you do that for?"

The trooper said, "You're in Texas, son. When we pull you over, you better have your license ready when we get to your car."

The driver said, "I'm sorry, officer; I'm not from around here."

The trooper ran a check on the man's license, and he was clean. So he returned his license and walked around to the passenger side and tapped on the window.

The passenger rolled down his window, and *whack*, the trooper smacked him with the nightstick too.

The passenger said, "What did you do that for?"

"Just making your wish come true," said the trooper.

"Huh?" replied the passenger.

The trooper said, "I know that two miles down the road you're gonna say, 'I wish that tough cop would have tried that routine with me.'"

Dates & Places Used:

TOPIC: Baptism

Broken Record

A minister kept boring his congregation with sermon after sermon about baptism. Finally, church leaders told him to preach on another subject the following Sunday. They chose the subject of pills. Certainly, they felt, there could be no connection between pills and baptism.

So the next Sunday the minister began, "There are big pills and little pills, also bitter pills and sweet pills, cheap pills and expensive pills. Another pill is the 'gos-pill'—and that brings me to my real subject, baptism."

Dates & Places Used:

76

TOPIC: Baptism

A New Name

A little boy went to his mother and asked her what the next-door neighbors were going to name their brand-new baby girl. The mother replied that she thought they were going to name the baby after her grandmother. The boy thought for a moment and then said, "Mom, you mean to say that they're going to call that tiny little baby 'Grandma'?"

Dates & Places Used:

77

TOPIC: Beauty

Lady Lied to Mom

A little girl was watching her mother apply some facial cream when she asked her mother what that stuff was that she was putting on her face.

Her mother answered, "This is facial cream, honey. The woman at the store told me it would make me beautiful."

The girl looked carefully at her mother's face and said, "Mommy, I think that lady at the store lied to you."

Dates & Places Used:

78

TOPIC: Beauty

Don't Kiss the Frog

An elderly man was taking his evening walk. He was enjoying the crisp night air and the sound of the wind blowing through the trees when, suddenly, he heard a little voice calling, "Help me! Help me!"

The man looked all around and saw no one, so he continued his walk. Again he heard the tiny little voice. "Help me! Help me!"

This time he looked down and saw a small frog. He gently lifted the frog and looked at it intently. The frog spoke: "I'm really a beautiful young princess. If you will kiss me, I will turn back into a princess and I will love you forever."

The man thought for a moment, placed the frog in his top pocket, and continued walking. The little frog looked up out of the pocket and asked, "Why don't you kiss me?"

The man responded, "Frankly, at this stage in my life, I would rather have a talking frog."

Dates & Places Used:

79

TOPIC: Beauty

Cheap Is Expensive

It takes a lot of money to make me look this cheap. *(Dolly Parton)*

Dates & Places Used:

80

TOPIC: Beauty

Ignored Warnings

Finding one of her students making faces at others on the playground, a teacher stopped to gently reprove the child. Smiling sweetly, she said, "Son, when I was a child, I was told that if I made ugly faces, my face would freeze, and I would stay like that."

The boy looked up into her face, looked intently for a moment, and then replied, "Well, teacher, you can't say you weren't warned."

Dates & Places Used:

TOPIC: Beauty

The Real Me

A woman was working in her front yard when a moving van pulled up next door. Her new neighbors drove up behind the moving van. While the movers were unloading the van, the new neighbors walked over and greeted the woman. She was a bit self-conscious because she had dirt on her hands and face and was wearing dirty, old clothes.

A few days later the new neighbors invited the woman and her husband to an open house. This was the woman's opportunity to make a better impression. She colored her hair, put on a girdle, glossed her lips, applied eye shadow and false eyelashes, polished her fingernails, and popped in her colored contact lenses. She stepped to the mirror and admiringly told her husband, "Now the new neighbors will get to see the *real me.*"

Dates & Places Used:

TOPIC: Beauty

Toward a More Colorful World

A ten-year-old art student had just completed the painting of a raspberry pink stag with one blue antler and one yellow antler. An adult visitor to the art class looked at the picture and remarked, "But people don't see pink stags with blue and yellow antlers!"

The young artist looked at his painting critically, thought about it for a minute, and then said, sincerely and soberly, "Isn't that too bad?"

Dates & Places Used:

83

Age-Old Problem

In an anthropology class the teacher was looking for an example of how ideas about beauty change over the years. Finally, he said, "Take the Miss America contest for example: Seventy years ago, the Miss America winner was only five feet tall. She weighed just over one hundred pounds, and her measurements were 30–25–32. How do you think she would be viewed by the judges in this year's contest?"

One student replied, "Not very well."

"Why not?" the teacher asked.

The student answered, "Because she's too old!"

Dates & Places Used:

84

Improvement Is Optional

A little boy was overheard praying: "Lord, if you can't make me a better boy, don't worry about it. I'm having a real good time like I am!"

Dates & Places Used:

85

Walk This Way

A man walked into a pharmacy and asked if they had any talcum powder. The pharmacist said, "Yes, we do. Just walk this way."

"I'm afraid I can't do that," the man answered. "If I could walk that way, I would not need any talcum powder."

Dates & Places Used:

86

Notify the Next of Kin

A preacher went to his church office on Monday morning and discovered a dead mule in the churchyard. He called the police. Since there did not appear to be any foul play, the police referred the preacher to the health department.

They said that since there was no health threat, he should call the sanitation department. The sanitation manager said he could not pick up the mule without authorization from the mayor.

Now the preacher knew the mayor and was not too eager to call him. The mayor had a bad temper and was generally hard to deal with, but the preacher had no choice, so he called him anyway.

The mayor did not disappoint. He immediately began to rant and rave at the pastor and finally said, "Why did you call me? Isn't it your job to bury the dead?"

The preacher paused for a brief prayer and asked the Lord to direct his response. He then answered, "Yes, your honor, it is my job to bury the dead, but I always like to notify the next of kin first."

Dates & Places Used:

87

TOPIC: Birth

Breech Birth

One day a cattle farmer heard one of his cows bellowing out in the north forty. She sounded like she was in hard labor. He went out and, sure enough, found that she was having a breech delivery. He tried to turn the calf around, but it was too late–the legs were already coming out. All he could do was pull on the legs to assist in the birth.

The farmer's field was right next to the interstate, and a red MG stopped. Out jumped a librarian type with glasses and a bun in her hair. She asked, "Is there anything I can do to assist?"

The farmer said, "Yes, please! Grab a leg and pull!"

So they both pulled, and they were able to get the calf out. The farmer, very grateful, said, "Wait a minute while I run back and get my wallet–I owe you for this."

"Oh no, I wouldn't dream of accepting any recompense for this service. However, there is one question you can answer for me."

"Anything!"

"How fast was the little one going when it ran into the big one?"

Dates & Places Used:

88

TOPIC: Birth

When God Overanswers

An Italian woman consulted her priest about her inability to conceive. Her priest assured her to rest in the comfort that he was going to Rome for ten years and would light a candle for her.

Ten years later the priest returned from Rome and went to visit the woman. As he entered the house, he saw the woman in the midst of eight young screaming children. "God answered our prayer! The candle worked!" the priest exclaimed. "Where is your husband? I wish to congratulate him and rejoice with him."

The exhausted woman answered, "He is not here; he went to Rome to blow out that stupid candle you lit!"

Dates & Places Used:

89

TOPIC: Birth

Greens Fee

An expectant mother was being rushed to the hospital but didn't quite make it. She gave birth to her baby on the hospital lawn.

Later the father received a bill listing "Delivery Room Fee: $500."

He wrote a letter to the hospital reminding them that the baby was born on the front lawn. A week passed and a corrected bill arrived: "Greens Fee: $200."

Dates & Places Used:

90

TOPIC: Birth

A Father's Compassion

A young father-to-be was pacing back and forth, wringing his hands in the hospital corridor while his wife was in labor. He was tied up in knots from fear and anxiety. Beads of perspiration dripped from his brow.

Finally, at 4:00 A.M. a nurse popped out of the delivery room door and said, "Congratulations, sir, you have a little girl!" The young father breathed a huge sigh of relief as he collapsed into a chair. He finally looked up at the nurse and said, "Oh, how I thank God it's a girl. She'll never have to go through the awful agony I've had tonight."

Dates & Places Used:

91

TOPIC: Blame

Shared Blame

A husband and wife were playing in the mixed foursomes. He hit a great drive down the middle, and she sliced the second shot into a grove of trees.

Unfazed, the husband played a brilliant recovery shot that went onto the green a meter from the pin. She poked at the putt and sent it five meters beyond the pin. He lined up the long putt and sank it.

To his wife he said, "We'll have to do better. That was a bogey five."

"Don't blame me," she snapped, "I only took two of them."

Dates & Places Used:

92

TOPIC: Blame

Whom to Blame

The reason people blame things on previous generations is that there is only one other choice.

Dates & Places Used:

48

93

TOPIC: Budgets

Budget Analysis

A well-planned budget is the best way to know why you went broke.

Dates & Places Used:

94

TOPIC: Budgets

Economic Equation

If your outgo exceeds your income, then your upkeep will be your downfall.

Dates & Places Used:

95

TOPIC: Budgets

Income for One

The young man asked his girlfriend, "If we get married, will you be able to live on my income?"

His girlfriend answered, "I think so, but what will you live on?"

Dates & Places Used:

96

TOPIC: Caution

Test with One Foot

No one tests the depth of a river with both feet.

Dates & Places Used:

97

TOPIC: Caution

Crocodile Confusion

Don't think there are no crocodiles because the water is calm.
Dates & Places Used:

98

TOPIC: Caution

Recalled by Maker

Drive carefully—it's not only cars that can be recalled by their maker.
Dates & Places Used:

99

TOPIC: Caution

Pandora's Box Lesson

From Greek mythology comes a great lesson. Pandora opened the box that unleashed all kinds of evil. The lesson is this: Don't open any box that you did not close.
Dates & Places Used:

100

TOPIC: Change

Creative Maturity

To exist is to change; to change is to mature; to mature is to create oneself endlessly. *(Henri Bergson)*
Dates & Places Used:

TOPIC: Change

Change the Coffee

A bachelor moved into his first apartment and asked a neighbor how to make coffee. She gave him step-by-step directions. A few days later they passed in the hall and she asked how his coffee making was coming along.

He said, "Well, to be truthful, it went okay at first. But lately it has been really terrible. By the way, how often should I change the coffee?"

Dates & Places Used:

TOPIC: Change

On the Right Track

Even if you're on the right track, you're going to get run over if you sit there. *(Will Rogers)*

Dates & Places Used:

TOPIC: Change

Confusing Conversion

A Jewish man moved into a Catholic neighborhood. Every Friday the Catholics went crazy because, while they were morosely eating fish, the Jew was outside barbecuing steaks. So the Catholics worked on the Jew to convert him.

Finally, by threats and pleading, the Catholics succeeded. They took the Jew to a priest who sprinkled holy water on him and intoned, "Born a Jew, raised a Jew, now a Catholic."

The Catholics were ecstatic. *No more delicious, maddening smells every Friday evening,* they thought. But the next Friday evening the scent of barbecue wafted through the neighborhood once again. The Catholics all rushed to the new convert's house to remind him of his new diet. They saw him standing over the grilled steak sprinkling it with water. As he did so he said, "Born a cow, raised a cow, now a fish."

Dates & Places Used:

104

TOPIC: Change

When Jesus Sticks Out

A seven-year-old boy went to evangelistic services on Monday night, Tuesday night, Wednesday night, Thursday night, and Friday night. He never did respond to the invitation, but on Friday night he ran out to the parking lot following the evangelist. He said, "Let me ask you something. You say I have to ask Jesus Christ into my life."

The evangelist replied, "That's right."

"I'm seven years old. How big is Jesus?"

"He's a pretty good size because he's a carpenter."

"That's what I thought. If I were to ask him into me, wouldn't he stick out?"

"Son, you've got the message. More and more he'd stick out."

You know, when you're seven, it's not hard to take God at his Word: "Except you become like a child and be converted, you'll never see the kingdom of heaven." That's his Word.

Dates & Places Used:

105

TOPIC: Character

Understandable Bias

A judge glared down from his bench at a prospective juror. "And just why is it," he asked, "that you don't want to serve on this jury?"

The man replied, "Well, Your Honor, I'm biased. One look at that man convinced me that he is guilty."

The judge scowled and replied, "That man is not the defendant; he's the district attorney."

Dates & Places Used:

TOPIC: Character

Close Scrutiny

A prosperous young Wall Street broker met, fell in love with, and was frequently seen escorting about town a rising actress of gentility and dignity. He wanted to marry her, but being a cautious man he decided that before proposing marriage he should have a private investigating agency check her background and present activities. *After all,* he reminded himself, *I have both a growing fortune and my reputation to protect against a marital misadventure.*

The young man requested that the agency not reveal his identity to the investigator reporting on the actress. In due time the investigator's report came back. It said the actress had an unblemished past and a spotless reputation. Her friends and associates were of the best repute. The report concluded, "The only shadow is that she is often seen around town in the company of a young broker of dubious business practices and principles."

Dates & Places Used:

TOPIC: Character

Converted Annoyance

A pearl is a garment of patience that enclosed an annoyance.

Dates & Places Used:

TOPIC: Cheating

Attorney in Heaven

A lawyer died and went to heaven. After a day or two he noticed that he was considerably younger than nearly everyone else. This began to bother him, and he wondered if his death had been a mistake. He found St. Peter and asked him about this concern. St. Peter said he would look into his case and see what he could find out.

The next day Peter came back and said to the lawyer, "Yes, after looking at your file, I realized a mistake had been made in your case. We had figured your age by the number of your billing hours!"

Dates & Places Used:

109

TOPIC: Cheating

Playing with a Cheater

The golf pro met Charlie in the clubhouse and said, "Charlie, you used to play golf with Pete all the time, but you don't anymore. Why?"

Charlie answered with a question of his own. "Would you play with a guy who tees the ball up in the rough, gives himself even the long putts, and cheats on the scorecard?"

The pro thought about this and then said, "No, I guess I wouldn't."

Charlie responded, "Well, neither will Pete!"

Dates & Places Used:

110

TOPIC: Cheating

Almost Identical Answers

Two young engineers applied for a single position at a computer company. They both had the same qualifications. In order to determine which individual to hire, the department manager asked both applicants to take a test.

Upon completion of the test, both men had missed only one of the questions. The manager went to the first applicant and said, "Thank you for your interest, but we've decided to give the job to the other applicant."

"And why would you be doing that? We both got nine questions correct," argued the rejected applicant.

"We have based our decision not on the correct answers, but on the question you missed," said the department manager.

"And just how would one incorrect answer be better than the other?" the rejected applicant inquired.

"Simple," said the department manager. "Your fellow applicant put down on question number five, 'I don't know.' You put down, 'Neither do I.'"
Dates & Places Used:

TOPIC: Cheating

111

Dishonest Golf Buddies

Sid and Barney headed out for a quick round of golf. Since they were short on time, they decided to play only nine holes.

Sid made Barney an offer. "Let's say we make the time worthwhile, at least for one of us, and spot five dollars on the lowest score for the day."

Barney agreed, and they enjoyed a great game. After the eighth hole, Barney was ahead by one stroke, but he cut his ball into the rough on the ninth. "Help me find my ball. You look over there," he told Sid.

After five minutes neither had had any luck, and since a lost ball carries a four-point penalty, Barney pulled a ball from his pocket and tossed it to the ground. "I've found my ball!" he announced triumphantly.

Sid looked at him forlornly. "After all the years we've been friends, you'd cheat me at golf for a measly five bucks?"

"What do you mean cheat? I found my ball sitting right here!"

"And a liar too!" Sid said with amazement. "I'll have you know I've been standing on your ball for the last five minutes!"
Dates & Places Used:

TOPIC: Cheating

112

One Dollar for Each Point

A college professor was giving a final exam to his students. He distributed the tests to the class and waited for his students to finish. When the students handed in their completed tests, one of the tests had a one-hundred-dollar bill attached with a note that explained, "One dollar for each point."

When the student got his exam back, he had a grade of forty-five with fifty-five dollars in change attached.

Dates & Places Used:

113 TOPIC: Cheating

Double Standards

If you copy anything out of one book, it is plagiarism. If you copy it out of two books, it is research. If you copy it out of six books, you are a professor. *(Bishop Fulton J. Sheen)*

Dates & Places Used:

114 TOPIC: Children

Pray for Me!

On a recent Sunday in a Midwest city a young child was acting up during the morning worship hour. The parents did their best to maintain some sense of order in the pew but were losing the battle. Finally, the father picked the little fellow up and walked sternly up the aisle on his way out. Just before reaching the safety of the foyer, the little one called loudly to the congregation, "Pray for me! Pray for me!"

Dates & Places Used:

115 TOPIC: Children

More Theology Needed

Children have a way of keeping all of us off balance. I read recently about a new salesman who worked door-to-door selling children's encyclopedias. He had concluded his presentation to the mother of a five-year-old boy. Although he sensed that he had already convinced her of the value of the books, he went on and used one more of his highly charged sales techniques.

"If the answer to any question your little boy asks can't be found in this encyclopedia, I will refuse to sell these books to you," he said to the mother. Then, turning to the five-year-old, he said, "Ask me a question, sonny. Just ask me anything you want to know, and I'll show your mother where she can find the answer in this wonderful encyclopedia."

The five-year-old thought only a moment before he asked, "What kind of car does God drive?"

That experience was educational for the salesman. He never used that sales technique again.

Dates & Places Used:

116

TOPIC: Children

The Honest Prayer

A woman invited some people to dinner. At the table she turned to her six-year-old daughter and said, "Would you like to say the blessing?"

"I wouldn't know what to say," the little girl replied.

"Just say what you hear Mommy say," the mother said.

The little girl bowed her head and said, "Dear Lord, why on earth did I invite all these stupid people to dinner?"

Dates & Places Used:

117

TOPIC: Children

Booger Blooper

The following is a true story reported by a mother.

As I was trying to pack for vacation, my three-year-old daughter was having a wonderful time playing on the bed.

At one point, she said, "Mom, look at this," and stuck out two of her fingers.

Trying to keep her entertained, I reached out and stuck her fingers in my mouth, pretending to eat them. Then I rushed out of the room again. When I returned, my daughter was standing

on the bed with a devastated look on her face. "Mommy, where's my booger?" she asked.
Dates & Places Used:

118

TOPIC: Children

Better to Mow Indoors

A little boy received a toy lawn mower for Christmas. He pretended to use it in the house but was well aware that he was not really mowing the carpet. He looked forward to the day he would get to take it outside and "mow" the real grass. When summer came the boy's father invited him out to help mow the lawn. The boy excitedly dragged his toy mower outside to assist his father. The boy lasted about two minutes and announced, "I think I'll go back inside and mow the carpet. It's too hot out here."
Dates & Places Used:

119

TOPIC: Children

Unpredictable Children

Children are unpredictable–you never know how far up the wall they're going to drive you.
Dates & Places Used:

120

TOPIC: Christmas

Born in a Barn

A four-year-old girl often forgot to close the door when coming in from outside. Finally, her father scolded her, "Shut that door! Were you born in a barn?"

She looked at her father and replied softly, "No, but Jesus was."
Dates & Places Used:

121

Turned Off Jesus

To show the splendor of the newborn Savior in the church Christmas pageant, an electric lightbulb was hidden in the manger. All the stage lights were to be turned off so only the brightness of the manger could be seen, but the boy who controlled the lights got confused, and suddenly all the lights went out.

The tense moment was broken by a little shepherd's loud whisper. "Hey, you just turned off Jesus!"

Dates & Places Used:

122

Not My Birthday

Five-year-old Billy was showing his Christmas presents to Grandma when she asked, "Did you get everything you wanted for Christmas?"

Billy thought for a moment before he answered, "No, I didn't, Grandma. But that's okay. It wasn't my birthday."

Dates & Places Used:

123

The Pushy Church

Just a few days before Christmas two women stood looking into a department store window at a large display of the manger scene with clay figures of the baby Jesus, Mary, Joseph, the shepherds, the wise men, and the animals. Disgustedly, one woman said, "Look at that, the church trying to horn in on Christmas!"

Dates & Places Used:

TOPIC: Christmas

The Christmas Tree

While I was getting my "Christmas haircut," my barber, Lou, shared with me an incident that had happened a few days before. He was cutting the hair of a little boy while the boy's father was waiting for him. The boy was fascinated by the barbershop's Christmas tree, which was adorned with lights and decorations. He turned to his father and asked, "Daddy, why can't we have a Christmas tree in our house?"

The father very gently said, "Jewish houses don't have Christmas trees."

The little boy thought for a moment and then with a frown on his face replied, "Daddy, why did we have to buy a Jewish house?"

Dates & Places Used:

TOPIC: Christmas

Watch Your Step

A small country church was having their yearly Christmas cantata. Part of the ritual of their cantata was that they always marched in singing "O Come, All Ye Faithful" and departed singing "Hark! The Herald Angels Sing."

A large floor furnace heated the building, and the grating for the furnace was right in the center of the aisle. As the choir began their processional, they marched precisely up the aisle, each person three pews behind the other. Just as the last alto got midway up the aisle, she stepped on the grating of the floor furnace. She had bought a new pair of heels to wear for the Christmas program, and unfortunately, the pencil-thin heel of her shoe went through the grating and stuck there. She shook her foot hard several times, but the shoe remained stuck. The man in line behind her was getting close. Even though she was stunned, she played it cool. She slipped her foot out of the shoe and went limping up the aisle with only one shoe on.

The man coming behind looked down and realized what had happened. He knew if the shoe was left sticking there, it would cause the congregation to break into laughter. Thinking quickly, he reached down, grabbed the shoe, and gave it a strong twist.

To his amazement, the entire floor grate came up with the shoe. He went into a mild state of shock and dazedly marched up the aisle in time with the music, with the floor grate and shoe in hand.

You guessed it! The next man in line fell into the hole.

Dates & Places Used:

126

TOPIC: Church

Which Side I Am On

A little old man was seen every Sunday morning walking to church. He was deaf, so he could not hear a word of the sermon, or the music of the choir, or the hymns sung by the congregation.

A scoffer asked him, "Why do you spend your Sundays in that church when you can't hear a word?"

He replied, "I want my neighbors to know which side I'm on."

Dates & Places Used:

127

TOPIC: Church

Church Growth Equation

Hot heads plus cold hearts equal empty churches.

Dates & Places Used:

128

TOPIC: Church

Your Niche

A man had visited church after church trying to find a congenial congregation, and finally he stopped at a little church just as the congregation read with the minister, "We have left undone those things we ought to have done, and we have done those things which we ought not to have done." The man slipped into

a pew with a sigh of relief and murmured, "Thank goodness, I've found my crowd at last."
Dates & Places Used:

---

129 **TOPIC:** Church

Fads and Popular Religions

Running after religious fanatics who come up with some new or "rediscovered" doctrine reminds me of the old farmer who, when asked what was the matter with his hogs, replied, "When I lost my voice a year ago I could not call them to their feed, so I got a big stick and hammered on the crib. They soon learned that was a call to their corn. They were doing well until three weeks ago when some woodpeckers came in here and went to pounding on the old dead trees. My hogs ran in the direction of the noise, thinking it was my call to their feed. When the hogs came running and squealing, the frightened woodpeckers would fly to another dead tree, and the hogs would run to that part of the woods. They have just about run my hogs to death." I hope the church will cease running after the religious woodpeckers. Much so-called "new thought" is old nonsense.
Dates & Places Used:

---

130 **TOPIC:** Clergy

Butchered Sermon

Back in the day when butchers made deliveries, a mother was waiting for the butcher, who was late. She told her son Johnny, "I'm going upstairs. If the butcher comes, let me know. I want to talk to him."

Johnny forgot whom his mother wanted to see, so when the minister came to the door, he shouted upstairs, "Ma, that man's here now."

The mother answered, "I can't come now. Give him the money out of my purse, and tell him we didn't like his tongue last week, so we're going to change!"
Dates & Places Used:

131

TOPIC: Clergy

God Does Not Blabber

A drunken man stumbled out of a bar and happened to bump into his pastor who was walking down the street. The man apologized, "I never meant for you to see me this way."

The man's pastor seized the opportunity and asked the man, "Why does it matter that I see you when the Lord sees you all the time?"

The drunken man answered, "God isn't a blabbermouth like you are."

Dates & Places Used:

132

TOPIC: Clergy

Private Prayer

A passenger jet was suffering through a severe thunderstorm. As the passengers were being bounced around by the turbulence, a young woman turned to a minister sitting next to her and with a nervous laugh asked, "Reverend, you're a man of God; can't you do something about this storm?"

He looked at her and replied, "Sorry, lady, I'm in sales, not management."

Dates & Places Used:

133

TOPIC: Clergy

Pastoral Preparation

A young man with a terrible stuttering problem determined to visit a renowned speech therapist in his city. The therapist had a very unconventional method (for modern times) of treating such problems. He had this young man talk with his mouth filled with marbles. Every week he would allow him to take one out. Amazingly, his speech began to improve. Finally, after he had lost all his marbles, he became a preacher.

Dates & Places Used:

134

TOPIC: Clergy

Who Is Asleep?

When people sleep in church, it may be the minister who needs waking up.
Dates & Places Used:

135

TOPIC: Comfort

House without Beds

An air force chaplain was transferred to another base and was allowed to decide between two houses. Along with his wife and four-year-old daughter, he inspected the two houses. As soon as they finished inspecting the first house, their four-year-old daughter told her parents that she did not like that house. No problem; they just went to the other house to inspect that one. The girl made it quite clear that she did not like that house either.

There were no more choices, so her confused parents asked, "What is it that you don't like about these houses?"

The disappointed girl answered, "Neither one of them has beds!"
Dates & Places Used:

136

TOPIC: Comfort

Wet Pants Comfort

Come with me to a third grade classroom. A nine-year-old boy is sitting at his desk when all of a sudden a puddle appears between his feet and the front of his pants are wet. He panics, because he cannot possibly imagine how this has happened. It has never happened before, and he knows that when the boys find out, he will never hear the end of it. When the girls find out, they will never speak to him again as long as he lives.

The boy believes his heart is going to stop, so he puts his head down and prays this prayer: "Dear God, this is an emergency! I need help now! Five minutes from now I'm dead meat." He looks up from his prayer, and here comes the teacher with a look in her eyes that says that he has been discovered. As the teacher is coming to snatch him up, a classmate named Susie is carrying a goldfish bowl filled with water. Susie trips in front of the teacher and inexplicably dumps the bowl in the boy's lap. The boy pretends to be angry, but all the while is saying, "Thank you, Jesus! Thank you, Jesus!" Now, instead of being the object of ridicule, this boy is the object of sympathy. The teacher rushes him downstairs and gives him gym shorts to put on while his pants dry out and brings him back up to the room. All the children are on their hands and knees cleaning up around this child's desk. Their sympathy is wonderful!

But as life would have it, the ridicule that should have been his has been transferred to someone else—Susie. She tries to help, but the other students tell her to get out. "You've done enough, you klutz!" As the day progresses, the sympathy gets better and better and the ridicule gets worse and worse. Finally, at the end of the day, the children are waiting for the bus, and once again Susie has been shunned by the other children. The boy walks over to Susie and whispers, "Susie, you did that on purpose, didn't you?" Susie whispers back, "I wet my pants once too."

The best comforters are those who have been comforted.

Dates & Places Used:

137

TOPIC: Comfort

Comfortable Quest

Money can't find happiness, but it can make the quest a bit more comfortable.

Dates & Places Used:

138

TOPIC: Commitment

Involved versus Committed

Football coach Lou Holtz points out the difference between being merely involved and being truly committed to a cause:

"The kamikaze pilot who was able to fly fifty missions was involved but not committed."
Dates & Places Used:

139

TOPIC: Commitment

Get a Second Opinion

A pastor was shaking hands with people as they left the church. A couple greeted him and said, "We listened carefully to every word you said."

The pastor thanked the couple and said that he looked forward to seeing them next week.

"Oh, we won't be here next week," the couple responded. "We're going to another church next week to get a second opinion."

Dates & Places Used:

140

TOPIC: Communication

Chandelier or Lights?

A pastor met with his board of trustees and requested they approve the purchase of a chandelier for the church sanctuary. The next month when the minutes were read there was no mention of the pastor's suggestion, so he requested it a second time.

The third month the pastor waited expectantly for a report of action taken, but there was absolutely no word in the minutes of his request. So after the meeting he went to the chairman of the board and asked for an explanation.

"Well, pastor, it was this way," explained the chairman. "First of all, the secretary of the trustees didn't know how to spell the word, and it would have embarrassed him if we had insisted on including it in the minutes. Second, if we got one of those things, we don't believe there is anyone in the church who knows how to play it. And third, we feel that the thing we really need is better lighting."

Dates & Places Used:

141

TOPIC: Communication

Babblespeak

The following notice was sent home with some high school students: "Our school's cross-graded, multiethnic, individualized learning program is designed to enhance the concept of an open-ended learning program on the continuum of multiethnic, academically enriched learning, using the identified intellectually gifted child as the agent of his own learning."

One parent sent back a note that read, "I have a college degree and speak two foreign languages and four Indian dialects …, but I haven't the faintest idea what you are talking about."

Has our communication become so loaded with babblespeak that no one understands what we are saying?

Dates & Places Used:

142

TOPIC: Communication

Care about Terminology

A psychiatrist was concerned about his nurse's office procedure so he said to her, "When you answer the phone, just say, 'We're terribly busy just now,' instead of 'It's a madhouse.'"

Dates & Places Used:

143

TOPIC: Communication

Floating Memo

From a principal's memo to the district superintendent: "On Tuesday a frozen water pipe broke and flooded four classrooms. Alternative arrangements were made by doubling classes and having special teachers float."

Dates & Places Used:

144

TOPIC: Communication

Humorous Headlines

Father of Nine Fined $100 for Failing to Stop
Dead Policeman on Force Twenty-Three Years
Twenty-Six-Year Friendship Ends at Altar
Man Found Dead in Cemetery
Nine Volunteers Put in New Church Furnace
Florist Asks Girls to Drop Strapless Gowns
Babies Flood Hospital
Escaped Leopard Believed Spotted
City Officials Talk Rubbish

Dates & Places Used:

145

TOPIC: Communication

Windy and Thirsty

Three senior citizens were out for a walk together and one made the comment, "It sure is windy!"

The second responded, "It's not Wednesday. It's Thursday."

Immediately the third chimed in, "I'm thirsty too!"

Dates & Places Used:

146

TOPIC: Communication

Unfriendly Phones

Some people are put off when they make a phone call and are greeted with someone spouting off the number they just called. When one such caller placed her call, the secretary at the other end picked up the phone and answered, "555-4664."

"May I speak to Mr. Barrier, please?"

"Certainly. May I tell him who's calling?" asked the secretary.

Impatiently the caller replied, "555-0779!"

Dates & Places Used:

147

Punctuation Makes the Difference

How you punctuate your writing is important. A woman who was concerned about her husband who had joined the navy handed a prayer request to her pastor that should have read: "George Bowen having gone to sea, his wife desires the prayers of the congregation for his safety." The pastor read the note to the congregation this way: "George Bowen, having gone to see his wife, desires the prayers of the congregation for his safety."

Dates & Places Used:

148

Above the Green Grass

If your neighbor's grass is greener, just be thankful that you are still above ground to see it.

Dates & Places Used:

149

Armadillo Crossroad

Here is a riddle from the southern United States.
Question: Why did the chicken cross the road?
Answer: To show the armadillo it could be done.

Dates & Places Used:

150

Twisted Toast

Here's to you, as good as you are.

Here's to me as bad as I am.
As good as you are and as bad as I am,
I'm as good as you are as bad as I am.
Dates & Places Used:

151

TOPIC: Comparison

Circular Forecasts

The Cree people asked their chief in the autumn if the winter was going to be cold. Not really knowing an answer, the Cree chief replied that the winter was going to be cold and that the members of the village were to collect wood to be prepared.

Being a good leader, he then went to the nearest phone booth and called the National Weather Service and asked, "Is this winter going to be cold?"

The man on the phone responded, "This winter is going to be quite cold indeed."

So the chief went back to speed up his people to collect even more wood to be prepared. A week later he called the National Weather Service again and asked, "Is it going to be a very cold winter?"

"Yes," the man replied, "it's going to be a very cold winter."

So the chief went back to his people and ordered them to go and find every scrap of wood they could find. Two weeks later he called the National Weather Service again: "Are you absolutely sure the winter is going to be very cold?"

"Absolutely," the man replied, "the Cree are collecting wood like crazy."

Dates & Places Used:

152

TOPIC: Complaints

The Perfect Broom

An annoying customer had handled almost every article in the hardware store, but nothing was worthy of her approval. Wearying of the customer's constant criticism, the clerk suggested that she inspect a new selection of brooms.

"These are very low quality," the customer observed. "Cheap straw, flimsily made, shoddy material, and the wooden handle is too rough. They aren't like the ones they used to make. This broom would not last long for sweeping. What is it good for, anyway?"

"Well," commented the exasperated clerk, "you could always ride it."

Dates & Places Used:

153

TOPIC: Complaints

Living with the Lions

A little girl was showing a friend around her new house. "This is the kitchen. Here's my bedroom. Here's the den. Do you have a den in your house?"

"No, we don't," her playmate replied. "My dad just growls all around the house."

Dates & Places Used:

154

TOPIC: Compliments

Confident Wife

Bob was in his usual place in the morning—sitting at the table reading the paper after breakfast. He came across an article about a beautiful actress who was about to marry a football player who was known primarily for his low IQ and lack of common knowledge.

He turned to his wife with a questioning look on his face. "I'll never understand why the biggest jerks get the most attractive wives."

She replied, "Why thank you, dear!"

Dates & Places Used:

155

TOPIC: Concern

Easy Objectivity

It's always easy to see both sides of an issue we are not particularly concerned about. *(Mark Twain)*
Dates & Places Used:

156

TOPIC: Concern

Pseudo Concern

A knock at the door brought the lady of the house face-to-face with a man of sad countenance. He said, "I am sorry to disturb you, but I'm collecting money for an unfortunate family in your neighborhood." He went on with great sympathy. "The husband is out of work, the kids are hungry, the utilities are soon to be cut off, and worst of all, they are going to be kicked out of their home if they cannot get the rent money by this afternoon."

The woman replied with great concern, "I will be happy to help, but who are you?"

He replied, "I'm their landlord."
Dates & Places Used:

157

TOPIC: Conclusions

Paratrooper's Jump to Conclusion

An army recruit was assigned to the paratroopers' outfit. The instructor explained the operation of parachutes to the recruits.

One of the recruits asked, "What if the chute doesn't open?"

The instructor answered, "That, Private, is what is known as jumping to a conclusion!"
Dates & Places Used:

158

TOPIC: Conclusions

Brilliant Deduction

Sherlock Holmes and Dr. Watson went on a camping trip. As they lay down for the night, Holmes said, "Watson, look up into the sky and tell me what you see."

Watson looked up and said, "I see millions and millions of stars."

Holmes asked, "And what does that tell you?"

Watson thoughtfully answered, "Astronomically, it tells me that there are millions of galaxies and potentially billions of planets. Theologically, it tells me that God is great and that we are small and insignificant. Meteorologically, it tells me that we will have a beautiful day tomorrow. What does it tell you, Holmes?"

Holmes deduced, "Someone stole our tent!"

Dates & Places Used:

159

TOPIC: Confession

A Rather Tenuous Forgiveness

A little boy said, "Look, there is a bear in our backyard!"

His mother looked outside and said, "That's not a bear. It's Joe Smith's dog. Now go to your room and ask God to forgive you for telling a lie."

The boy went to his room and later came back downstairs. His mother asked, "Did you ask God to forgive you?"

The little fellow said, "Yes, and God said it was all right. He said the first time he saw Joe Smith's dog, he thought it was a bear too."

Dates & Places Used:

160

Fallen into Adultery

An old priest got sick of all the people in his parish who kept confessing adultery. One Sunday he said from the pulpit, "If I hear one more person confess to adultery, I'll quit!"

Well, everyone liked him, so they came up with a code word. Someone who had committed adultery would say they had "fallen."

This seemed to satisfy the old priest, and things went well until the priest died. About a week after the new priest arrived, he visited the mayor of the town and seemed very concerned. The priest told the mayor, "You have to do something about the sidewalks in town. When people come to the confessional, they keep talking about having 'fallen.'"

The mayor started to laugh, realizing that no one had told the new priest about the code word. But before he could explain, the priest shook an accusing finger at him and said, "I don't know what you're laughing about! Your wife fell three times this week."

Dates & Places Used:

161

Sin or Mistake

A girl knelt in the confessional and said, "Bless me, Father, for I have sinned."

"What is it, child?" asked the priest.

"Father, I have committed the sin of vanity. Twice a day I gaze at myself in the mirror and tell myself how beautiful I am."

The priest turned, took a good look at the girl, and said, "My dear, I have good news. That isn't a sin—it's only a mistake."

Dates & Places Used:

162

TOPIC: Confession

Throwing Peanuts

Three boys came to confession. The first ended by saying
"... and I threw peanuts in the river." He was scolded for wasting good food.

The second boy came in and admitted that he too had thrown peanuts into the river.

The third little boy didn't say a thing about peanuts.

The priest, wanting to show that he was aware of little boys and what was going on in the neighborhood, asked, "Didn't you throw peanuts in the river?"

The boy replied, "No, I'm Peanuts."

Dates & Places Used:

163

TOPIC: Confidence

Half the Confidence

I wish I could be half as sure of anything as some people are of everything.

Dates & Places Used:

164

TOPIC: Conflict

Final Observation

A lawyer was trying to console a weeping widow. Her husband had passed away without a will. "Did the deceased have any last words?" asked the lawyer.

"You mean right before he died?" sobbed the widow.

"Yes," replied the lawyer. "They might be helpful if it's not too painful for you to recall."

"Well," she began, "he said, 'Don't try to scare me! You couldn't hit the broad side of a barn with that gun.'"

Dates & Places Used:

165

Tied Down

A henpecked husband went to a psychologist to learn to assert himself. The psychologist told him, "You do not have to accept your wife's bullying. You need to go home right now and let her know that you are your own boss."

The husband was encouraged to take the doctor's advice. He went home and slammed the door on his way in. He shook his fist in his wife's face and shouted, "From now on you'll do what I say, woman! Go get my supper, then go upstairs and lay out my clothes. After I eat, I'm going out with the boys. You can stay here where you belong. By the way, do you know who is going to tie my tie for me?"

"I sure do," said his wife calmly. "The undertaker."

Dates & Places Used:

166

Her Own Way

Only two things are necessary to keep one's wife happy: One is to let her think she is having her own way; the other is to let her have it.

Dates & Places Used:

167

On the Losing Side

A ten-year-old boy answered the doorbell at his home one day. When he opened it, he discovered a strange man on the porch.

The man said, "Son, you don't know me, do you?"

The boy agreed that he did not know the man.

The man replied, "Well, I am your uncle on your father's side."

To this the young fellow replied, "Well, I'm glad to meet you, but you are certainly on the losing side."

Dates & Places Used:

168

TOPIC: Conflict

Unfair Advantage

Never wrestle with a pig. You both get all dirty – and the pig likes it.

Dates & Places Used:

169

TOPIC: Consequences

Convince Them They Are Wrong

Sometimes the best way to convince people that they are wrong is to let them have their own way.

Dates & Places Used:

170

TOPIC: Consequences

Which Foot in Mouth?

I don't mind so much saying something and putting my foot in my mouth as I do saying something and having someone else put his foot in my mouth.

Dates & Places Used:

171

TOPIC: Consequences

Cancer Cures

Cancer cures smoking.

Dates & Places Used:

172

When He Came to Himself

Here is a new twist on the prodigal son story: The rebellious young man wasted all that he had. He became so destitute that he had to sell his coat to buy bread. Then he had to sell his shirt to buy bread. The young man was still hungry, so he was forced to sell the rest of his clothing. And that is when he came to himself.

Dates & Places Used:

173

Perfect Example

A man was approached by a homeless man who asked for two dollars.

"Are you going to use this to buy booze?" the man asked.

"No, I'm not," the homeless man replied.

"Are you going to use it for gambling?"

The homeless man shook his head and said, "No."

"Are you going to use it to make bets at the golf course?"

"No, I don't golf," he answered.

The man was elated and asked the homeless man to come home with him and meet his wife. He then explained, "My wife needs to see what happens to a man who doesn't drink, gamble, or play golf."

Dates & Places Used:

174

Cheap Giving

The world's stingiest man went Christmas shopping, but everything he saw was too expensive except for a fifty-dollar vase that was on sale for two dollars because the handle had been broken off. He bought it and had the salesman ship it by mail so that his friend would think he had paid fifty dollars for it and that it had been broken in shipment.

A week after Christmas he received a thank you note from his friend. "Thank you for the lovely vase," the letter read. "It was so nice of you to wrap each piece separately."

Dates & Places Used:

175

TOPIC: Consideration

Too Many Barking Dogs

An apartment manager was showing a prospective tenant an apartment. The prospective tenant asked, "Are there any barking dogs in the adjoining apartments?"

The manager assured her, "Oh no! I would never allow such a thing."

The relieved woman sighed, "That's good, because I have two barking dogs of my own, and I don't think I could stand to hear any others."

Dates & Places Used:

176

TOPIC: Consideration

Nothing Good Enough

"Before we were married," remarked a wife, "you kept saying 'nothing is good enough for you.'"

"Yes dear," said the husband, "and I still think *nothing* is good enough for you."

Dates & Places Used:

177

TOPIC: Consideration

Tee Time for the Blind

A priest, a doctor, and an engineer were waiting one morning for a particularly slow group of golfers.

The engineer asked, "What's with these guys? We must have been waiting for fifteen minutes."

The doctor agreed. "I don't know, but I've never seen such ineptitude!"

The priest noted, "Hey, here comes the greens keeper. Let's have a word with him."

The priest called out to the greens keeper, "Say, George, what's with that group ahead of us?"

"They are rather slow, aren't they?" he answered. "Oh yes, that's a group of blind firefighters. They lost their sight saving our clubhouse from a fire last year, so we always let them play for free."

The group was silent for a moment.

The priest sympathized, "That's so sad. I think I'll say a special prayer for them tonight."

The doctor added, "That's a good idea. I'm going to contact my ophthalmologist buddy and see if there is anything we can do for those guys."

The engineer suggested, "Well, in the meantime, why can't these guys play at night?"

Dates & Places Used:

178 TOPIC: Consideration

Finding Your Way

A couple were returning to their seats in a theater after the intermission. The man asked a man at the end of the row, "Did I step on your toes as I went out?"

"You certainly did," the man answered grimly, waiting for an apology.

The man turned to his wife and exclaimed, "Here, honey, this is our row."

Dates & Places Used:

179

TOPIC: Consideration

All Taste the Same

A Persian in the market in Old Jerusalem bought a packet of pecans and handed a pecan to his wife, who was dutifully following him around.

After a while, she asked for another.

"What for?" he replied. "They all taste the same."

Dates & Places Used:

180

TOPIC: Consistency

Plant Doctor

Never go to a doctor whose office plants have died. *(Erma Bombeck)*

Dates & Places Used:

181

TOPIC: Consistency

Lost Golf Ball

Two guys were playing golf. One never lost his ball, but the other kept losing one ball after another. The second fellow complained that the game was getting too expensive.

"Then you should get one of these balls," said the first fellow. "It's a ball that you can't lose. If you hit this ball into the rough, it makes a beeping noise that leads you right to it. If you hit this ball into the water, it floats. If it's getting late, this ball glows in the dark! I tell you, you can't lose it."

The man's golfing partner was indeed impressed and asked where the man got that wonderful golf ball.

The man answered him, "Oh, I just found it."

Dates & Places Used:

182

Trash Teamwork

Maybe you heard the story about the woman who was away for a few days at a teachers' convention. In the middle of the convention she suddenly remembered it was trash day, and she expressed her concern to her friend.

Her friend tried to calm her fears and reminded her that her husband was still at home and could certainly put out the trash by himself.

But the woman said, "You don't understand, it takes both of us to take out the trash. I can't carry it, and he can't remember it."

Dates & Places Used:

183

TOPIC: Cooperation

Wake-up Balls

A preacher was well into his sermon when he noticed his young son standing at the edge of the balcony. The boy was throwing little balls of paper onto the heads of people in the congregation.

The alarmed pastor was about to command his son to stop when the boy called out to his father encouragingly, "Don't worry, Dad; you just keep preaching, and I'll keep them awake!"

Dates & Places Used:

184

TOPIC: Courage

What You Need to Have Courage

There is an apocryphal account of two skeletons in the corner of a closet who were grumbling about the heat, the dust, and the boredom. "What are we staying here for anyhow?" one asked.

"I don't know," the second skeleton answered. "I'd leave here in a minute if I had any guts."

Dates & Places Used:

185

TOPIC: Courage

Wild Adventures

A little boy came running into the kitchen and hurriedly asked his mother if he could watch a wildlife special on the public television station. "Hurry, Mom! It's got lions and tigers and snakes and all kinds of wild animals. Please, Mom, can I watch it?"

"Well, sure, son," his mother answered. "You know it's all right to watch that station. And that sounds like a wonderful show for a brave little guy like you to watch."

"Will you come watch it with me?" the little boy asked.

"I'm sorry, but Mommy is kind of busy right now."

"But Mom, you've got to watch it with me – I'm too scared to watch it by myself."

That's the way with life. There are a lot of exciting things to do out there. There are many unique and adventurous opportunities. It's just that we want someone to keep us company throughout the adventure. God has not forgotten us; God has not left us.

Dates & Places Used:

186

TOPIC: Courage

Ostrich Safety

Two ostriches were standing side by side, their heads in holes in the ground. One ostrich said to the other, "How should I know if it's safe yet?"

How prophetic. Denial never gets you anywhere. No matter what the problem in your life, if you keep your head buried in the sand and fail to admit that there is a problem, you will never find a solution. It takes courage and faith to look the problems of life in the eye. Christ helps us face our personal problems and overcome them.

Dates & Places Used:

187

TOPIC: Credibility

Chocolate Advantage

A report from the Princeton Dental Resource Center said chocolate is actually beneficial in fighting plaque and cavities. Before you get all excited, further investigation showed that 90 percent of the funds for this particular study were provided by M&M Mars candy company.

Dates & Places Used:

188

TOPIC: Credibility

Suspicious Mother

In the cartoon *Herman*, by James Unger, we see the husband handing the phone to his wife and saying, "Here, tell your mother we're out. She won't believe me."

Dates & Places Used:

189

TOPIC: Criticism

Taking Advice

If one person calls you a jackass or a donkey, pay no attention to him. But if five people call you one, go out and buy yourself a saddle.

Dates & Places Used:

TOPIC: Criticism

Variable Temperatures

A restaurant patron seemed particularly bothered about the temperature in a restaurant. He complained to his waiter that it was too cold and asked the waiter to turn down the air conditioner. The waiter told the patron he would do so immediately. A few minutes later the patron complained that it was now too hot. The waiter apologized and told the irate patron that he would make a slighter adjustment to the air conditioner.

These temperature complaints and slight adjustments happened several more times during the course of the evening. A man at another table asked the waiter how he could be so patient with the constantly changing whims of this dissatisfied patron.

The waiter shrugged his shoulders and said that it was simple. "By the way," the waiter added, "this restaurant does not even have an air conditioner!"

Dates & Places Used:

TOPIC: Criticism

Qualified to Complain

When reaching his plane seat, a man was surprised to see a parrot strapped in next to him. He asked the flight attendant for a coffee, whereupon the parrot squawked, "And get me a whiskey, you lazy woman!" The flight attendant, flustered, brought back a whiskey for the parrot and forgot the coffee.

When her omission was pointed out to her, the parrot drained its glass and bawled, "Get me another whiskey—and make it snappy!"

Quite upset, the poor woman came back shaking with another whiskey but still no coffee.

Unaccustomed to such slackness, the man tried the parrot's approach. "I've asked you twice for a coffee! Go and get me that coffee or I'm going to throw you out of this plane!"

A moment later two burly flight attendants ran back to the man and the parrot. They took hold of them and threw them out of the airplane. As the parrot and the man plummeted toward the ground, the parrot said, "What's the matter with you, mister? I've never seen such rudeness from someone who can't fly!"

The parrot then flew away.

Dates & Places Used:

TOPIC: Dating

The Ideal Male Combination

"I'd be the happiest girl in the world if only I could combine the two men I'm dating," one girl said to a friend. "One of them is incredibly handsome, filthy rich, and wonderful to be around."

"And the other one?" her friend asked.

The girl concluded, "The other one wants to marry me."

Dates & Places Used:

TOPIC: Death

Child's Logic

A five-year-old girl came home from her grandmother's funeral in a car with her other grandmother. "Where did Grandma go?" she asked.

"We believe she went to be with God," the other grandmother replied.

"How old was she?" asked the girl.

"She was eighty years old," her grandmother replied.

"How old are you?"

"Eighty-three," said the grandmother.

The little girl thought a bit, then said, "I hope God hasn't forgotten you!"

Dates & Places Used:

194

TOPIC: Death

At the Noose

St. Thomas More, on the way to his execution, came to the scaffold and turned to the executioner and said, "Would you mind helping me up? I can get down by myself."
Dates & Places Used:

195

TOPIC: Death

Subscriber Expired

The editor of a small Missouri newspaper sent a notice to one Bill Jenkins that his subscription had expired. Back came a note with the reply, "So has Bill."
Dates & Places Used:

196

TOPIC: Death

What the Problem Was

A man had become quite sick and was now lying home in bed. His doctor had come to examine him and had brought with him another doctor for a consultation. After the examination, the doctors retired to the next room to discuss the sick man's condition. Quickly the man called for his young son and asked him to eavesdrop at the door and tell him what the doctors said. Later the man asked his son, "Well, son, what did they say?"

The boy, somewhat perplexed, replied, "Dad, I can't tell you that. I listened as hard as I could, but they used such big words that I can't remember much of it. All I could catch was when one doctor said, 'Well, I guess we'll find out what the problem really was at the autopsy.'"
Dates & Places Used:

197

TOPIC: Debts

Solution for Unpaid Bills

A husband and wife going through a pile of unpaid bills were unsure how they would ever get them paid off. The wife finally offered a solution: "The only fair thing to do is to flip a coin. Heads I spend less; tails you earn more."
Dates & Places Used:

198

TOPIC: Debts

Credit Philosophy

One Alaska storekeeper's philosophy regarding credit: "You ask for credit, we don't give it to you, you get mad. We give you credit, you don't pay, we get mad. Better that you get mad."
Dates & Places Used:

199

TOPIC: Debts

Revocable Award

When Brian McKnight was given a Blockbuster award for best male rhythm and blues artist, he said that he hoped Blockbuster would not change their minds and take the award back when they found out he owed about five hundred dollars in late charges.
Dates & Places Used:

200

TOPIC: Debts

Sliding Fees

When a lawyer tells you he has a sliding fee schedule, what he means is that after he bills you, it is financially hard to get back on your feet.
Dates & Places Used:

201

TOPIC: Debts

Another Collection Agency

A woman has finally figured out how to stop unsolicited "chance-of-a-lifetime" offers by telemarketers. She enthusiastically welcomes these calls by saying, "Oh, thank you so much for calling! I am so grateful that someone is still willing to sell me something. I thought you were just another collection agency."

Dates & Places Used:

202

TOPIC: Debts

Costly Advice

A lawyer's dog ran into a butcher shop and stole a roast. The butcher went to the lawyer's office and asked him, "If a dog is without a leash and steals a roast from my store, do I have the legal right to require payment for the meat that was taken from me?"

The lawyer answered the butcher, "Oh yes, absolutely."

"The dog was your dog, the meat was my meat, and–according to your own advice–you owe me ten dollars for the meat your dog took from me today."

The lawyer agreed with the butcher and immediately wrote the butcher a check for ten dollars.

A few days later the butcher received a letter from the lawyer. The butcher opened the envelope and found an invoice for sixty dollars for the lawyer's consultation fee.

Dates & Places Used:

203

TOPIC: Debts

Really Dead Debtors

My sermon for the morning was on the fifth petition of the Lord's Prayer: "Forgive us our debts as we forgive our debtors." The children are always excused just before my sermon for their own children's church, where the leaders use my text for their lesson. So during the course of the session they asked the children, "What is a debtor?"

Rachel, a five-year-old, responded, "It's someone who is really, really dead. There's dead and then there's really, really dead."
Dates & Places Used:

204

TOPIC: Deception

Best Liars

A little boy had a bad habit of lying. His mother had tried everything she knew to make him stop, but nothing seemed to work. The problem came to a head one day when he came home from school about an hour late. When questioned about his tardiness, the boy said he had stopped at the lake near his school to fish.

"Did you catch any fish?" his mother asked.

"Yes, about fifty," came the reply.

"Where are the fish?" the mother questioned.

"Well," he said, "some people were sitting on their porch, and they looked hungry, so I gave the fish to them."

The mother exploded, "You know that's not true! I've had it– we're going to talk to the preacher about this!"

So they went to the preacher's office, and the mother explained the problem to the minister while the boy waited outside.

"I think I have an idea," the pastor said. "I'll show him just how absurd it sounds to lie like that. Bring him in."

After the boy was seated, the pastor said, "Son, I want to tell you a story. After the service last Sunday, I was at the altar when suddenly I heard a strange sound. When I turned around to look, I saw a five-hundred-pound grizzly bear walking down the aisle toward me. He came right up to me and started choking the very life out of me. I would have been a goner, but just then from the side door came a five-pound Chihuahua. He ran up to the bear and started choking the life out of him. He then dragged the bear outside, dug a big hole, threw the bear into it, covered it up, and sat on top of that grave wagging his tail. Now son, do you believe that story?"

"Yes, sir," said the boy. "That was my dog!"
Dates & Places Used:

205

TOPIC: Deception

Distortion Details

Get your facts first, and then you can distort them as much as
you please. *(Mark Twain)*
Dates & Places Used:

206

TOPIC: Deception

Sand Smuggler

A man rode up to the border on his bicycle with two large
bags. The border patrol stopped the man to check his bags. The
bags contained sand. The border guards were confused and
asked, "What else is in the bags?"

The man answered, "Just sand."

The guards were not so sure. "We'll figure out what else is in
those bags. Get off the bike."

The border patrol took the bags and thoroughly searched
through them. They ripped the bags apart, emptied them, and
found nothing in them except sand.

The patrol detained the cyclist overnight and ran a chemical
analysis on the bags but determined that there was only common sand in the bags. The guards finally released the man.
They put the sand in new bags, returned the bags to the man,
and let him cross the border.

A week later the same thing happened. The patrol stopped the
cyclist and asked, "What's in the bags?"

"More sand," said the cyclist. The patrol made a thorough
investigation and discovered that these bags contained nothing
but sand. He gave the bags back to the man and sent him on his
way across the border on his bicycle. This routine continued
every day for several years. And then one day the cyclist never
returned.

Ten years later one of the guards happened to see the man on
the street. The guard approached the man and identified himself
in hopes of finding out what he had been carrying so many
years before. "I know you were smuggling something," said the

guard. "Now that it doesn't matter anymore, please tell me, what were you carrying in those bags?"

The man smiled at the guard and answered, "All those bags had in them was sand. I was smuggling bicycles."

Dates & Places Used:

207

TOPIC: Deception

Murder or Perjury

At a trial, the prosecuting attorney asked the defendant if he committed the murder.

The defendant said he did not.

The attorney then asked the man if he understood the penalty for perjury.

The man said, "I sure do! I understand the penalty for perjury is a lot less than the penalty for murder!"

Dates & Places Used:

208

TOPIC: Deception

Designated Decoy

A police officer was waiting across the street from a bar parking lot late on a Saturday night watching for drunks trying to drive home. After a short wait, one particularly sad case stumbled out the door with the front of his shirt soaked. He was bleary-eyed and confused as he wandered to the parking lot looking for his car. He finally located his car, fumbled for his keys, bumped his head while getting into the car, and drove off, bumping the curb on the way.

Of course the man didn't get very far before the police officer was on him, and he immediately pulled over. The police officer had him step out of the car and proceeded to administer several sobriety field tests. The driver seemed to have considerable difficulty understanding some of the tests. In fact, he failed all the tests miserably: he couldn't touch his nose, he couldn't walk straight, he couldn't stand on one foot, and he couldn't recite the alphabet quickly. The final legal step, of course, was the Breath-alyzer, so the police officer asked his subject to blow into the tube. The green light indicated that the man was not drunk. In disbelief, the police officer checked the Breathalyzer and had the suspect try again. Another green light–the guy's blood-alcohol level was legal.

"All right," said the police officer, "how can you pass a breath test when you're so obviously falling-down drunk?"

"Well, it's like this," replied the man. "I'm the designated decoy."

Dates & Places Used:

209

TOPIC: Deception

What Fish?

A man carrying two buckets of fish was stopped by a game warden while leaving a northern Michigan lake well known for its fishing. The game warden asked the man, "Do you have a license to catch those fish?"

The man replied, "No, sir. These are my pet fish."

"Pet fish," the warden repeated.

"Yes, sir. Every night I take these here fish down to the lake and let them swim around for a while. I whistle, they jump back into their buckets, and I take them home."

"That's a bunch of hooey! Fish can't do that!"

The man looked at the game warden for a moment and then said, "Here, I'll show you. It really works."

"Okay, I've got to see this!" The game warden was curious now.

The man poured the fish into the lake; then he stood patiently and waited. After several minutes the game warden turned to the man and said, "Well?"

"Well, what?" the man responded.

"When are you going to call them back?" the game warden prompted.

"Call what back?" the man inquired.

"The fish."

"What fish?" the man asked.

Dates & Places Used:

TOPIC: Deception

Bad Mommy!

A young man was walking through a supermarket to pick up a few items when he noticed an old lady following him around. Thinking nothing of it, he ignored her and continued on. Finally, he went to the checkout line, but she got in front of him.

"Pardon me," she said. "I'm sorry if my staring at you has made you feel uncomfortable. It's just that you look just like my son who died recently."

"I'm very sorry," replied the young man. "Is there anything I can do for you?"

"Yes," she said. "As I'm leaving, can you say, 'Good-bye, Mother'? It would make me feel so much better."

"Sure," answered the young man. As the old woman was leaving, he called out, "Good-bye, Mother!"

Then as he stepped back to the checkout counter, he saw that his total was $127.50. "How can that be?" he asked. "I only purchased a few things!"

"Your mother said that you would pay for her," said the clerk.

Dates & Places Used:

TOPIC: Decisions

Yes or No

During a flight on a commercial airline, the flight attendant asked a passenger if he would like dinner.

The passenger asked, "What are my choices?"

The flight attendant answered, "Your choices are 'yes' and 'no.'"

Dates & Places Used:

212

Dismal Crossroads

Civilization stands at the crossroads. Down one road is despondency and despair, and down the other is total annihilation. Let us pray that we choose the right road. *(Woody Allen)*
Dates & Places Used:

213

Bread and Water with Ketchup

Two little boys were visiting their grandfather, and the grandfather took them to a restaurant for lunch. They couldn't make up their minds about what they wanted to eat. Finally, the grandfather grinned at the server and said, "Just bring them bread and water."

One of the little boys looked up and asked, "Can I have ketchup on it?"
Dates & Places Used:

214

Perspective Helps Decisions

The easiest thing to decide is what you'd do if you were in someone else's shoes.
Dates & Places Used:

215

TOPIC: Denominations

Bury All the Baptists

Years ago there were two churches in a certain community, a Methodist church and a Baptist church.

The Baptists were temporarily without a pastor when a church deacon died. The family asked the Methodist pastor if he would conduct the funeral service.

This was the Methodist pastor's first year in the ministry, and he felt he needed approval from the bishop of the area. So he sent a telegram asking, "May I have approval to bury a Baptist deacon?"

The bishop quickly replied with a telegram that read, "Bury all the Baptists you can!"

Dates & Places Used:

216

TOPIC: Denominations

Private Prayer

The Catholic church's air conditioning broke down, so they had to hire a man to crawl around in the ducts and figure out what was wrong. As the man peeked down through one of the vents above the sanctuary, he saw his elderly neighbor kneeling by the altar apparently saying her rosary. The man just could not resist the temptation to mess with this poor woman's mind. In his most authoritative voice, he said, "This is Jesus. Your prayers will be answered."

The little old lady didn't even blink; she just kept on saying her prayers. The man decided maybe she didn't hear him, and so he tried again. "This is Jesus, the Son of God! Your prayers will be answered!"

Again, she didn't react at all. Mustering up a big breath of air, the man decided to try one more time. He loudly repeated, "This is Jesus Christ, the Son of God! Your prayers will be answered!"

The elderly woman looked up and said, "Young man, I am trying to talk to your mother!"

Dates & Places Used:

217

TOPIC: Denominations

Rabbi's Ham at the Priest's Wedding

A Catholic priest and a Jewish rabbi were sitting together at a banquet. The priest asked the rabbi, "Tell me, when are you going to break down and eat a little ham?"

The rabbi answered, "At your wedding!"

Dates & Places Used:

218

TOPIC: Denominations

Bingo Prayer

Two atheists were flying in a single-engine airplane when it was struck by lightning. Faced with certain death, the atheists grasped for hope and turned to God. Their problem was that they didn't know how to reach out to God. One asked the other, "How are we going to have God help us if we do not know how to pray?"

The other atheist answered, "Listen, I live next to a Catholic church. I've listened to them pray many times. Let's pray one of their prayers." So he began praying: "B5 ... N14 ... B1 ..."

Dates & Places Used:

219

TOPIC: Desire

Too Long until Sundae

A little girl was asked by her mother if she would like an ice cream sundae. The daughter replied, "I don't want to wait until Sunday. I want ice cream *now!*"

Dates & Places Used:

220

Getting What You Want

"Be careful," runs the old saying, "or you may get what you want."

One who would agree was a tailor who lived in a squalid tenement on a side street in East Boston. He worked long hours each day to eke out a meager existence. He allowed himself but one luxury–a ticket each year to the Irish Sweepstakes. And each year he prayed fervently that this would be the winning ticket that would bring him his fortune.

For fourteen years this man's life continued in the same impoverished vein, until one day there came a loud knocking on his door. Two well-dressed gentlemen entered his shop and informed him that he had just won the Irish Sweepstakes. The grand prize was $250,000!

The tailor could hardly believe his ears. He was rich! No longer would he have to slave away cuffing pants and hemming dresses. Now he could really live! He locked his shop and threw the key into the Charles River. He bought himself a wardrobe fit for a king, a new Rolls Royce, and a suite of rooms at the Ritz. And soon he was dating a string of attractive women.

Night after night the man partied until dawn, spending his money as if each day were his last. Of course the inevitable happened: He ran out of money and nearly destroyed his health. Disillusioned, ridden with fever, and exhausted, he returned to his little shop and set up business once more. And from force of habit, once again each year he set aside from his meager savings the price of a sweepstakes ticket.

Two years later there came a second knock at his door. The same two gentlemen stood there once again. "This is the most incredible thing in the history of the sweepstakes!" exclaimed one. "You have won again!"

The tailor staggered to his feet with a groan. "Oh no!" he protested. "Do you mean I have to go through all that again?"

Dates & Places Used:

221

Slightly Wrong

Two farmers were chatting in front of the bank. "I hear you made sixty thousand dollars in alfalfa," said the first.

Not wishing to be impolite, his friend replied, "Well, that isn't quite right. It wasn't me; it was my brother. It wasn't alfalfa; it was oats. It wasn't sixty thousand dollars; it was six thousand dollars. And he didn't make it; he lost it."

Dates & Places Used:

222

Blow the Dents Out

A young driver was driving his car home and got caught in a bad hailstorm. His car was covered with dents. He took the car to the body shop to see how much it would cost to repair. He was dismayed with the news. The cost of repairs was just too high. He told the estimator that he could not afford the cost of the body work and asked if there was any other way to fix the car.

The estimator thought he would have a little fun with the young fellow. He told him that there was a possibility that he could take the dents out by blowing into the tailpipe as hard as he could. The pressure might just pop out the dents.

So the young man went home, waited for the car to cool off, and then blew into the tailpipe as hard as he could. He hoped the pressure would pop out the dents. He kept trying, but no dents seemed to be popping out.

The young man's father came home and saw him blowing on the tailpipe and asked what he was doing. The boy explained to his father what the estimator had told him. The father started laughing and told his son that he had been fooled by the estimator.

The young man was embarrassed and asked what was wrong with trying to fix the car this way. His father answered, "That should be obvious, son. You can't pop the dents out by blowing through the tailpipe like that. First you have to roll up the windows!"

Dates & Places Used:

223

First Golf Lesson

A retiree was given a set of golf clubs by his coworkers. Thinking he would try the game, he asked the local pro for lessons, explaining that he knew nothing about the game.

The pro showed him the stance and swing, then said, "Just hit the ball toward the flag on the first green."

The novice teed up and smacked the ball straight down the fairway and onto the green, where it stopped inches from the hole.

"Now what?" the fellow asked the speechless pro.

"Uh ... you're supposed to hit the ball into the cup," the pro finally said after he was able to speak again.

"Oh great! *Now* you tell me!" said the beginner in a disgusted tone.

Dates & Places Used:

224

Crash Course in Integration

Making a right turn off the main highway onto a narrow two-lane road, I skidded on the gravel and wound up just short of hitting a stopped car. I expected an angry reaction from the occupants, a group of African American laborers leaving a nearby construction job. But the driver's comment was good-humored: "Man, we do want to integrate, but not quite that fast!"

Dates & Places Used:

225

Heaven or Hell

Heaven is where the Germans run the factories, the Italians are the police, the French do the cooking, the Dutch sweep the floors, and the British write the poetry and love songs.

Hell is where the Italians run the factories, the Germans are the police, the French sweep the floors, the British do the cooking, and the Dutch write the poetry and love songs.
Dates & Places Used:

226

TOPIC: Direction

Bat Turn

Two vampire bats were ready to go out feeding for the night. The first bat took off to get an early start. Moments later he returned with blood all over his mouth. The second bat was astounded and asked, "How did you find so much blood so quickly?"

The first bat responded, "You know how when you leave the cave you fly to the right and are gone for the rest of the evening?"

"Sure," said the second bat.

"Well," continued the first bat, "if you turn to the left, there is a wall!"
Dates & Places Used:

227

TOPIC: Direction

Misplaced Mountain

After a half day of climbing a range of mountains, a party of climbers came to the realization that they were lost. They took turns studying the map, and each tried to figure out where they were. One of the climbers began to match up the surrounding landmarks with the ones shown on the map as he confirmed his findings with his compass. After careful charting, he announced to the others, "See that big mountain over there?"

"Yes," answered his fellow climbers eagerly.

"According to the map, we're standing on top of it."
Dates & Places Used:

228

Height or Length

Two men were measuring a pole. One was holding it up, and the other was trying to run the tape up it. A man driving by saw what these two were trying to do, and he pulled up alongside them and asked, "Why don't you lay the pole down so it will be easier to measure?"

So the two men laid down the pole and began measuring. As soon as the man drove off, one of the fellows said to the other, "Put that pole back up the way it was; I wanted to measure the height of the pole, not the length."

Dates & Places Used:

229

TOPIC: Direction

Easier Direction

Two Georgia hunters were dragging their dead deer back to their car. A South Carolina hunter approached pulling his along too. "Hey, I don't want to tell you fellows what to do, but I can tell you that it's easier if you drag the deer in the other direction. Then the antlers won't dig into the ground."

After the third hunter left, the two decided to try it. A little while later one hunter said to the other, "You know, that guy was right. This is a lot easier!"

"Yeah," the other added, "but we're getting farther away from the truck!"

Dates & Places Used:

230

TOPIC: Direction

Direction Prioritized

It is more important to know where you are going than to see how fast you can get there.

Dates & Places Used:

231

Tie Up Loose Ends

A guest speaker was speaking at a small church. Prior to the adult sermon, he gave the children's message. He asked the children to tell some of the ways they were disciplined when they misbehaved.

The speaker was not sure what one of the boys in the group said, but it may have been "time out." At the time, however, it sounded like the boy said, "They tie me up."

The speaker was taken by surprise by what he thought he had heard. He turned to the boy and gasped, "What–they tie you up?"

The congregation was laughing so loudly that the speaker never did learn what the boy really said. Maybe the boy did get tied up.

Dates & Places Used:

232

TOPIC: Discipline

Strategic Name Change

I had just put my little boy to bed for the umpteenth time and my patience was running out. When I heard him cry "Mama" again, I yelled to him, "If I hear you say 'Mama' one more time, I'm going to spank you."

For a little while, all was quiet. Then I heard a little voice whisper, "Mrs. Green, can I have a drink?"

Dates & Places Used:

233

TOPIC: Discipline

Familial Enemies

Little Anne had been exceedingly naughty, and during the dinner hour she was forced to eat alone in the corner at a card table. When everyone was seated, Father bowed his head and gave thanks.

Then little Anne gravely bowed her head and said, "Thank you, dear Lord, for preparing a table before me in the presence of my enemies."
Dates & Places Used:

234

TOPIC: Discovery

Disorderly Delights

One of the advantages of being disorderly is that one is constantly making exciting discoveries. *(A. A. Milne)*
Dates & Places Used:

235

TOPIC: Discovery

Federal Ostrich Studies

Word has it there was a federally funded grant to discover why ostriches have such long necks. After thousands of dollars were spent, the discovery was made: The reason ostriches have such long necks is that their heads are so far from their bodies!
Dates & Places Used:

236

TOPIC: Divorce

Marriage Enlistment

Marriage is like the army. Everybody complains, but you would be surprised at how many reenlist.
Dates & Places Used:

237

TOPIC: Divorce

Barbie Gets Divorced

A man was driving home from work and suddenly remembered that it was his daughter's birthday and that he had not bought her a gift. He turned his car around and headed for the store. He asked the store clerk how much a Barbie doll costs. The store clerk inquired, "It depends. Do you want the Barbie Goes to the Gym for $19.95, the Barbie Goes to the Beach for $19.95, the Barbie Goes Shopping for $24.95, the Barbie Goes to the Ball for $19.95, or the Barbie Gets Divorced for $249.95?"

"Wait a minute!" the father exclaimed. "Why is the Barbie Gets Divorced selling for so much more than the others?"

The clerk answered, "The Barbie Gets Divorced comes with Ken's car, Ken's house, Ken's boat, and Ken's furniture."

Dates & Places Used:

238

TOPIC: Divorce

Never Hated That Much

I never hated a man enough to give him his diamonds back. *(Zsa Zsa Gabor)*

Dates & Places Used:

239

TOPIC: Doctors

Death from Waiting

An elderly man went to the doctor's office for his 2:00 P.M. appointment. After three hours of waiting, he got up to leave. As he passed the nurse, he told her, "I guess I'll go home and just die a natural death."

Dates & Places Used:

240

TOPIC: Doctors

Second Opinion

My doctor gave me six months to live, but when I couldn't pay the bill, he gave me six months more. *(Walter Matthau)*
Dates & Places Used:

241

TOPIC: Doctors

Doctors, Professors, and Mechanics

A professor watched while a mechanic removed engine parts from his car to get to the valves. A surgeon waiting for his car being repaired walked over to observe the process.

After the two introduced themselves, they began to chat and the conversation turned to their lines of work. "You know, Doctor," said the professor, "I sometimes believe this type of work is as complicated as the work we do."

"Perhaps, but let's see him do it when the engine is running."
Dates & Places Used:

242

TOPIC: Doctors

Doctors and Shingles

One man walked into a doctor's office, and the receptionist asked him what he had. He told her he had shingles. So the receptionist took down his name, address, and medical insurance information and told him to have a seat.

A little while later a nurse's aide came out and asked the man what he had. He told her he had shingles. She wrote down his vital statistics such as height, weight, and medical history and then told him to wait in an examining room.

A long while later a nurse entered the examining room and asked the man what he had. He told the nurse that he had shingles. So the nurse took the man's blood pressure and drew some of his blood for a blood test. She then told him to take off all his clothes and wait for the doctor.

About an hour later the doctor came into the room and asked the man what he had. The man told the doctor that he had shingles. The doctor examined the man and found no such symptoms. The bewildered doctor asked the man where he had shingles.

The man answered, "They're out in the truck. Where do you want me to put them?"

Dates & Places Used:

243

TOPIC: Doctors

Standing for the Doctor

A little girl went to the doctor for a preschool physical examination. The doctor examined her and then did some coordination tests. While testing the girl's coordination, the doctor asked, "Could you stand on one foot for me now?"

"Sure!" the girl answered as she stood on the doctor's foot.

Dates & Places Used:

244

TOPIC: Drinking

Unrighteous Indignation

A pastor answered his telephone and heard a woman's voice request, "Please have six cases of whiskey sent to my house. We're having a party."

Inadvertently, she had dialed the wrong number, and the pastor recognized the voice as that of one of his parishioners. Gently he replied, "I am your pastor."

He had expected an apology for her dialing the wrong number. Instead, she retorted in an angry voice, "Well, pastor, what are you doing at the liquor store?"

Dates & Places Used:

245

TOPIC: Drinking

Whiskey and a Snake

W. C. Fields once said, "Always carry a flagon of whiskey in case of snakebite, and furthermore always carry a small snake."
Dates & Places Used:

246

TOPIC: Drinking

Mommy Hits the Bottle

While a woman was attempting to get ketchup out of a bottle, the phone rang. She asked her four-year-old daughter to answer the phone for her.

"Mommy, it's the pastor," the child told her mother.

The woman told her daughter to tell the pastor she would call him back.

The little girl told the pastor what her mother had said, and then she added, "She can't come to the phone right now because she's hitting the bottle."
Dates & Places Used:

247

TOPIC: Drinking

Wake-up Call

A man was pulled over by a police officer for speeding. As the officer was explaining to the driver that he was speeding, she noticed several large daggers in the backseat.

"What are you doing with those?" she asked suspiciously.

"I'm a juggler," said the man. "I need those daggers in my act."

Still suspicious, the officer requested, "Well, show me." So the juggler reached for the daggers and started juggling them. He stood in front of his car juggling six daggers at one time—overhand, underhand, behind the back. He was putting on quite a show for the amazed officer.

While he was performing, another car passed by. The driver did a double take and then said, "I'm not ever drinking again for the rest of my life! I could never pass these new sobriety tests!"

Dates & Places Used:

248

TOPIC: Drinking

Unhealthy Drunk

A man left a bar, got into his car, and drove away. He was soon stopped by a police officer.

The officer explained that he was testing drivers to determine whether they were driving under the influence of alcohol. "Would you please blow into this machine?"

The driver answered, "I'm sorry, I can't do that. I have asthma. If I blow into that machine, I'll have an asthma attack."

The officer then said, "Then please come along with me to the station so I can give you a blood test."

The man still protested, "I can't do that. I'm a hemophiliac. If you stick a needle in me, I will bleed to death."

The officer suggested a third alternative: "Then just get out of the car and walk five yards along this white line."

The man responded, "I'm afraid I can't do that either."

The officer asked, "And why can't you do that?"

The man answered, "Because I'm too drunk."

Dates & Places Used:

249

TOPIC: Drinking

Golf and Scotch

The people of Scotland invented golf, which might explain why they also invented Scotch.

Dates & Places Used:

250

Spiritual Gatherings

A preacher was finishing a temperance sermon, and with passion he concluded, "If I had all the beer in the world, I'd take it and throw it into the river."

With even greater emphasis he said, "And if I had all the wine in the world, I'd take it and throw it into the river."

Then finally, he said, "And if I had all the whiskey in the world, I'd take it and throw it into the river."

As the preacher sat down, the song leader stood very cautiously and announced with a smile, "In closing, let's all stand and sing the hymn 'Shall We Gather at the River?'"

Dates & Places Used:

251

TOPIC: Drinking

An Inopportune Drink

Two cars collided on a curving country road. The drivers got out and exchanged information in a gentlemanly way. Then one driver took out a flask and said, "Look, fellow, you seem pretty shaken up. How about a drink to steady your nerves?"

The other man took a big swig and asked, "Aren't you going to have any?"

The other driver responded, "Not now. Not until after the police get here."

Dates & Places Used:

252

TOPIC: Driving

Peaceful Way to Go

A group of junior high students was asked to write down their thoughts about death. One student wrote, "When it is my time to die, I want to die in my sleep like my grandfather did. I would

hate to die screaming in panic like the passengers in Grandfather's car did."
Dates & Places Used:

253 TOPIC: Driving

Night Driver

Two older women were talking about a mutual friend who had recently married.

One woman asked, "Is he rich?"

The other woman said, "No, she told me he was not well-off at all."

"Is he good-looking?" the woman asked.

"No, he is rather plain."

"Well, then, why did she marry him?"

"The best I can figure, she married him because he can drive at night."

Dates & Places Used:

254 TOPIC: Easter

Make Room for the Easter Crowd

Two women dressed to the hilt in their Easter finery were making slow progress in the crowd headed for the church entrance. Finally, one of them burst out impatiently, "Now wouldn't you think that these people who do nothing but go to church Sunday after Sunday would stay home on Easter and leave room for the rest of us?"

Dates & Places Used:

255

Signs of Our Times

In case you don't think we live in times of spiritual ignorance, note this item from *Leadership* magazine. A Denver woman told her pastor of a recent experience that she felt was indicative of the times in which we live. She was in a jewelry store looking for a necklace and said to the clerk, "I'd like a gold cross." The man behind the counter looked over the stock in the display case and said, "Do you want a plain one or one with a little man on it?"

Dates & Places Used:

256

TOPIC: Education

Education or Experience

The difference between education and experience: Education is what you get from reading the small print. Experience is what you get from not reading it.

Dates & Places Used:

257

TOPIC: Education

Education or Ignorance

If you think a good education is too expensive, consider the alternative: ignorance.

Dates & Places Used:

258

TOPIC: Education

Hitting the Books

Two fathers were discussing how each of their sons was doing in college. One father said, "My son is so smart that when he writes home I have to go to the dictionary."

"You're lucky," the other father replied. "When my son writes home, I have to go to the checkbook."

Dates & Places Used:

TOPIC: Education

259

Ignorance Is Bliss

Shortly before his death, former Chief Justice Melville W. Fuller was presiding at a church conference. During the heated debate, a delegate rose and began a tirade against universities and education, giving thanks to God that he had not been corrupted by contact with any college.

"Do I understand the speaker to be thanking God for his ignorance?" interrupted Chief Justice Fuller.

"Well, yes, if you want to put it that way," the man answered.

"All I have to say then," responded the chief justice, "is that you have a great deal to be thankful for."

Dates & Places Used:

TOPIC: Education

260

Sweep the Store

A young man applied for a job at a supermarket. The manager said, "Yes, I'll give you a job. Sweep out the store."

"But," said the young applicant, "I'm a college graduate."

The manager quietly replied, "Oh, that's all right. I'll show you how."

Dates & Places Used:

TOPIC: Education

261

Halfway Through

Once while preaching in David Spencer's church in Long Beach, Mississippi, New Orleans Seminary professor Dr. Vernon

Stanfield said, "I studied to be a wit while I was in school, but, as my wife will tell you, I only got halfway through."
Dates & Places Used:

262

TOPIC: Education

College Teaches Everyone

Sending a youngster to college these days is very educational. It teaches parents how to do without a lot of things.
Dates & Places Used:

263

TOPIC: Education

Self-Taught Teachers

Self-taught people may be very successful, but only if they have excellent teachers.
Dates & Places Used:

264

TOPIC: Effectiveness

Quite Organized

A soldier smashed his thumb and went to the infirmary. He went through a series of doors: Illness/Injury–External/Internal; Surgery/Therapy–Major/Minor. The last door put him out back behind the infirmary.

A friend asked him, "Did they help you?"

The soldier answered, "No, but they sure are organized!"
Dates & Places Used:

265

Revealing Photo

The following incident was reported as a true story by an embarrassed mother:

I was taking a shower when my two-year-old son came into the bathroom and wrapped himself in toilet paper. Although he made a mess, he looked adorable, so I ran for my camera and took a few shots. They came out so well that I had copies made and included one with each of our Christmas cards. Days later, a relative called about the picture, laughing hysterically and suggesting I take a closer look. Puzzled, I stared at the photo and was shocked to discover that in addition to my son, I had captured my reflection in the mirror—wearing nothing but a camera!

Dates & Places Used:

TOPIC: Embarrassment

266

Sock in the Mouth

A young couple decided to wed. As the big day approached, they grew apprehensive. Each had a problem he or she had never before shared with anyone, not even each other.

The groom-to-be, overcoming his fear, decided to ask his father for advice. "Dad," he said, "I am deeply concerned about the success of my marriage."

His father replied, "Don't you love this girl?"

"Oh yes, very much," he said. "But you see, I have very smelly feet, and I'm afraid she won't want to sleep in the same room with me."

"No problem," said the dad. "All you have to do is never take off your shoes until right before bed, and then always put on new clean socks and wear them to bed."

Well, this seemed to the son to be a workable solution.

The bride-to-be, overcoming her fear, decided to take up her problem with her mother. "Mom," she said, "when I wake up in the morning my breath is truly awful."

"Honey," her mother consoled, "everyone has bad breath in the morning."

"No, you don't understand. My morning breath is so bad, I'm afraid my husband won't want to sleep in the same room with me."

Her mother said simply, "Try this: In the morning, get straight out of bed and head for the kitchen and make coffee. While your husband is busy, move on to the bathroom and brush your teeth. The key is not to say a word until you've brushed your teeth."

"I shouldn't say good morning or anything?" the daughter asked.

"Not a word," her mother affirmed.

Well, it's certainly worth a try, the daughter thought.

The loving couple were finally married. Not forgetting the advice each had received—he with his perpetual socks and she with her morning silence—they managed quite well. That is, until about six months later.

Shortly before dawn one morning, the husband awakened with a start to find that one of his socks had come off. Fearful of the consequences, he frantically searched the bed. This, of course, awakened his bride, and without thinking, she asked, "What on earth are you doing?"

"Oh no," he replied, "you've swallowed my sock!"

Dates & Places Used:

267

TOPIC: Encouragement

How's Your Wife?

Randy and Dan hadn't seen each other for over a year. They bumped into each other after a football game.

Randy: "And how is your wife?"

Dan: "My wife has gone to heaven."

Randy: "Oh, I'm so sorry." Then realizing that wasn't the appropriate response, he countered by saying, "I guess I mean I'm glad." That didn't sound quite right either, so he said, "I mean I'm so surprised!"

Dates & Places Used:

268

TOPIC: Enthusiasm

Excitement or Resurrection

A preacher was visiting with his congregation after the Sunday morning service when a determined-looking woman approached him. Obviously displeased, she said, "Pastor, as a member of the pulpit committee, I was hoping that your sermons would excite our congregation."

The new pastor replied, "You're right, I did say I could excite this congregation, but I did not say I could raise them from the dead!"

Dates & Places Used:

269

TOPIC: Evangelism

Waiting Too Long

A minister waited in line to have his car filled with gas just before a long holiday weekend. The attendant worked quickly, but there were many cars ahead of the minister.

Finally, the attendant motioned him toward a vacant pump. "Reverend," said the young man, "sorry about the delay. It seems as if everyone waits until the last minute to get ready for a long trip."

The minister chuckled, "I know what you mean. It's the same in my business."

Dates & Places Used:

270

TOPIC: Exaggeration

An Oral Exaggeration

A man with a toothache went to the dentist. "I have a huge cavity!" he said. The doctor, seeing only a moderate amount of decay, assured him, "It will only be a small filling."

"But why does it feel so large?" the patient asked.

"Just the natural tendency of the tongue to exaggerate, I guess," replied the dentist with a twinkle in his eye.

Dates & Places Used:

271

TOPIC: Exaggeration

A Car like That

A Texan drove into a gas station in the hills of Tennessee. He was wearing a ten-gallon hat and fancy cowboy boots, he had diamond rings on both hands, and he was puffing a king-sized cigar. "Fill 'er up!" he yelled at the attendant as he strolled inside.

Sitting over to one side of the room on a keg was a Tennessee farmer.

"Live around here?" asked the Texan.

"Yep," the farmer answered, "that's my place across the road."

"Oh, it is?" said the Texan condescendingly. "Well, tell me, how many acres have you got?"

"Oh, about eighty acres, more or less."

"Only eighty acres?" scoffed the Texan. "Well, let me tell you about my place. Why, I get in my car early in the morning and start driving in a straight line, and by noon I haven't even reached the other side! Now what about that?"

"Yep, I know what you mean," the Tennessee farmer replied. "I used to have a car like that myself."

Dates & Places Used:

272

TOPIC: Excellence

The Way They Used To

Another thing they don't make like they used to is people who can fix 'em like they used to!

Dates & Places Used:

273

TOPIC: Excellence

Anything for a Grade

Early in the semester a student stopped by during the professor's office hours.

He bid her enter.

She glanced up and down the hall, stepped in, closed the door, and said, "I would do anything to pass this class."

She stepped closer to his desk, flipped back her hair, and gazed into his eyes. "I mean," she whispered, "I would do ... anything."

He returned her gaze. "Anything?"

"Anything!" she replied.

The professor's voice dropped to a whisper, and he said, "Would you ... study?"

Dates & Places Used:

274

TOPIC: Excuses

Dead Excuse

A young Palermo man arrested for stealing a car had the year's most novel excuse. He'd found the automobile in front of a cemetery, he explained, and thought the owner was dead.

Dates & Places Used:

275

TOPIC: Excuses

Previous Giving

Here's the perfect answer when you are hit up for a donation by a Hare Krishna at the airport: "I gave in a previous lifetime."

Dates & Places Used:

276

Clever Excuses

As a teenage boy was trying to sneak his date back into her home—very late—they were met by a very angry father at the head of the stairs. He boomed out, "Young man, didn't I hear the clock strike four when you brought my daughter home?"

The clever boy replied, "Yes, sir, you did. It was going to strike eleven, but I grabbed it and held the gong so it wouldn't disturb you."

The father muttered, "Doggone it! Why didn't I think of that in my day?"

Dates & Places Used:

277

Defensive Speeding

One man gave the perfect reason for speeding when he was pulled over by a state highway patrolman. He said, "But officer, I wasn't speeding; I was just trying to stay a safe distance ahead of that truck in back of me."

Dates & Places Used:

278

Can We Deceive God?

When our son was in grade school, his route home from school each day took him by an irrigation canal. Because it is not uncommon for youngsters to drown in open waterways, he had been instructed repeatedly not to play around the canal on his way home. One afternoon Jimmy came in later than usual. His pants were wet and muddy, and he was carrying his shoes. He obviously had been in the forbidden canal.

His mother asked the expected question: "Have you been in the canal?"

He had obviously prepared himself for this interrogation and answered, "Yes, ma'am, but I didn't do it on purpose. I just fell in accidentally."

Based on the evidence at hand, his mother then asked, "How is it that if you fell in accidentally, you didn't get your shoes and socks wet?" Quick as a wink, he came back, "Well, I just barely had time to get 'em off before I hit the water!"

Dates & Places Used:

279

TOPIC: Excuses

Seeing-Eye Chihuahua

A guy with a Doberman pinscher said to a guy with a Chihuahua, "Let's go over to that restaurant and get something to eat."

The guy with the Chihuahua said, "We can't go in there. We have dogs with us."

"Just follow my lead," said the guy with the Doberman.

So they walked over to the restaurant, and the guy with the Doberman put on a pair of dark glasses and started to enter.

"Sorry, no pets allowed," said the doorman.

The Doberman owner said, "You don't understand. This is my seeing-eye dog."

"A Doberman pinscher?"

"Yes, they're using them now; they're very good."

"Come on in, then," said the doorman.

The guy with the Chihuahua figured, "Oh well, why not?" So he put on a pair of dark glasses and started to walk in.

"Sorry, pal, no pets allowed," said the doorman.

The Chihuahua owner said, "You don't understand. This is my seeing-eye dog."

"A Chihuahua?"

"What?" said the guy. "You mean they gave me a Chihuahua?"

Dates & Places Used:

280

TOPIC: Excuses

We All Manufacture

We are all manufacturers–some make good, others make trouble, and still others make excuses.
Dates & Places Used:

281

TOPIC: Exercise

Tai Chi

Tai Chi is a popular Chinese exercise that is similar to standing still, only faster.
Dates & Places Used:

282

TOPIC: Exercise

Age-Old Bargain

A woman was more athletically inclined than her husband and frequently engaged in biking, canoeing, and other strenuous activities. Several years ago, when her husband was sixty, he came inside after a day of yard work and collapsed into his favorite easy chair, bemoaning the aches and pains of his advancing age.

Attempting to comfort him, the woman reminded her husband that when they were newlyweds, they had looked forward to growing old together.

"Yes," he replied, "but you haven't kept your end of the bargain."
Dates & Places Used:

283

TOPIC: Exercise

Far-Reaching Weight Loss

A doctor recommended a way to lose weight to his patient–run five miles a day for the next hundred days and lose fifty pounds.

One hundred days later, the patient called his doctor and complained that he did not like this weight-loss program.

The doctor asked the patient if he had lost fifty pounds.

The patient said that he had.

"So what's the problem?" asked the doctor.

The patient answered, "The problem is that I am five hundred miles from home."

Dates & Places Used:

284

TOPIC: Exercise

Working Out Revenge

Those who are "workout-challenged" can take comfort in the fact that every five minutes of every single day someone in an exercise class pulls a muscle.

Dates & Places Used:

285

TOPIC: Exercise

Folly of Fitness

My grandmother started walking five miles a day when she was sixty. She's ninety-seven now, and we don't know where she is.

The only reason I would take up jogging is so that I could hear heavy breathing again.

I joined a health club last year. Spent about four hundred bucks. Haven't lost a pound. Apparently you have to show up.

I have to exercise in the morning before my brain figures out what I'm doing.

I like long walks, especially when they are taken by people who annoy me.

I have flabby thighs, but fortunately my stomach covers them.

The advantage of exercising every day is that you die healthier.

If you are going to try cross-country skiing, start with a small country.

I don't jog. It makes the ice jump right out of my glass.

Dates & Places Used:

286

TOPIC: Expectations

Not Too Picky

A woman went into a restaurant and ordered the breakfast special. "I want my pancakes well done," she said. "You need to cook them all the way through and golden brown on both sides. Use the light syrup, because the regular syrup is too sweet. Make the bacon crisp and thin, not oily or soggy, and put it on a separate plate. The eggs must be over-easy, not broken or runny."

"And would you like butter or margarine?" asked the waitress.

The woman answered, "Oh, it doesn't matter; I'm not that picky."

Dates & Places Used:

287

TOPIC: Experts

Economic Employment

Economics is extremely useful as a form of employment for economists.

Dates & Places Used:

288

TOPIC: Experts

Bird Expert

A man had two parrots, and he wanted to know which was male and which was female. A man standing nearby said, "I'm a bird expert, and I can tell you. If you will notice, every time the birds eat worms, the male bird always eats the male worms and the female bird always eats the female worms."

"Well, how do you know which is the male worm and which is the female worm?"

"I don't know that. I'm just a bird expert."

Dates & Places Used:

289

Confidence Builder

Overheard from a physician to a patient following surgery: "I had to remove one of your livers, but you'll be up and around in no time or I don't know my medicine."

Dates & Places Used:

290

Weather Logic

Tourist: "What's that you have there?"

Old-timer: "That there's a weather gauge."

Tourist: "How can you possibly tell the weather with a piece of rope?"

Old-timer: "It's simple. When it swings back and forth, it's windy, and when it gets wet, it's raining."

Dates & Places Used:

291

Native American Meteorology

An old Native American chief was famous for predicting what the weather would do. A group of people would go to the chief and ask him, "What will the weather be like tomorrow?"

The chief would reply, "Much rain. Very wet."

The next day it would rain and be very wet.

Others from the tribe would go to the chief and ask, "What will the weather be like tomorrow?"

"Much snow. Very cold," he would reply.

Sure enough, it snowed, and it was very cold.

On one such occasion, the people of the tribe asked, "Chief, what will the weather do tomorrow?"

The chief replied, "I dunno. Radio broken."

Dates & Places Used:

292

Four Engineers and One Broken Car

Four engineers—a mechanical engineer, a chemical engineer, an electrical engineer, and a computer engineer—were traveling in a car when it broke down.

"Sounds to me as if the pistons have seized. We'll have to strip down the engine before we can get the car working again," said the mechanical engineer.

"Well," said the chemical engineer, "it sounded to me as if the fuel might be contaminated. I think we should clear out the fuel system."

"I thought it might be a grounding problem," said the electrical engineer, "or maybe a faulty plug lead."

They all turned to the computer engineer, who had said nothing, and said, "Well, what do you think?"

"Hmm—perhaps if we all get out of the car and get back in again?"

Dates & Places Used:

293

Definition of an Auditor

An auditor is the person who shows up at the end of the battle and bayonets all of the wounded.

Dates & Places Used:

294

Build It or Plan It

Sometimes putting the cart before the horse is the right thing to do. During World War II, General Douglas MacArthur asked one of his army engineers how long it would take to "throw a bridge across this river."

"Three days," said the engineer.

"Good!" snapped the general. "Have your draftsmen make the drawing right away."

Three days later the general asked the engineer how the bridge was progressing.

"It's all ready," reported the engineer. "You can send your troops across right now if you don't have to wait for plans. They aren't done yet."

Dates & Places Used:

295

TOPIC: Failure

Just Missed by Plenty

A golfer returned to the clubhouse and announced that he had just missed a hole-in-one on the fourteenth hole. The guys in the clubhouse were impressed. One of them said, "But the fourteenth hole is a par four. How did you get so close to a hole-in-one?"

The golfer thought for a moment and answered, "How did I get so close? I only missed it by four strokes."

Dates & Places Used:

296

TOPIC: Failure

Equal Opportunity Robbers

A pair of robbers entered a record shop nervously waving revolvers. The first one shouted, "Nobody move!" When his partner moved, the startled first bandit shot him.

Dates & Places Used:

297

TOPIC: Failure

Pitcher's Predicament

The rookie pitcher had just walked a third straight batter, and the manager went to the mound. "Son," he told the pitcher, "I think it's time to replace you."

"Don't replace me now," the pitcher protested. "Last time this guy was up, I struck him out."

"That's true," agreed the manager. "But we are still in the same inning."

Dates & Places Used:

298

TOPIC: Failure

Winning Point

Johnny's father called home during a business trip to see how his son's basketball game had gone. Johnny came to the phone and told his dad, "I finally made a basket today."

His father was excited. "Did it help the team, Johnny?"

"Well," Johnny answered, "it was the winning point."

Now Johnny's dad was ecstatic. "Son, that's wonderful. You are a hero with your very first basket!"

"Not exactly, Dad," Johnny explained. "I made the basket for the other team."

Dates & Places Used:

299

TOPIC: Faith

Christian Jargon

After hearing his dad preach on "justification," "sanctification," and all the other "-ations," a minister's son was ready when his Sunday school teacher asked if anybody knew what "procrastination" meant. The boy said, "I'm not sure what it means, but I know our church believes in it!"

Dates & Places Used:

300

TOPIC: Faith

Get Ready

When a farmer prays for a good crop, God expects him to say amen with a hoe. *(J. Vernon McGee)*
Dates & Places Used:

301

TOPIC: Faith

Loch Ness Monster and God

An atheist was spending a quiet day fishing when suddenly his boat was attacked by the Loch Ness monster. In one easy flip, the beast tossed him and his boat high into the air. Then it opened its mouth to swallow both.

As the man sailed head over heels, he cried out, "Oh, my God! Help me!"

At once, the ferocious attack scene froze in place, and as the atheist hung in midair, a booming voice came down from the clouds. "I thought you didn't believe in me!"

"Come on, God, give me a break!" the man pleaded. "Two minutes ago I didn't believe in the Loch Ness monster either!"
Dates & Places Used:

302

TOPIC: Faithfulness

Found Someone Else

A minister told about a function he attended at his church, which his wife was unable to attend. During the function, he struck up a conversation with a woman who was attending the church for the first time. As they talked, they learned that the woman had a great deal in common with his wife–same birthplace, background, and interests. The minister told the woman he would be sure to mention this to his wife.

At the end of the function, as the woman was preparing to leave, she turned toward the minister from the other side of the room and spoke so all could hear: "Be sure to tell your wife that you have found someone else."
Dates & Places Used:

303

TOPIC: Faithfulness

Mommy's Victory

Have you ever noticed the times in which a four-year-old's voice is louder than a hundred adult voices?

Several years ago a man returned home from a trip just when a storm hit with crashing thunder and severe lightning. As he entered the bedroom at about 2:00 A.M., he found his two children in bed with his wife, apparently scared by the loud storm. He reluctantly resigned himself to sleeping in the guest room. The next day he spoke to his children and explained that it was okay to sleep with Mom when the storm was bad, but when he was expected home, he did not want them to sleep with Mom. They said that was okay.

After his next trip a few weeks later, this man's wife and children went to pick him up at the airport terminal, and since the plane was late, a crowd of people waited at the gate for its arrival. As the father entered the waiting area, his son saw him and came running. As he ran, he shouted, "Hi, Dad! I've got some good news!"

As the father waved back, he shouted, "What is the good news?"

"Nobody slept with Mommy while you were away this time!"

The noisy airport became very quiet as everyone in the waiting area looked at the boy, then at his dad, and then scanned the area to find his poor, embarrassed mother.

Dates & Places Used:

304

TOPIC: Family

No Single Virtues

Family life teaches you loyalty, patience, understanding, perseverance, and a lot of other things you wouldn't need if you had stayed single.

Dates & Places Used:

305

TOPIC: Fathers

Ideal Father

The father of five children had won a toy at a raffle. He called his kids together to ask which one should have the present. "Who is the most obedient?" he asked. "Who never talks back to Mother? Who does everything she says?"

Five small voices answered in unison, "You play with it, Daddy!"

Dates & Places Used:

306

TOPIC: Fathers

Devil Dad

Asked by a friend if she thought the devil was real, a little girl replied, "He's probably like Santa Claus—my father."

Dates & Places Used:

307

TOPIC: Fathers

Picture of a Father

A father is a man who carries photographs where his money used to be.

Dates & Places Used:

308

TOPIC: Fathers

Dad's Favorite Gift

Fatherhood is pretending the present you love most is soap-on-a-rope. *(Bill Cosby)*
Dates & Places Used:

309

TOPIC: Fathers

Daddy Got Two Shots

The cold and flu season had come to our church, and I was talking to one of the first graders after she and her father had missed a Sunday due to illness. I asked her if she was feeling better, and she replied with a proud voice, "Yes, I'm all better now, but Daddy and I had to go to the doctor."

Sensing there was more to the story, I asked, "And what did you think about visiting the doctor?"

She answered with a small, sad voice, "I didn't like it very much. I had to get a shot, and it hurt."

But before I could begin to comfort her, she suddenly looked up with a great big, beaming smile and said, "Yep, I had to get a shot, but my daddy had to get two shots, and that made me feel lots better!"

Dates & Places Used:

310

TOPIC: Fathers

Dad's Math

The first grade teacher asked one of her students if he knew his numbers. He said he did—that his father had taught him.

"Okay," the teacher said, "let's see how much he taught you."

The boy agreed, so the teacher asked, "What number comes after two?"

"Three," answered the boy.

"What comes after five?"

"Six."

"What comes after eight?"

"Nine."

The teacher was pleased with the boy. "Very good," praised the teacher. "It looks like your father did a great job. So, tell me, what comes after ten?"

"A jack," the boy answered.

Dates & Places Used:

311

Not Fit to Drink

One day Gramma sent her grandson Johnny down to the water hole to get some water for cooking dinner. As he was dipping the bucket into the water, he saw two big eyes looking back at him. He dropped the bucket and hightailed it for Gramma's kitchen.

"Well now, where's my bucket and where's my water?" Gramma asked him.

"I can't get any water from that water hole, Gramma," exclaimed Johnny. "There's a big ol' alligator down there!"

"Now don't you mind that ol' alligator, Johnny. He's been there for a few years now, and he's never hurt no one. Why, he's probably as scared of you as you are of him!"

"Well, Gramma," replied Johnny, "if he's as scared of me as I am of him, then that water ain't fit to drink!"

Dates & Places Used:

312

We Need One Another

A young woman was waiting for a bus in a slum area one evening when a rookie policeman approached her. "Want me to wait with you?" he asked.

She replied "Thank you, but that's not necessary. I'm not afraid."

"Well, then," he grinned, "would you mind waiting with me?"

Dates & Places Used:

313

TOPIC: Fear

Afraid of Only Mom

A little girl asked her father if he was afraid of the dark. He told her he was not. She asked if he was afraid of snakes. He said he was not. The little girl asked if he was afraid of long, slimy worms. Her father again told her he was not afraid—not even of long, slimy worms.

The girl thought for a moment and then concluded, "Then the only thing you're afraid of is Mom!"

Dates & Places Used:

314

TOPIC: Finances

Budget Ring

Angela was thrilled with her engagement ring and lost no time showing it to the girls at the office. "It must be reassuring for you to know," meowed one of them, "that he's the kind of man who doesn't throw his money around foolishly."

Dates & Places Used:

315

TOPIC: Finances

Save a Little Money

Save a little money each month, and at the end of the year you'll be surprised at how little you have.

Dates & Places Used:

316

TOPIC: Finances

Simple Rules for Investing

Don't gamble. Take all your savings and buy some good stock and hold it until it goes up, then sell it. If it don't go up, don't buy it. *(Will Rogers)*

Dates & Places Used:

317

TOPIC: Fishing

Shark Fishing

A priest was walking along the cliffs at Dover when he came upon two locals pulling another man ashore on the end of a rope. "That's what I like to see," said the priest, "a man helping his fellow man."

As he was walking away, one local remarked to the other, "Well, he sure doesn't know the first thing about shark fishing."

Dates & Places Used:

318

TOPIC: Fishing

Pews Harder Than Rocks?

As a woman watched her husband fishing for hours, sitting on the rocky shoreline of the lake, she commented to her friend, "Can that possibly be the same man who complains every Sunday about uncomfortable pews?"

Dates & Places Used:

319

He's Got a License to Run

Two men were fishing when a game warden slipped up on them and asked to see their fishing licenses. One of the men took off running. The warden started chasing the man along the river through the brush and marshes. After about ten minutes he caught the man and asked him for his fishing license. The man reached into his wallet and produced a current fishing license. The game warden inspected the license carefully and asked the man why he had run away. The man smiled at the warden and answered, "So you wouldn't ask to see the other guy's license."

Dates & Places Used:

320

TOPIC: Fishing

Teaching Worms to Swim

A man saw a young boy who was fishing without permission in his private lake. He approached the boy. "This lake is clearly posted with No FISHING signs. So why are you fishing in my private lake?"

"I'm not fishing, sir," the boy politely answered. "I'm just teaching these worms how to swim!"

Dates & Places Used:

321

TOPIC: Fishing

Special Scales for Fisherman

When President Cleveland's second child was born, the doctor asked Cleveland for a scale to determine the baby's weight. Cleveland searched through the house without success. Finally, he remembered that he had an old scale in the basement that he always used on his fishing trips. He got it and brought it upstairs.

Carefully, the doctor placed the infant on the scale and was amazed to learn that the newborn weighed twenty-five pounds.
Dates & Places Used:

322

TOPIC: Fishing

Slow Boat to Ice Fishing

A couple of fellows from Alabama loved to fish. They had heard that ice fishing was a great sport, and they wanted to give it a try. If they were going to do it, though, they were going to do it in Canada to get the full effect of the sport. When they arrived at a frozen lake in Canada that was famous for its ice fishing, they stopped at a bait shop to get the very best bait and tackle for the lake. The shop owner told them that they would need an ice auger. It was a bit expensive, but the men did not hesitate; they purchased the auger to drill holes in the ice.

In a short while they had gathered their equipment and arrived on the ice. They began to prepare for a great day of ice fishing.

About two hours later they returned to the shop and asked the shop owner for another ice auger.

The shop owner was confused. "What's wrong with the one I sold you?"

"Nothing," the men answered, "it works fine."

"Then why do you need another one?" the owner asked.

"It's cold out there. The holes keep freezing after a while, and we haven't been able to fish yet. At the rate we're going, we're not even going to get the boat in the water before dark!"
Dates & Places Used:

323

TOPIC: Fishing

Not Going Fishing

An old woman saw a young boy with a fishing pole over his shoulder and a jar of tadpoles in his hand. He was walking through the park on a Sunday afternoon. "Son," she called out, "don't you know you shouldn't go fishing on Sunday?"

"I'm not going fishing," the boy answered. "I'm going home."
Dates & Places Used:

324

Magnetic Fishing

Three fishermen were sitting on a riverbank holding fishing poles with the lines in the water. A game warden came up behind them, tapped them on the shoulder, and said, "Excuse me, I'd like to see your fishing licenses."

"We don't have licenses," replied the first fisherman.

"Well, if you're going to fish, you need fishing licenses," said the game warden.

"But, Officer," replied the second fisherman, "we aren't fishing. We all have magnets at the end of our lines, and we're collecting debris off the bottom of the river."

The game warden lifted up all the lines and, sure enough, there were horseshoe magnets tied on the end of each line. "Well, I know of no law against it," said the game warden. "Take all the debris you want." And with that, the game warden left.

As soon as the game warden was out of sight, the three fishermen started laughing hysterically. "What a stupid fish cop!" the second fisherman said to the other two. "Doesn't he know that there are steelhead salmon in this river?"

Dates & Places Used:

325

Business Is Business

A young Jewish boy started attending public school in a small town. The teacher of the one-room school decided to use her position to try to influence the new student. She asked the class, "Who was the greatest man who ever lived?"

A girl raised her hand and said, "I think George Washington was the greatest man who ever lived because he is the father of our country."

The teacher replied, "Well, that's a good answer, but that's not the answer I'm looking for."

Another young student raised his hand and said, "I think Abraham Lincoln was the greatest man who lived because he freed the slaves and helped end the Civil War."

"Well, that's another good answer, but that's not the one I was looking for."

Then the new Jewish boy raised his hand and said, "I think Jesus Christ was the greatest man who ever lived."

The teacher's mouth dropped open in astonishment. "Yes!" she said. "That's the answer I was looking for." She then brought him up to the front of the classroom and gave him a lollipop.

Later, during recess, another Jewish boy approached him as he was licking his lollipop. He said, "Why did you say, 'Jesus Christ'?"

The boy stopped licking his lollipop and replied, "I know it's Moses, and you know it's Moses, but business is business."

Dates & Places Used:

326

TOPIC: Focus

Fanatic Focus

A fanatic is someone who can't change his mind and won't change the subject. *(Winston Churchill)*

Dates & Places Used:

327

TOPIC: Focus

Am I Driving?

Two elderly women were out driving in a large car—both could barely see over the dashboard. As they were cruising along, they came to an intersection. The stoplight was red, but they just went on through. The woman in the passenger seat thought to herself, "I must be losing it, but I could have sworn we just went through a red light."

After a few more minutes they came to another intersection, and the light was red again, and again they went right through. This time the woman in the passenger seat was almost sure that the light had been red but was really very concerned that she was losing her mind. She was getting nervous and decided to pay very close attention to the road and the next intersection to see what was going on.

At the next intersection, sure enough, the light was definitely red, and they did go right through it! She turned to the other woman and said, "Mildred! Did you know we just ran through three red lights in a row? You could have killed us!"

Mildred turned to her and said, "Oh, am I driving?"

Dates & Places Used:

328

TOPIC: Food

Miss Piggy on Eating

Muppet star Miss Piggy shared her considerable wisdom and experience concerning food: "You should never eat more at one sitting than you can lift."

Dates & Places Used:

329

TOPIC: Food

Source of Stress

If you have ever struggled with a diet, then you probably know that *stressed* is just *desserts* spelled backwards.

Dates & Places Used:

330

TOPIC: Food

Baskin' Robins

Two robins were sitting in a tree. "I'm really hungry," said the first one.

"Me too," said the second. "Let's fly down and find some lunch."

They flew to the ground and found a nice plot of plowed ground full of worms. They ate and ate and ate until they could eat no more.

"I'm so full I don't think I can fly back up to the tree," said the first one.

"Me either. Let's just lie here and rest in the warm sun," said the second.

"Okay," said the first.

They plopped down, basking in the sun. No sooner had they fallen asleep than a big fat tomcat snuck up and gobbled up both of them. As he sat washing his face after his meal, he thought, *I just love baskin' robins.*

Dates & Places Used:

331

TOPIC: Food

Both Pieces of Pie

A boy brought a friend over for supper. His friend seemed to enjoy the food all right, even though his mother was not the best cook around.

Then it came time for dessert. The mother asked her son's friend, "Would you like some of my famous apple pie?"

The boy told her that he would. When the boy had finished the pie, he thanked his friend's mother.

The mother was pleased with the boy's manners. "Did you like my pie?"

"Ma'am, I just want to thank you for both pieces."

"But you only ate one piece of my pie."

The boy explained, "Not exactly. That piece of your pie was my first and my last."

Dates & Places Used:

332

Hear the Onion Rings

You can be sure you are hungry if you can hear the onion rings.
Dates & Places Used:

333

A Fly a Day

A thought for the day in the booklet "A Clarification of Questions": Iran's Ayatollah Ruhollah Khomeini wrote that "if a fly gets into the throat of one who is fasting, it is not necessary to pull it out."
Dates & Places Used:

334

Daddy's Decimal Points

A young boy watched as his dad finished a heavy meal and then loosened his belt.

"Look, Mom," he said, "Pop has just moved his decimal point over two places."
Dates & Places Used:

335

Cajun Zoos

Question: What's the difference between Cajun zoos and other zoos?

Answer: In front of each exhibit, other zoos have a plaque with the name of the animal, its habitat, etc. Cajun zoos have a plaque with the name of the animal and its recipe.
Dates & Places Used:

336

TOPIC: Food

Peanuts without Chocolate

A preacher visited an elderly woman from his congregation. As he sat on the couch, he noticed a large bowl of peanuts on the coffee table.

"Mind if I have a few?" he asked.

"No, not at all," the woman replied.

They chatted for an hour, and as the preacher stood to leave, he realized that instead of eating just a few peanuts, he had nearly emptied the bowl. "I'm sorry for eating all your peanuts; I really just meant to eat a few," he said.

"Oh, that's all right," replied the woman. "Ever since I lost my teeth, all I can do is suck the chocolate off them."

Dates & Places Used:

337

TOPIC: Food

Blinding Sweets

Two young boys were taking their first train ride. Their grandmother had bought them a new kind of superfizzy candy that would practically explode when eaten.

One of the boys ate his candy before his brother. Just as he began to eat, the train went through a tunnel.

A little while later, his brother reached for his candy to eat it. The boy who had already eaten his candy felt it necessary to warn the other. He said, "I'd be real careful with that candy if I were you. When I ate my candy, I went blind for a minute."

Dates & Places Used:

338

TOPIC: Foolishness

Fool's Money

How did a fool and his money get together in the first place?

Dates & Places Used:

339

TOPIC: Foolishness

Specialty Nails

Two novices were trying to build a garage, and one was attaching the siding. He would pick up a nail, look at it, then hammer it in. Then he would pick up another nail, look at it, and throw it away. His friend watched as over and over he looked at each nail and either hammered it in or tossed it over his shoulder. Finally, the friend walked over and asked, "Hey, why are you throwing away half our nails?"

"The points were on the wrong end," the man explained.

"You idiot," bellowed the friend, "those are for the other side of the house!"

How you see things depends on your perspective.

Dates & Places Used:

340

TOPIC: Foolishness

Double or Nothing

A man who was never known for his intelligence returned home after a night out with his friends. He seemed quite disgruntled. His wife asked him what was troubling him.

"Oh, I lost a hundred dollars," the man answered.

His surprised wife asked, "How did you lose that much money?"

"We were watching the football game," he told her, "and I thought they were going to win the game with a field goal on the final play of the game. I was so sure, I bet Bill fifty dollars that they would score. They didn't score."

His wife thought for a moment and said, "But that's only fifty dollars; I thought you said one hundred dollars."

"Yeah, I know. I was so disgusted that I lost fifty dollars, I made a second double-or-nothing bet with Bill."

"I thought you said it was the final play of the game," his wife responded.

"It was," said the man, "so we bet on the instant replay."

Dates & Places Used:

144

341

Naive Water

Ever wonder about those who spend two dollars for a little bottle of Evian water? Just spell Evian backwards.

Dates & Places Used:

342

Even Better Than Mother

A little boy disobeyed his mother, but his conscience began to hurt him, and he was sneaking up to his room when his mother saw him. "Where are you going, Frank?" she asked.

"To my room to talk to God."

"Is it something you can't tell me?"

Frank explained, "Yes, it is. You'll just scold and punish me while God will forgive me and forget all about it."

Out of the mouths of babes.

Dates & Places Used:

343

Complete Forgiveness

In teaching my boys, ages four and three, the Lord's Prayer, I was startled to hear my oldest boy say, "As we forgive those who pass gas against us."

Dates & Places Used:

344

Good Sam Strategy

When we bought our new television set, the neighbors gathered one Saturday to help us put up the antenna. Since we had only the simplest tools, we weren't making much progress—until a man who was new on the block appeared with an elaborate toolbox, with everything we needed to get the antenna up in record time.

As we stood around congratulating ourselves on this piece of good luck, we asked our new neighbor what he made with such fancy tools. Looking at us all, he smiled and answered, "Friends, mostly."

Dates & Places Used:

345

Affair with Toupee

On *The Phil Donahue Show* on January 13, 1992, a number of reporters and anchor persons from twenty years of the *Today* show were being interviewed by Phil Donahue.

Bryant Gumble commented on his reconciliation with Willard Scott. He said they now had an excellent relationship. In fact, one of the staff found Willard's toupee in Bryant's dressing room and accused them of having an affair. Willard Scott jumped up in surprise and exclaimed, "You're having an affair with my toupee?"

Dates & Places Used:

346

Gum Sisters

My daughter Kelly (age six) grew to be close friends with Michelle (age eleven). Michelle had recently learned about covenant love and persuaded Kelly to become a covenant sister.

They got all excited about "having all things in common," that is, toys, games, secrets, etc. But then they realized that in order to become true bonded covenant sisters they would have to allow their blood to mingle together. Horrors! Feeling quite dismayed, the idea was about to die when suddenly Michelle blurted, "I've got an idea." She ran to her bedroom, grabbed a pack of gum, took one piece and gave another to Kelly. They chewed their gum until it was soft–and permeated with saliva. "Now, let's trade," she said. They traded those mushy, germ-filled, already-been-chewed pieces of gum. They bit into them and they chomped on them. Then they proudly announced to family and friends, "We're gum sisters; we stick together!"

Dates & Places Used:

347

TOPIC: Frugality

Air Glutton

It has been said that the first Scotsman to use free air at a service station blew out four tires.

Dates & Places Used:

348

TOPIC: Frugality

Choose Your Friends Very Carefully

Three friends were having lunch together–Jack Benny, George Burns, and Edgar Bergen. Jack Benny had a reputation for being tight. George Burns said Benny had a "reach impediment" when it came to picking up the bill, so Burns was therefore surprised to hear Benny ask for the check. On the way out he complimented Benny. "That was good of you to ask for the check," he told him. Benny replied, "I did not ask for the check, and that's the last time I'll have lunch with a ventriloquist."

Dates & Places Used:

349

TOPIC: Frugality

Let's Talk Aggravation

Hardly anything is as upsetting as picking up a lunch check for someone who is too rich to carry money.

Dates & Places Used:

350

TOPIC: Frugality

Why Jesus Walked on Water

A Scotsman was traveling in the Holy Land on a vacation when he came to the Sea of Galilee. Inquiring the price of a pleasure boat in which he might see the sights, he found it was five dollars per hour.

"Five dollars per hour?" he exclaimed. "Why, I rent a boat in Aberdeen for less than half as much."

"Ah, but this is Palestine," replied the boatman, "and these are the waters on which our Lord walked."

"No wonder he walked!" said the Scotsman in disgust.

Dates & Places Used:

351

TOPIC: Future

Psychic Frog Line

It is not always in our best interest to know the future. A frog called a psychic hotline for frogs. The phone psychic told the frog that he was about to meet a beautiful young woman who would want to know all she could about him.

The frog was excited to hear this news and asked the psychic, "When will I meet this beautiful woman?"

The psychic answered, "You will meet her next week."

"And where will we meet?" the frog probed.

The psychic hesitated and then told the frog, "You will meet this woman in her biology class."

Dates & Places Used:

352

Math Tax

The lottery is a tax on people who are bad at math.
Dates & Places Used:

353

TOPIC: Gambling

The Loser Is Five Bucks Richer

Two old men were sitting around talking, and the first one said, "Let's go get some lottery tickets. The jackpot is up to thirty million."

The second old guy said, "I don't buy those things."

"But that's a whole pile of money. Don't you think it's worth spending five bucks to win?" asked the first.

The second old guy said, "No! You've only got a 1 in 5.4 million chance to win. That puts the odds of proving you're a loser at almost 100 percent."

"Well, not playing at all makes you an automatic loser," answered the first.

"That's okay," said the second guy. "At least I'll still have my five bucks."
Dates & Places Used:

354

TOPIC: Gambling

Psychic Limitations

How come you never see a headline that reads: "PSYCHIC WINS LOTTERY"?
Dates & Places Used:

355

TOPIC: Gambling

Were You Gambling?

A rabbi, a minister, and a priest were playing poker when the police raided the game. Turning to the priest, a police officer asked, "Father O'Connor, were you gambling?"

Turning his eyes to heaven, the priest whispered, "Lord, forgive me for what I am about to do." To the police officer, he then said, "No, Officer; I was not gambling."

The officer then asked the Protestant minister, "Pastor Thompson, were you gambling?"

Again, after an appeal to heaven, the minister replied, "No, Officer; I was not gambling."

Turning to the rabbi, the officer asked, "Rabbi Epstein, were you gambling?"

Shrugging his shoulders, the rabbi replied, "With whom?"

Dates & Places Used:

356

TOPIC: Gambling

ATM Winnings

A young girl went with her mother to get some money from an automated teller machine. The mother helped her daughter push the correct account numbers and personal identification numbers. When she finished entering the numbers, the money came out of the tray.

This was the first time the young girl had seen this, and she was quite excited. She screamed, "Look, Mommy! We hit the jackpot!"

Dates & Places Used:

357

TOPIC: Gender

Heart of a True Father

One day a mother chanced by the nursery and noticed her husband standing in rapt contemplation by the crib of his sleep-

150

ing son. Silently, she watched him for a while, wondering what thoughts were going through his mind as he looked at his own flesh and blood asleep in the crib. At last she slipped into the room and put her arm through his and asked, "What are you thinking of, dear?"

He came to with a start. "Oh, I was just wondering how in the world they can make a crib like this for $24.95."

Dates & Places Used:

358

TOPIC: Gender

Men and Computers

Men are like computers: hard to figure out and never have enough memory.

Dates & Places Used:

359

TOPIC: Gender

Simply Irresistible

A guy was walking along the beach when he came across a lamp. He picked it up, rubbed it, and, of course, a genie popped out. The genie told his new master he would grant the man three wishes.

"First," the guy began, "I'd like a million dollars." *Poof!* A million dollars was suddenly showing on his checkbook balance.

"Second," he continued, "I'd like a new Mercedes." *Poof!* A Mercedes appeared right in front of him.

"Third," the guy smirked, "I'd like to be irresistible to women." *Poof!* He turned into a box of chocolates.

Dates & Places Used:

360

Of Cats and Men

I've never understood why women love cats. Cats are independent; they don't listen; and they don't come in when you call. They like to stay out all night, and when they do come home, they expect to be fed and stroked; then want to be left alone to sleep. In other words, every quality that women hate in a man, they love in a cat.

Dates & Places Used:

361

Better Verbal Skills

A study in *The Washington Post* says that women have better verbal skills than men. I just want to say to the authors of that study: Duh! *(Conan O'Brien)*

Dates & Places Used:

362

Quick Wit

A tourist traveling down a country road in the Deep South passed a young boy walking down the road wearing only one shoe.

The tourist stopped the car and asked the boy, "You lose a shoe?"

"Nope," the boy replied, "just found one."

Dates & Places Used:

363

TOPIC: Gifts

Gift Wrap It?

After spending over three hours enduring the long lines, surly clerks, and insane regulations at the Department of Motor Vehicles, I stopped at a toy store to pick up a gift for my son. I brought my selection—a baseball bat—to the cash register.

"Cash or charge?" the clerk asked.

"Cash," I snapped. Then apologizing for my rudeness, I explained, "I've spent the afternoon at the motor vehicle bureau."

"Shall I gift wrap the bat?" the clerk asked sweetly. "Or are you going back there?"

Dates & Places Used:

364

TOPIC: Gifts

Looking for a Gun

A woman went to a gun shop and told the clerk, "I'm looking for a gun for my husband."

The clerk asked the woman, "Did your husband tell you what kind of gun he wants?"

"Oh no," the woman answered, "he doesn't even know that I'm going to shoot him."

Dates & Places Used:

365

TOPIC: Giving

Give Them Our Aunt

A mother appealed to her children to care for orphan children. "These poor children don't have a mother, a father, or even aunts and uncles. Would you children like to give anything to them?"

The children discussed this among themselves and then announced their decision: "Let's give them Aunt Martha!"

Dates & Places Used:

366

TOPIC: Giving

Tied Up in Five Brooms

A church member angrily complained to the pastor that the church had wastefully purchased five new brooms, and he felt the expenditure to be unnecessary.

The pastor mentioned it to the church treasurer, who responded, "No wonder he was upset. How would you feel if you saw everything you gave in the past year tied up in five brooms?"

Dates & Places Used:

367

TOPIC: Giving

Story behind the Gift

The minister was greeted at the door of the church after Sunday morning worship by a young boy. The boy looked up at the preacher and said, "Pastor, we were going to bring you a chicken for dinner, but he got well!"

Dates & Places Used:

368

TOPIC: Goals

Chasing Two Hares

If you chase two hares, both will escape you.

Dates & Places Used:

369

TOPIC: Goals

Lost Faster

Pilot over intercom to passengers: "I have good news and bad news. The good news is we are ahead of schedule. The bad news is we are lost."

Dates & Places Used:

TOPIC: Goals

Realistic Goals

Two friends went camping in the woods. They woke up the first morning and were standing by their tent having their first cup of coffee when they suddenly spotted a grizzly bear heading for them at full speed. Quickly, the one man reached down and grabbed his sneakers and started putting them on.

The other man looked at him and said, "What are you doing? Do you think you can outrun that grizzly bear?"

The first man said, "No, and I don't need to. All I need to do is outrun you!"

Dates & Places Used:

TOPIC: God

God's Picture

A little boy was so engrossed in drawing that his mother finally asked him what it was he was drawing.

"God," he said.

"But nobody has ever seen God," said his mom.

"Well, they will when I'm finished," the little boy responded.

Dates & Places Used:

TOPIC: God

On Hold with God

As a mother and daughter walked out of church one Sunday morning, the mother said, "That was a nice service. I really liked the soft piano music during the prayer."

The little girl turned and asked her mother, "That was a piano?"

The mother nodded, and the little girl said, "Oh. I thought God had put us on hold."

We need never fear that God will put us on hold. Our God reaches down and enters our trials and struggles with us. Our

God is with us to the ends of the earth through the power and presence of the Holy Spirit.
Dates & Places Used:

373

TOPIC: God

What God Can Do

A young boy going to see his grandfather was traveling by train. He took a seat beside a man who happened to be a seminary professor. The boy was reading a Sunday school take-home paper, and the professor thought he would have some fun with the boy, so he said, "Young man, if you can tell me something that God can do, I'll give you a big shiny apple."

Thoughtfully the boy replied, "Mister, if you can tell me something that God can't do, I'll give you a whole barrel of apples."
Dates & Places Used:

374

TOPIC: Golf

Secret of Good Golf

The secret of good golf is to hit the ball hard, straight, and not too often.
Dates & Places Used:

375

TOPIC: Golf

Good Golf Day

I've had a good day when I don't fall out of the golf cart.
(Buddy Hackett)
Dates & Places Used:

376

Taking a Second Shot

It was a sunny Saturday morning, just perfect for golf, and a man was beginning his preswing routine, visualizing his upcoming shot, when a voice came over the clubhouse loud-speaker: "Would the gentleman on the ladies' tee back up to the men's tee, please!"

The man was still deep in his routine, seemingly impervious to the interruption. Again the announcement: "Would the *man* on the *women's* tee kindly back up to the men's tee!"

That was too much for the man. He broke his stance, lowered his club back to the ground, and raised his voice: "Would the announcer in the clubhouse kindly be quiet and let me play my second shot?"

Dates & Places Used:

377

TOPIC: Golf

Hitting Fewer Spectators

I know I am getting better at golf because I am hitting fewer spectators. *(Gerald Ford)*
Dates & Places Used:

378

TOPIC: Golf

No Game like Golf

Golf is a simple sport. All you do is go out with three friends, play eighteen holes, and return with three enemies.
Dates & Places Used:

379

Extra Golf Pants

A man was golfing with his buddies. He reached into his bag for a club, and an extra pair of pants fell out of the bag. His friends were curious why he had an extra pair of pants in his golf bag.

The man explained, "Oh, I always bring an extra pair of pants when I golf ... just in case I get a hole in one."

Dates & Places Used:

380

Doctor's Privilege

A man and his wife were playing golf on the ninth green when she collapsed from what appeared to be a heart attack.

"I need help!" the woman gasped.

Her husband ran off and told her he would get help. A few minutes later the man returned and began to make his putt into the ninth hole.

His wife looked up from the ground and asked him what he thought he was doing.

The man told his wife, "Don't worry, I found a doctor. I'm just finishing my putt while we wait."

"But where is the doctor?" the woman asked with all the strength she could muster.

The man walked a short distance to the next tee, teed his ball, and drove it toward the tenth hole. He then answered, "I found a doctor on the sixth hole."

The woman probed, "You found a doctor on the sixth hole and came back by yourself. Where is that doctor?"

"He won't be very long," the man answered confidently. "The guys on the seventh and eighth holes agreed to let him play through."

Dates & Places Used:

381

Golf Speed

Golf is a game in which the slowest people in the world are in front of you and the fastest are behind you.
Dates & Places Used:

382

Patience in Golfing

It's good sportsmanship to not pick up lost golf balls while they are still rolling. *(Mark Twain)*
Dates & Places Used:

383

Too Many Golf Strokes

"Uff-da, Hans! Golfing must be bad for da heart," remarked Hilda.

"Vat makes yew say dat?" asked Hans.

"Vell," replied Hilda, "I yust heard a golfer say dat he had four strokes on da very first hole."
Dates & Places Used:

384

Golf Sermons

How can you tell when a preacher is about to give a short sermon?

He has his golf shoes on.
Dates & Places Used:

385

TOPIC: Golf

Tossing for Tee Time

Perkins was twenty minutes late at the first tee one Sunday morning, and the other three members of the regular foursome were almost ready to drive off without him.

"I agreed with my wife," explained Perkins, "that this Sunday I'd toss to see whether I played golf or went to church. And you know, I had to toss twenty-four times."

Dates & Places Used:

386

TOPIC: Golf

Put or Putt

Golfers were surveyed to determine what the difference is between the words *put* and *putt*. The most common definition given was that *put* means to place an object where you intend for it to be. In contrast *putt* means to unsuccessfully attempt to do the same thing with a golf ball.

Dates & Places Used:

387

TOPIC: Golf

Perfect Shot Too Short

Four work associates were golfing together on a Saturday morning. One of the men took his turn to tee off. He stood at his tee for an extended length of time, looking up and down and calculating and recalculating the distance of the shot. He even figured the wind velocity and direction.

His golfing partners were growing more and more impatient with his behavior. One of his buddies finally interrupted him. "Why are you taking so long for one stupid shot? Just hurry up and hit the ball!"

The golfer turned to his buddy and explained, "Look straight ahead at the clubhouse. The owner of our company is sitting outside on the clubhouse patio, and he's watching us with binoculars. I want to make this a perfect shot."

His friend answered, "You may as well forget it; even with a perfect shot, you'll never hit him from here."

Dates & Places Used:

388

TOPIC: Gossip

Gossip Confusion

The things that go in one ear and out the other don't hurt as much as the things that go in one ear, get all mixed up, and then slip out the mouth.

Dates & Places Used:

389

TOPIC: Gossip

As a Matter of Fact

"As a matter of fact" is an expression that precedes many an expression that isn't.

Dates & Places Used:

390

TOPIC: Gossip

Squashing Rumors

Trying to squash a rumor is like trying to unring a bell.

Dates & Places Used:

391

TOPIC: Gossip

Interesting Gossip

The more interesting the gossip is, the more likely it is that the gossip is untrue.

Dates & Places Used:

392

TOPIC: Gossip

Shorter Story

Nothing makes a long story short like the arrival of the person you happen to be talking about.

Dates & Places Used:

393

TOPIC: Government

Bureaucratic Accomplishments

Bureaucracy is the art of making the possible impossible. *(Javier Pascual Salcedo)*

Dates & Places Used:

394

TOPIC: Government

On the Committee

If you ever live in a country run by a committee, be on the committee. *(William Graham Sumner)*

Dates & Places Used:

395

TOPIC: Government

Political Economy

"Political economy" are two words that need a divorce on grounds of incompatibility.

Dates & Places Used:

396

TOPIC: Grace

Getting What She Deserves

A woman with a very nasty attitude had spent almost two hours browsing through the store. The longer she shopped, the more she complained and criticized. Finally, she said, "Why is it that I never get what I ask for in here?"

"Perhaps, madam," said the exhausted clerk, "it's because we are too polite."

Dates & Places Used:

397

TOPIC: Grace

God Is Watching the Apples

At a recent church luncheon buffet line, next to the apples was a sign that read: "Apples–take one per person. Remember, God is watching."

A little further down the line next to the cookies, someone had scrawled with a crayon: "Cookies–take all you want. God is watching the apples."

Dates & Places Used:

398

If You Think about It, Things Are Tough

Henry was looking so glum and depressed that a friend asked, "Henry, what's the matter with you? You look like you've lost your last friend."

Henry responded, "What's the matter? I'll tell you. Remember two weeks ago, my Aunt Molly died and left me fifty thousand dollars?"

His friend said, "Yes, I remember. What's so awful?"

"What's so awful, you ask! Remember last week, my Uncle David died and left me a hundred thousand dollars?"

His friend said he remembered that too and asked, "What's so bad about that?"

With a sad face Henry responded, "What's bad about it? This week I inherited nothing."

The Lord gives us many gifts each day. We have many reasons to be joyful and happy. Yet many times we are not happy with what we have because we are disappointed that we do not have more.

Dates & Places Used:

399

We're in the Money

A couple had installed a fancy horn system on their car that played various tunes. This unfortunate couple had the embarrassment of having their fancy horn system get stuck at a most inopportune time, while in a procession of cars that had come to a stop all at the same time. Their horn inadvertently began to play the tune "We're in the Money." The circumstance was the graveside service of their grandmother. The crowd was not amused.

Dates & Places Used:

400

TOPIC: Greed

Owning a Man's Company

She is the kind of girl who does not care for a man's company—unless he owns it.
Dates & Places Used:

401

TOPIC: Greed

Source Not Important

The grandfather of William Jackson III died and left him twenty million dollars. A few days later Willam's girlfriend Roxanne suggested that they get married.

After just a few weeks of marriage, William felt that Roxanne was growing more and more distant and less affectionate. After a few months of marriage, William wondered if Roxanne cared about him at all. She seemed completely indifferent toward him. He felt that he needed to confront her.

When William finally got Roxanne to agree to speak with him, he said, "I'm beginning to think that the only reason you married me is that I inherited twenty million dollars from my grandfather."

Roxanne was slightly amused at William and assured him that this was not the case at all. "That's a ridiculous notion," she told him. "It would *not* have mattered to me who gave you the money!"
Dates & Places Used:

402

TOPIC: Guidance

Not Dead Yet

A man's plane crashed in the heart of the darkest jungle of Africa. He pried himself from the wreckage and began to work his way through the dense jungle. As he entered a clearing, he found himself face-to-face with what looked like a hunting party of cannibals. His response was immediate: "I'm a dead man now!"

And then he heard a voice saying, "You're not a dead man. There is a spear at your feet. Pick it up and thrust it through the heart of the chief."

The man did as he was told. He looked down at the ground, and indeed, there was a spear. He picked it up and thrust it through the heart of the chief.

The voice spoke to him once more: "*Now* you're a dead man!"
Dates & Places Used:

TOPIC: Guidance

403 Golfing Tips

As the golfer approached the first tee, a hazardous hole with a green surrounded by water, he debated whether he should use his new golf ball. Deciding that the hole was too treacherous, he pulled out an old ball and placed it on the tee. Just then he heard a voice from above say loudly, "Use the new ball!"

Frightened, he replaced the old ball with the new one and approached the tee. Now the voice from above shouted, "Take a practice swing!"

With this, the golfer stepped backward and took a swing. Again he approached the tee, only to hear the voice shout, "Use the old ball!"
Dates & Places Used:

TOPIC: Guidance

404 The Voice from Above

Two big city coaches from the University of Washington were snooping around in Washington State country. It was winter, and they heard that one of the specialties of the area was ice fishing, so they decided to try their hand at it. They went to a sporting goods store and bought all the necessary paraphernalia–lines, poles, lures, bait, a small power saw, a tent, a camp stove–the whole bit–and then they found some ice, pitched their tent, and started to cut a hole in the ice. Just as they got into the spirit of the thing, a loud, awesome voice from above proclaimed, "There's no fish under the ice."

Well, that stopped them for a minute, and they looked quizzically at each other; but then, embarrassed to acknowledge this eerie voice to each other, they turned back to their saw and the ice. Just as they got going again they heard the voice again: "There's no fish under the ice."

They stole embarrassed looks at each other but kept on sawing. Now, a third time, even louder than before, the booming voice thundered at them: "There's no fish under the ice."

Finally, one of them could stand it no longer, stood up, and cried out, "Is that you, Lord?"

And the voice boomed out, "No, this is the manager of the ice skating rink."

[Note: When Mark Neuenswander told this story at Westminster Chapel in Bellevue, Washington, he had the sound man supply the awesome voice from above.]

Dates & Places Used:

405

TOPIC: Guilt

Principal's Daughter

"Isn't the principal a dummy!" said a boy to a girl.
"Say, do you know who I am?" asked the girl.
"No."
"I'm the principal's daughter."
"And do you know who I am?" asked the boy.
"No," she replied.
"Good, let's keep it that way!"

Dates & Places Used:

406

TOPIC: Guilt

Maternal Guilt

God invented guilt so mothers could be everywhere at once.

Dates & Places Used:

407

TOPIC: Guilt

Due Process

A thief picked a man's pocket on a crowded elevator. As the result of quick police action, he was arrested and brought before the local magistrate. "You are charged with stealing another person's wallet," said the magistrate. "How do you plead: guilty or not guilty?"

The pickpocket replied, "How can I tell, Your Honor, until I have heard the evidence?"

Dates & Places Used:

408

TOPIC: Habits

Getting Off the Tiger

He who rides a tiger must make plans for dismounting.
(William R. Inge)
Dates & Places Used:

409

TOPIC: Habits

Overactive Fork

"What are you planning to do about that excess weight you're carrying around?" the doctor asked the patient.

"I just can't seem to lose the weight," the patient said. "Must be an overactive thyroid."

"The tests show your thyroid is perfectly normal," the doctor said. "If anything is overactive, it's your fork."

Dates & Places Used:

410

TOPIC: Habits

Just One Drink

A man went into the same bar every day and ordered two drinks. He'd drink one, then slide to the other side of the table and drink the other. When asked about this, the man told the bartender, "One drink is for me; the other I drink for my friend who lives in Texas." One day the man came into the bar but only ordered one drink.

"Oh," asked the bartender, "did your friend in Texas pass away?"

"No," the man responded, "I'm just on the wagon."

Dates & Places Used:

411

TOPIC: Habits

Addictions and Stopping Them

One day a mechanic was working late under a car and some brake fluid dripped into his mouth. *Wow! That stuff isn't too bad tasting,* he thought.

The next day he told his buddy about tasting the brake fluid. "Not bad," he said. "Think I'll have a little more today." His friend got a little concerned but didn't say anything.

The next day he told about drinking a cupful of the brake fluid. "Great stuff! Think I'll have some more today." And so he did.

A few days later he was up to a bottle a day, and his friend was now very worried. "You know that brake fluid is poisonous and really bad for you. You had better stop drinking it."

"Hey, no problem," he said. "I can stop anytime."

Dates & Places Used:

412

TOPIC: Happiness

Man without Mirth

A man without mirth is like a wagon without springs: He is jolted disagreeably by every pebble in the road. *(Henry Ward Beecher)*

Dates & Places Used:

413

TOPIC: Happiness

Make Someone Happy

The late Congressman Sol Bloom would habitually drop a coin into the street. When someone asked why, he said, laughingly, "Oh, somebody is sure to find it and be happy the rest of the day."

Dates & Places Used:

414

TOPIC: Happiness

Happiness and Marriage

At a wedding reception a woman and her friend watched the newly married couple cut their cake. As they watched, the woman remarked to her friend, "I never knew what true happiness was until I got married, but by then it was too late."

Dates & Places Used:

415

TOPIC: Happiness

Too Much Good

Excess: Too much of a good thing is wonderful!

Dates & Places Used:

416

TOPIC: Happiness

Delighted Lightning Bug

Here is a "bright" opening: "I am delighted to speak to you today. Like the lightening bug who backed into a fan."
Dates & Places Used:

417

TOPIC: Hatred

Disliked Dictator

The dictator of a small country was bitterly disappointed that nobody would use the newly issued postage stamps bearing his portrait. He questioned his postmaster, who explained that the stamps were not sticking.

Seizing a stamp, the dictator licked it and stuck it on an envelope. "Look!" he shouted. "It sticks perfectly!"

The postmaster faltered for a moment, then explained, "Well, sir, the truth is that the people have been spitting on the wrong side."
Dates & Places Used:

418

TOPIC: Healing

Acupuncture and Porcupines

Many have not given acupuncture enough credibility. Those who doubt its effectiveness need only look at the porcupine. Rarely does one see a sick porcupine.
Dates & Places Used:

TOPIC: Healing

Destructive Healing

One nice morning two men were out fishing on a large lake. It was a beautiful morning–seventy-eight degrees and sunny with a light breeze–and the fish were biting. They had caught their limit and were enjoying the day. One fisherman noticed a man walking on the shore. He could not believe his eyes. He said to his friend, "If I did not know any better, I'd say that was Jesus over there."

The man on the shore waved them in. They rowed to the shore, and indeed it was Jesus. They began talking with him, and one man asked him if he really could heal sick people.

Jesus said, "Yes, of course, I'm good at that."

The man then asked him to heal some chronic physical problems he had. Jesus touched the affected areas, and one by one each place was restored to healthy functioning. The man never felt better. He was more alive than he had ever felt and had a renewal of youthful energy.

Jesus then looked at the other fisherman.

The man's eyes got wide, and he said, "Don't you come near me. I'm on 100 percent disability."

Dates & Places Used:

420

TOPIC: Healing

Pray Informed Prayers

Rev. Arley Fadness of Harrisburg, South Dakota, told of being a student at Augustana Academy in Sioux Falls, South Dakota. On Sunday afternoons the students would go in small groups to a nearby hospital to visit the sick and take turns praying for their recovery. Finally, it was Fadness's turn. Nervously he prayed for God to heal the woman and spare her any recurrence of the illness. After his "Amen" he went back into the hall, only to be told that they were in the maternity ward!

Dates & Places Used:

421

TOPIC: Healing

Something for the Cough

A teacher walked over to a student who was coughing uncontrollably and said, "That's quite a cough you have there! What are you taking for that cough?"

The student, between coughs, answered, "I don't know, teacher. What will you give me for it?"

Dates & Places Used:

422

TOPIC: Health

Diet to Die For

Eat right, exercise regularly, die anyway.

Dates & Places Used:

423

TOPIC: Health

Realistic Dental Care

In health class a teacher asked a six-year-old what he did to protect his teeth. "I watch out for kids pushing at the drinking fountain," he said.

Dates & Places Used:

424

TOPIC: Health

Tooth Fairy Nightmare

While working for an organization that delivers lunches to elderly shut-ins, I used to take my four-year-old daughter on my afternoon rounds. She was unfailingly intrigued by the various appliances of old age, particularly canes, walkers, and wheelchairs.

One day I found her staring at a pair of false teeth soaking in a glass. As I braced myself for the inevitable barrage of questions, she merely turned and whispered, "The tooth fairy will never believe this!"

Dates & Places Used:

425

TOPIC: Health

Finely Tuned Body

Your body is a great deal like a finely tuned automobile: Even if you take good care of it, eventually it will break down anyway.

Dates & Places Used:

426

TOPIC: Health

Smooth Cupcakes

A man was visiting his brother and sister-in-law and found his young nephew helping them bake cupcakes. The parents went into the living room and let the boy finish frosting the cupcakes by himself. When the boy finished, he brought the cupcakes into the living room and served them to his parents and his uncle.

"These cupcakes look wonderful!" his uncle exclaimed. He then took a couple more bites while looking at the other cupcakes. "And they are delicious too."

The boy's parents were still eating their first cupcake when the uncle had finished, so he took another. As he began his second cupcake, he thanked his nephew again and asked, "How did you get the icing to spread so smoothly?"

His nephew answered, "I licked them."

Dates & Places Used:

427

Toothbrush Hygiene

A little boy came out of the bathroom screaming. He ran to his mother and told her that he had dropped his toothbrush in the toilet.

His mother fished the toothbrush out of the toilet and threw it in the garbage. The boy watched carefully as his mother did this. He then ran to his mother's bathroom and came back with her toothbrush.

He held the toothbrush up for his mother to see and then told her, "We had better throw this one away too; it fell in the toilet a few days ago."

Dates & Places Used:

428

Killer in the Cure

A medical student was doing a rotation in toxicology at the poison control center. A woman called in and was quite upset. She had caught her little daughter eating ants.

The medical student quickly reassured her that ants are not harmful and there would be no need to bring her daughter into the hospital. The woman calmed down and at the end of the conversation happened to mention that she had taken precautions and had given her daughter some ant poison to eat to make sure the ants were dead.

The medical student told the woman to bring her daughter to the emergency room—*right away!*

Dates & Places Used:

429

Human Self-Sufficiency

I was home alone in bed with the flu one year while our church was having its annual Thanksgiving dinner. When the family began to arrive home afterward, one of the first ones into the house was our youngest daughter, Marie, age four. She led her sister, Bev, into the bedroom to check on me. She said, "Daddy, do you know who took care of you while we were at the dinner?"

I said, "No, who?"

"God." And then she added, "But you don't need God anymore—me and Bev are home now."

Dates & Places Used:

430

TOPIC: Health

Wealth or Health

Many people spend their health for wealth and then try to spend their wealth for health.

Dates & Places Used:

431

TOPIC: Heaven

The Sure Sign

Early in my career as a doctor, I went to see a patient who was just coming out of anesthesia. Church chimes were sounding in the distance. The woman murmured, "I must be in heaven." Then she saw me. She said, "No, I can't be. There's Dr. Campbell."

Dates & Places Used:

432

TOPIC: Hell

Enough, Already

A man was giving such unbelievable testimony in a court case that the judge warned him he was in danger of perjuring himself. "Are you aware," the judge asked, "of what will happen to you if you are caught lying under oath?"

"Yes, Your Honor," replied the witness. "When I die, I'll go to hell."

"But what else?"

The puzzled man thought for a moment. "You mean there's more?"

Dates & Places Used:

433

TOPIC: Hell

Anything Is Better

A woman hired a medium to bring back the spirit of her dead husband. When he appeared in a ghostly form, she asked, "Honey, is it better up there than it was here with me?"

Her husband answered, "Oh yes, it is much better. But I'm not up there!"

Dates & Places Used:

434

TOPIC: Hell

Wrong Bus

A man staggered onto a bus late at night and sat down next to an elderly woman. The woman piously looked at the man and told him, "I'm afraid I have bad news for you, young man. You're going to hell!"

The man jumped up from the seat and exclaimed, "Oh no! I must be on the wrong bus!"

Dates & Places Used:

435

TOPIC: Honesty

When a Man Keeps His Word

A man is forced to keep his word when no one else will take it.

Dates & Places Used:

436

Candor by the Dentist

A dentist was overheard speaking to his patient as he bent over him with a hypodermic needle in hand: "You might feel a little sting. On the other hand, it might feel as though you've been kicked in the mouth by a mule."

Dates & Places Used:

437

Ethics Test

A young woman was soaking up the sun's rays on a Florida beach when a little boy in his swimming trunks, carrying a towel, came up to her and asked her, "Do you believe in God?"

She was surprised by the question but replied, "Why, yes, I do."

Then he asked her, "Do you go to church every Sunday?"

Again, her answer was "Yes!"

Then he asked, "Do you read your Bible and pray every day?"

Again she said, "Yes!" But by now her curiosity was very much aroused. At last the boy sighed and said with obvious relief, "Will you hold my quarter while I go in swimming?"

Dates & Places Used:

438

Relative Honesty

A school teacher was trying to impress her students with the importance of honesty. She asked her class, "Suppose you found a briefcase with a half million dollars in it. What would you do?"

Johnny raised his hand immediately and replied, "If it belonged to a poor family, I'd return it."

Dates & Places Used:

439

Hard Dress to Iron

A little girl went up to the front of the church to listen to the pastor's children's sermon. The pastor gathered the children around himself and noticed the beautiful new dress on this little girl. The pastor complimented the girl for her pretty dress and asked if it was new.

The little girl leaned toward the pastor and spoke directly into his lapel microphone: "Yes, pastor, this is my brand-new dress. And my mommy says that it is even harder to iron this dress than to listen to one of your sermons."

Dates & Places Used:

440

False Hope

Nothing gives you more false hope than the first day of a diet.

Dates & Places Used:

441

Shoveling for a Horse

There were two rooms—one full of brand-new toys, the other full of hay and horse manure. Two children were taken into them, one a pessimist, the other an optimist. The pessimist looked at the first room and cried because all those wonderful toys would soon be broken. The optimist was in the other room shoveling. "I know there has to be a horse in here somewhere," he said.

Dates & Places Used:

442

Veal Cutlets and Pancakes

A man went into the hospital for tests, where he learned that he had several highly contagious incurable illnesses. He was quite upset and asked the doctor what he was to do. The doctor informed him there was only one way to treat him at this point— he would receive a private room and would need to eat veal cutlets and pancakes every day.

The patient liked pancakes and veal cutlets but asked, "Why do you want me to eat the same things every day? How will they help me?"

The doctor answered, "Oh, they won't really help you. They're just easy to slide under the door to your room."

Dates & Places Used:

443

Who Goes First?

The following incident happened when Patrick was four years old and his brother, Luke, was five. Already a half year in kindergarten had made Luke wiser.

Luke and Patrick were fighting over who would go first in a game. They had quite a debate that almost ended in a fight.

Luke changed his strategy and reasoned with his brother: "You know, Patrick, Jesus says that the first will be last and the last will be first, so it is better to be last."

Patrick thought about that for a moment and then answered, "Then I'll go last."

"Okay, then I'll go first," said a suddenly worldly-wise Luke.

Dates & Places Used:

444

TOPIC: Humility

World Was Here First

The world owes you nothing; it was here first. *(Mark Twain)*
Dates & Places Used:

445

TOPIC: Humility

Can You Top This?

An old minister who survived the great Johnstown flood loved to tell the story over and over in great detail. Everywhere he went he would talk about this great historic event in his life. One day he died and went to heaven, and in a meeting there all the saints gathered together to share their life experiences. The old minister got all excited and ran to Peter (who, naturally, was in charge) and asked if he might tell the exciting story of his survival of the Johnstown flood. Peter hesitated for a moment and then said, "Yes, you may share, but just remember that in our audience tonight will be Brother Noah."
Dates & Places Used:

446

TOPIC: Humility

Too Clean or Not Too Clean

A couple I know came at last to the level of financial success where they felt they could afford help with housework. They went to an agency and hired a woman to come in once a week to clean. She was scheduled to come for the first time the following Friday.

On Thursday the husband came home unexpectedly in the middle of the day to pick up some papers he had forgotten and found his wife home early from work, dressed in her oldest cleaning clothes, surrounded by mops, buckets, sponges, rags, and a lot of spray bottles. "What are you doing?" he asked.

"Well, the new cleaning lady is coming tomorrow," she replied, "and I couldn't stand to have her see the house a mess."
Dates & Places Used:

447

TOPIC: Humility

Wiser Today

A person should never be ashamed to own [say] that he is wrong, which is but saying in other words that he is wiser today than he was yesterday. *(Alexander Pope)*
Dates & Places Used:

448

TOPIC: Humility

Standing Room Only

When Mark Twain was on one of his lecture tours, he was getting a haircut in a small town, and the barber asked him if he planned to attend the lecture that evening by "Mr. Mark Twain."

Twain said he thought he might.

The barber said, "It's sold out, so if you don't already have a ticket, you'll have to stand."

Twain said, "Just my luck! I always have to stand when that fellow lectures!"
Dates & Places Used:

449

TOPIC: Humor

So Easily Provoked

A sense of humor enables us not so much to laugh at the people who provoke us as to laugh at ourselves for being so easily provoked.
Dates & Places Used:

TOPIC: Humor

Ha, Ha, Ha, Plop

Question: What goes Ha, ha, ha, plop?
Answer: Someone who laughs his head off!
Dates & Places Used:

TOPIC: Hunting

Follow the Tracks

Two experienced bear hunters and a friend who wanted to learn how to hunt bears went hunting. At the end of the first day, one of the experienced bear hunters brought back a large grizzly bear. The inexperienced bear hunter asked how the grizzly bear was bagged. The successful hunter explained, "I followed the tracks, I went into a cave, and I shot the bear."

The next day the three hunters went after some more bears. At the end of the day, the second experienced hunter dragged a black bear back into camp. When asked how he had shot the black bear, he told them, "I followed the tracks into the cave, and then I shot the bear."

The third day the three hunters went out to hunt and returned at the end of the day. Neither of the experienced hunters had a bear. When the inexperienced bear hunter returned to camp, he had no bear, but he was all cut up and bloody. The two other hunters asked what had happened. The inexperienced hunter explained, "I too followed the tracks, I went into the cave, and I got hit by a train."
Dates & Places Used:

TOPIC: Hunting

Meatless Definition

Vegetarian is an old Native American word meaning terrible hunter!
Dates & Places Used:

453

TOPIC: Hunting

Bird Calls Attract Cats

Hunters, the way to tell if your new bird calls really work is to try them and see if any hungry cats come running.

Dates & Places Used:

454

TOPIC: Hunting

Dynamic Retriever

Things could be worse. For example, you could have been the hapless victim of the faithful dog who played a good game of fetch the stick. Here is the story.

A fellow wanted to take his male relatives hunting, so he bought a brand-new Jeep Cherokee, gathered all the necessary hunting equipment, and then took off with his relatives to hunt some ducks. When the men arrived at the place where they wanted to hunt, they drove onto the frozen Michigan lake. They needed to make a hole for their decoys to float and for the ducks to land, so they had a stick of dynamite to create their swimming hole. The fuse on the dynamite took about twenty seconds to burn, and the men did not want to take the chance of falling on the ice after the dynamite was lit. The men chose to light the dynamite and throw it as far as they could from the Jeep where they stood.

As soon as they threw the lit dynamite, their hunting dog misread their intentions and perceived that they had initiated a game of fetch the stick. Despite the men's shouts, the dog retrieved the stick. The men panicked and shot at the dog. Although the shotgun blasts did not kill the dog, they did confuse him. Still holding the dynamite in his mouth, the dog ran under the Jeep Cherokee.

In moments the dog and the Cherokee were at the bottom of the lake. Insurance would not pay for the vehicle, because its destruction was the result of an illegal activity. The first of sixty payments was due a few days after the accident. There would still be fifty-nine payments more to go.

Dates & Places Used:

184

455

TOPIC: Hunting

Bearly Hunting

Two men were on an Alaskan bear hunt. On opening morning a light snow fell, and one man stayed in the cabin while the other went out hunting.

The one who went out to hunt found a huge grizzly bear, shot at it, but only wounded it. The enraged bear charged toward him, and the man dropped his rifle and started running for the cabin as fast as he could.

He ran fast, but the bear was faster and gained on him with every step. Just as he reached the open cabin door, he tripped and fell flat on his face. Too close behind to stop, the bear tripped over him and went rolling into the cabin. The man jumped up, closed the cabin door, and yelled to his friend inside, "You skin this one while I go and get another!"

Dates & Places Used:

456

TOPIC: Husbands

First Baby or Husband

The phone in the maternity ward rang, and a very excited voice came through: "This is Harold Smith, and I'm bringing my wife in—she's about to have a baby!"

"Calm down," the nurse said. "Tell me, is this her first baby?"

"No," the frantic voice replied, "this is her husband!"

Dates & Places Used:

457

TOPIC: Husbands

Husband Role

A little girl and a little boy were at day care one day. The girl approached the boy and said, "Hey, Stevie, wanna play house?"

"Sure! What do you want me to do?"

"I want you to communicate," replied the girl.

"That word is too big," said the boy. "I have no idea what it means."

The little girl smirked and said, "Perfect. You can be the husband."

Dates & Places Used:

458

TOPIC: Hypocrisy

Acting like Orphans

Some people who say "Our Father" on Sunday go around the rest of the week acting like orphans.

Dates & Places Used:

459

TOPIC: Hypocrisy

Hypocrisy Defined

Hypocrite defined: One who complains about the sex and violence in the videos he watches.

Dates & Places Used:

460

TOPIC: Hypocrisy

Hypocrite

A hypocrite is a man who writes a book praising atheism and then prays that it will sell. *(Leighton Ford)*

Dates & Places Used:

TOPIC: Identity

Old Sherman

A young father and his boy who lived in New York regularly jogged together through the city early in the morning. Their normal course took them by a statue of General William Tecumseh Sherman seated on a horse. One of their regular rituals was to pause for a breather at the foot of familiar old Sherman. Then the father took a job on the West Coast and the day came for their last jog and their last rest at the foot of the famous Civil War general. The father pointed out the significance of this last stop before Sherman. The next day they would be gone. "Take one good long last look at old Sherman," he said to his son. Then, as they stood and were about to resume their morning run, the boy said, "By the way, Dad, who is that fellow sitting up on the back of old Sherman?"

Dates & Places Used:

TOPIC: Identity

Obvious Clues

A French taxicab driver once played a joke on Sir Arthur Conan Doyle. The man had driven Sir Arthur from the station to a hotel, and when he received his fare, he said, "Merci, Monsieur Conan Doyle."

"Why, how do you know my name?" asked Sir Arthur.

"Well, sir," replied the taxi driver, "I read in the papers that you were coming from the south of France to Paris. Your general appearance told me that you were English. Your hair has been clearly last cut by a barber in the south of France. I put these indications together and guessed at once that it was you."

"That is very remarkable," replied Sir Arthur. "You have no other evidence to go on?"

"Well," hesitated the man, "there was also the fact that your name was on your luggage."

Dates & Places Used:

463

TOPIC: Identity

Old Enough but Not Smart Enough

A young man walked into a corner store with a shotgun and demanded all the cash from the cash drawer. After the cashier put the cash in a bag, the robber saw a bottle of scotch that he wanted behind the counter on the shelf. He told the cashier to put it in the bag as well, but the cashier refused and explained, "I don't believe you are over twenty-one."

The robber said he was, but the clerk still refused to give it to him because he didn't believe him. The robber took his driver's license out of his wallet and gave it to the clerk. The clerk looked it over and agreed that the man was indeed over twenty-one, and he put the scotch in the bag. The robber then ran from the store with his loot. The cashier promptly called the police and gave the name and address that he got off the license. The police arrested the robber two hours later at his home.

Dates & Places Used:

464

TOPIC: Identity

Parrot and the Plumber

A woman owned a parrot that could say only one thing–"Who is it?" For years and years she had been trying to teach the bird to extend its vocabulary, but it refused to utter anything other than "Who is it?"

One day the woman had sent for the plumber, and because she had to go out shopping, she arranged for him to find the key under the mat outside the front door. The plumber duly arrived, found the key, let himself in, and set to work. Naturally the parrot, hearing someone in the house with an unfamiliar tread, decided to give a recital. "Who is it?" called the parrot.

"The plumber!" called the workman.

Hearing a strange voice the parrot again decided to utter his one and only phrase: "Who is it?"

"The plumber!" came the response.

The parrot was not satisfied; he wanted to see who the stranger was. "Who is it?" he called again, and again the plumber yelled out, "It's the plumber!" Again and again the bird called out, "Who is it?" and again and again the poor bewildered plumber responded, "It's the plumber! It's the plumber! *It's the plumber!*"

Eventually in a fury the man roamed the house, going from room to room trying to find out who was calling him, but he failed to realize that it was the parrot. For a whole hour he dashed around the house, growing increasingly desperate and shouting out, "It's the plumber!" Finally, the exhausted man fainted in the hall.

Just at that moment the woman of the house entered, saw the unconscious figure on the carpet, and said, "Who is it?"

The parrot replied, "It's the plumber!"

Dates & Places Used:

465

TOPIC: Identity

False Impressions

I arrived in Toronto at ten in the morning for a meeting with two of my colleagues. We were to meet in the home of my associate's parents.

As I approached the home, I saw my colleague's car parked on the street, so I pulled into the driveway. As I grabbed my briefcase and started walking toward the house, an older gentleman came out of the house and warmly greeted me. I didn't recognize him, but I thought, "That's okay; I've only been here once before."

I entered the house, where I was introduced to the man's wife. We chatted briefly and the gentleman began to tell me the problem he was having with the dishwasher. I found it all fascinating. Then I was asked, "Would you like to see the electrical panel?"

"Sure, why not?" was my reply. (I thought it might be on the way to my meeting.)

We walked down to the basement where the electrical panel was pointed out. "Do you see the problem?" I was asked.

"No, not really," I responded.

"Look, see where it's burned out," my gracious host pointed out.

"Yes, I see it," I said enthusiastically.

"What do you recommend?" he asked.

"I'm not sure," I said naively.

"Should I replace the panel?" he continued.

"Well, how old is it?" I inquired. I was informed that it was about twenty-five years old, so I ventured to say that it might not be a bad idea.

At this point, I sensed something was not quite right. So I blurted out, "Would you mind telling me your name?" When he responded, I told him I was very embarrassed that I was in the wrong house. Then I told him the name of the people I was looking for.

"Oh, they live across the street," he said with a smile.

"That will be seventy-five dollars," I said sheepishly as I left for my meeting in the house across the road.

Dates & Places Used:

466

TOPIC: Identity

Early Identity

A story is told of a grandmother who proudly presented her two young grandchildren to her friend.

"Oh," remarked the friend, "They're so cute. How old are they?"

The question brought a definite response: "The lawyer is two and the doctor is four."

Dates & Places Used:

467

TOPIC: Identity

Small Phone Holes

A little boy ran to answer the phone for his mother. His mother called from the other room, "Who is it?"

The boy answered, "I can't tell who it is, Mommy. The holes in the phone are too small."

Dates & Places Used:

468

TOPIC: Impact/Influence

Self-Made the Easy Way

If you want to write your own ticket, then print it yourself.

If you want to make a name for yourself, then change the one you have.

If you want a place in the sun, then don't forget your sunscreen.

Dates & Places Used:

469

TOPIC: Impact/Influence

Not a Bit of Influence

A market research interviewer was surveying people in the grocery store after they picked up their bread. One man picked up a loaf of Wonder Bread, and the interviewer asked him, "Sir, would you be willing to answer a couple of questions about your choice of bread?"

The man responded, "Yes, I'd be happy to."

"Fine," the man said. "The question I'd like to ask you is this: Do you feel that your choice of Wonder Bread has been at all influenced by their advertising program?"

The fellow looked shocked and said, "Of course not. I'm not influenced by that sort of thing at all!"

"Well then," he said, "could you tell me just why you did choose Wonder Bread?"

He replied, "Of course I can. Because it builds strong bodies in eight ways!"

Dates & Places Used:

470

TOPIC: Impact/Influence

Evaluating Your Efforts

A young boy was excited when he successfully pulled a cornstalk out by its roots. When his father patted him on the back,

the boy beamed and said, "Just think, the whole world had hold of the other end of it."
Dates & Places Used:

471

TOPIC: Impact/Influence

Pig in the Parlor

An old proverb says, "You can bring a pig into the parlor, but that doesn't change the pig"–but it certainly changes the parlor!
Dates & Places Used:

472

TOPIC: In-laws

Pigs in the Family

A couple drove several miles down a country road, not saying a word. An earlier discussion had led to an argument, and neither wanted to concede his or her position. As they passed a barnyard of mules and pigs, the wife sarcastically asked, "Relatives of yours?"

"Yep," the husband replied, "in-laws."
Dates & Places Used:

473

TOPIC: In-laws

Outlaws Don't Promise

One big difference between outlaws and in-laws is that outlaws don't promise to pay it back.
Dates & Places Used:

474

TOPIC: In-laws

Convincing Proof of Hell

A young woman returned home early from a date with a long look on her face. Her mother asked her what was bothering her. The girl explained, "My boyfriend just proposed marriage."

Her mother asked, "What's so bad about that?"

The girl answered, "He also told me he is an atheist. He said there is no way he could ever believe there was a hell."

The mother consoled her daughter: "Don't let this bother you. Marry him anyway. With a little time and between the two of us, we will be able to convince him there is a hell."

Dates & Places Used:

475

TOPIC: Insults

Fine Line Called the Rio Grande

A Texan was visiting south of the border when he heard a Mexican say, "¡Loco Gringo!"

"You have to remember," he replied, "that there's a fine line between genius and insanity."

"¡Si, señor! We call it the Rio Grande."

Dates & Places Used:

476

TOPIC: Insults

Comparative Thankfulness

Eight-year-old Tommy was invited to a neighbor's home for supper. The neighbor asked little Tommy, "Are you sure you can cut your meat, Tommy?"

Tommy answered, "Yes, thank you. We often have it just as tough as this at home."

Dates & Places Used:

477

Wrong Man—Wrong Finger

A woman who had been married for just over a year was visiting her mother-in-law, who noticed that this woman was wearing her wedding ring on the wrong finger. When asked why this was, the daughter-in-law said, "For the first six months of our marriage I wore the ring on the right finger, but after that I started wearing the ring on the wrong finger."

"Why did you change?" her mother-in-law asked.

The young woman answered, "I changed my ring to the wrong finger when I realized that I was married to the wrong man."

Dates & Places Used:

478

Insulting Alligators

Never insult an alligator until you've crossed the river.
(Cordell Hull)
Dates & Places Used:

479

Apology Included

An elderly gentleman was in the post office and was unable to address the postcard he wanted to send to a friend. He asked a young man if he would address the postcard for him.

The man gladly agreed to do so and even offered to write a short note on the card for the elderly gentleman. After a short note was dictated, the young man handed the postcard to the old fellow. The elderly gentleman looked at the postcard, handed it back to the young man, and asked, "Would you mind doing one more thing for me?"

The young man had thoroughly enjoyed this act of kindness and answered, "Certainly, what else may I do for you?"

The elderly gentleman replied, "At the end of the note could you add, 'Please excuse me for the sloppy handwriting'?"
Dates & Places Used:

480

TOPIC: Insurance

Replacement Insurance

A farmer's barn burned down, and his wife called the insurance company. She told the agent, "We had that barn insured for fifty thousand dollars, and I want my money."

The agent replied, "Whoa there, just a minute. Insurance doesn't work quite like that. First, we will ascertain the value of what was insured and then provide you with a new one of comparable worth."

There was a long pause before the woman replied, "If that's the way insurance works, then I'd like to cancel the policy I have on my husband."

Dates & Places Used:

481

TOPIC: Insurance

How Do You Start a Flood?

A doctor vacationing on the Riviera met an old lawyer friend and asked him what he was doing there. The lawyer replied, "Remember that lousy real estate I bought? Well, it caught fire, so here I am with the fire insurance proceeds. What are you doing here?"

The doctor replied, "Remember that lousy real estate I had in Mississippi? Well, the river overflowed, and here I am with the flood insurance proceeds."

The lawyer looked puzzled. "Gee," he asked, "how do you start a flood?"

Dates & Places Used:

482

TOPIC: Insurance

Blessed Insurance

A teenager, pointing to the crumpled fender on the family car, said, "Good news, Dad! You haven't been pouring those insurance payments down the drain!"

Dates & Places Used:

483

TOPIC: Insurance

Preexisting Idiot

A man went on a ski trip and was knocked unconscious by the chairlift. He called his insurance company from the hospital, but they refused to cover his injury.

"Why is the injury not covered?" he asked.

"You got hit in the head by a chairlift," the insurance rep said. "That makes you an idiot, and we consider that a preexisting condition!"

Dates & Places Used:

484

TOPIC: Intelligence

Slow Laugh

He who laughs last thinks slowest!

Dates & Places Used:

485

TOPIC: Intelligence

Losing His Load

On a cold winter day a trucker pulled to a stop at a stoplight. The woman behind him jumped out of her car, ran up to his truck, and knocked on his door. The trucker lowered the window, and she said, "Hi, my name is Heidi, and you are losing some of your load."

The trucker ignored her and proceeded down the street. When the truck stopped for another red light, the woman once again caught up, jumped out of her car, and ran up and knocked on his door. And again the trucker lowered the window. As if they had never spoken, the woman said brightly, "Hi, my name is Heidi, and you are losing some of your load!"

Shaking his head, the trucker ignored her again and continued down the street. At the third red light, the same thing happened. All out of breath, the woman got out of her car, ran up, and knocked on the truck door. The trucker lowered the window. Again she said, "Hi, my name is Heidi, and you are losing some of your load!"

When the light turned green, the trucker revved up and raced to the next light. When he stopped this time, he hurriedly got out of the truck and ran back to the woman. He knocked on her window, and as she lowered it, he said, "Hi, my name is Bob, and I'm driving the *salt truck!*"

Dates & Places Used:

486

TOPIC: Intelligence

Primate Intelligence

Question: If you are in a room with three monkeys, and one holds a banana, one has a book, and the other has a pencil, which one is the smartest primate in the room?

Answer: Hopefully, you!

Dates & Places Used:

487

TOPIC: Intelligence

Length of Life

Man can live without air for a very few minutes, without water for a number of days, without food for about two months, without a new thought for years on end.

Dates & Places Used:

488

TOPIC: Intelligence

Really a Blonde

A blonde went to the appliance store sale and found a bargain. "I would like to buy this TV," she told the salesman.

"Sorry, we don't sell to blondes," he replied.

She hurried home and dyed her hair, then came back and again told the salesman, "I would like to buy this TV."

"Sorry, we don't sell to blondes," he replied.

"Oh, he recognized me," she thought. She went for a complete disguise this time—haircut and new color, new outfit, big sunglasses—then waited a few days before she again approached the salesman. "I would like to buy this TV."

"Sorry, we don't sell to blondes," he replied.

Frustrated, she exclaimed, "How do you know I'm a blonde?"

"Because that's a microwave," he replied.

Dates & Places Used:

489

TOPIC: Intelligence

Anatomical Vowels

According to former line coach Pat Boland of the Iowa Hawkeyes, a football player taking an anatomy test wrote, "The anatomy is divided into three parts: the head, the chest, and the abdomen. The head houses the brain and eyes; the chest houses the lungs, heart, and liver; the abdomen houses the vowels, of which there are five—A, E, I, O, and U."

Dates & Places Used:

490

TOPIC: Interpretation

Wine versus Grape Juice

A teetotalling mother was very vocal from time to time about her theory that only grape juice—not wine—was served at the Last Supper. During one of these discussions her daughter said,

"But, Mother, don't you remember that at Cana Jesus turned the water into wine?"

The mother, eyes blazing, said, "Yes! And he never should have done it, either!"

Dates & Places Used:

491

TOPIC: Interpretation

Out of the Mouths of Babes

My sister and her children moved to my city not long ago and began attending church for the first time in their lives. They particularly loved the singing and the Communion service. One day while babysitting, I fixed the children their favorite lunch of burritos and apple juice. As I left the room, I heard four-year-old Alisha begin to celebrate Communion with her lunch items. She seemed to have memorized the words of institution quite well, except when it came to the cup. I heard her say, "And Jesus took the cup, and he blessed it, and he gave God thanks for it, and he said, 'Fill it with Folgers and wake 'em up!'" What wonderful theology!

Dates & Places Used:

492

TOPIC: Interpretation

Lot's Flea

A father was reading Bible stories to his young son. He read, "The man named Lot was warned to take his wife and flee out of the city, but his wife looked back and was turned to salt."

His son asked, "What happened to the flea?"

Dates & Places Used:

493

TOPIC: Interpretation

Matzo Braille

A Jewish man took his Passover lunch to eat outside in the park. He sat down on a bench and began eating. A blind man came by and sat down next to him. Feeling neighborly, the Jew passed a sheet of matzo to the blind man.

The blind man handled the matzo for a few minutes, looked puzzled, and finally exclaimed, "Who wrote this nonsense?"

Dates & Places Used:

494

TOPIC: Interpretation

Wrong First Lady

A teacher was discussing a news item about the president and the first lady with her class. The teacher asked the class if anyone knew who the "first lady" was.

One student hesitantly answered, "Eve?"

Dates & Places Used:

495

TOPIC: Interpretation

Lopsided Tale of Two Cities

A Minneapolis man told his pastor that he was leaving the church because he finally looked into that book the pastor was always citing, and he noted, "It has all that stuff about St. Paul and not a word about Minneapolis!"

Dates & Places Used:

496

TOPIC: Interpretation

Tarzan and the Lion's Den

A little girl was getting quizzed by her Sunday school teacher to determine how well she knew the Bible. The teacher had asked several questions, and the poor girl had not answered any of the questions correctly. The sympathetic teacher, trying to come up with an easier question, asked the girl who had been thrown into the den of lions and had survived.

The girl paused and carefully thought for a moment. Her eyes brightened, and she then exclaimed, "Oh, I know that one; it was Tarzan!"

Dates & Places Used:

497

TOPIC: Interpretation

Flipping the Presidents

A low-achieving man was explaining why he was fired as an investigator for the treasury department. "I arrested a couple of alleged counterfeiters, but it turned out they were not counterfeiting at all."

His friend asked why he thought they were counterfeiting. He explained, "The bills they were passing looked suspicious."

"What was suspicious about them?" his friend asked.

He answered, "Some of the bills were printed upside down. So some of the presidents were on one side of the bills, and some were on the other side."

No wonder the man was fired!

Dates & Places Used:

498

TOPIC: Interpretation

Whole East Coast

A churchgoing family took a girl who was visiting with them to church one Sunday. This girl had never gone to church in her life but seemed to enjoy the experience. When they returned home, they asked the girl what she thought about the experience. She said she liked it, but she was confused about one thing. She asked why the whole West Coast was not included. No one in the family new what she was talking about. She explained, "The man in the front kept talking about the Father, Son, and whole East Coast."

Dates & Places Used:

499

Logic Lapses

Letter from a Dutch mother to her son, Hans:

Dear Son,

I'm writing this letter very slow 'cause I know that you can't read fast. You should also know that we don't live any longer where we used to live. You see, your father read in the paper that most accidents happen within twenty miles of home, so we moved. Our new house has a washing machine. The first day I put four shirts in it for my wash, and then I pulled the handle, and I haven't seen hide nor hair of them since.

It only rained twice this week. The first time it rained for three days, and the second time it rained for four days. You said that you wanted us to send you your coat. Well, when we talked to Aunt Sue about it, she said that it would be too heavy to mail with those big, heavy buttons, so we cut them off and put them in the pockets.

We got a bill from the funeral home today, and it said that if we didn't pay for Grandma's funeral then up she comes.

The other day your Uncle John was at the brewery and fell into the whiskey vat. Some people tried to pull him out, but he fought them off so long that he finally drowned. We had him cremated, and he burned for three days.

Three of your friends went off a bridge in their pickup the other day. The driver got out okay, but the two in the

*back drowned. It seems that they couldn't get the tailgate
down. That's all for now.*

Love,
Mom

*P.S. Was going to send some money but already had the
letter sealed.*

Dates & Places Used:

500

TOPIC: Interpretation

The Bible Says Jump

One of the fathers in our congregation related to me how he
and his five-year-old daughter had been jumping together on
their backyard trampoline. She was having a great time.

Finally, her father stopped for a rest and quoted a Scripture
verse: "You know, the Bible says, 'Be still and know that I am
God.'"

His daughter quickly grew tired of her father's inactivity and
retorted, "The Bible says, 'Jump, jump, jump!'"

Dates & Places Used:

501

TOPIC: Interpretation

Noah's Business Venture

An industrial executive who knew his Bible agreed to teach a
few sessions of Sunday school. He asked the children, "Why was
Noah the first businessman?"

There was silence. Nobody knew.

"Well," said the executive, "it's because he floated the first
joint stock company and forced all his competitors into involun-
tary liquidation."

Dates & Places Used:

502

TOPIC: Jobs

Job Insecurity

Insecurity is finding on your new job that your name is written on the door in chalk—and that there's a wet sponge hanging next to it.

Dates & Places Used:

503

TOPIC: Jobs

Church Staff Job Descriptions

Pastor: Able to leap tall buildings in a single bound. More powerful than a locomotive. Faster than a speeding bullet. Walks on water. Gives counsel to God.

Associate Pastor: Able to leap short buildings in a single bound. As powerful as a switch engine. Just as fast as a speeding bullet. Walks on water when the sea is calm. Talks with God.

Minister of Music: Leaps short buildings with a running start. Almost as powerful as a switch engine. Faster than a speeding BB. Walks on water if he or she knows where the stumps are. Sings to God.

Minister of Youth: Runs around buildings. Powerful enough to chase a locomotive with a handcar. Uses a squirt gun. Spends a lot of time around the water fountain. Mumbles to himself or herself.

Church Secretary: Lifts buildings to walk under them. Kicks locomotives off the track. Catches speeding bullets in her teeth. Freezes water with a single glance. When God speaks, she says, "May I ask who's calling?"

Dates & Places Used:

504

Sunday School Hours

Two children were walking home after Sunday school. One of the boys turned to the other and informed him, "I think I'll be a Sunday school teacher when I grow up; I like the hours."
Dates & Places Used:

505

Be Sure Your Sins Will Boomerang

When A. Phillip Johnson of Union City, California, was almost eighty-six years old and had been serving for eight years as chaplain of the Masonic Homes, he related this story from his own experience:

In a bilingual church I pastored many years ago in Massachusetts, a Mrs. Johnson was well known for her simple faith in God. Her husband was unemployed and, prayerfully she walked the streets helping him look for work. One day she saw a section gang working at a railroad crossing and walked up to one of the men, asking if there was any possibility for her husband's employment. He told her, rather irreverently, that she would have to talk to the foreman, calling him a son-of-a-so-and-so. Being from the old country and unfamiliar with foul names, she thought this was his designation. Addressing him as such, she repeated her request. Realizing her ignorance, the foreman asked who had sent her to him. She pointed out the man, and the foreman said, "Yes, your husband is hired and that man is fired."
Dates & Places Used:

506

What New Job Lingo Really Means

"Join our fast-paced company": We have no time to train you.

"Casual work atmosphere": We don't pay enough to expect that you'll dress up.

"Must be deadline oriented": You'll be six months behind schedule on your first day.

"Some overtime required": Some time each night and some time each weekend.

"Duties will vary": Anyone in the office can boss you around.

"Must have an eye for detail": We have no quality control.

"Career-minded": Female applicants must be childless (and remain that way).

"No phone calls please": We've filled the job; our call for resumes is just a legal formality.

"Seeking candidates with a wide variety of experience": You'll need it to replace three people who just left.

"Problem-solving skills a must": You're walking into a company in perpetual chaos.

"Requires team leadership skills": You'll have the responsibilities of a manager without the pay or respect.

"Good communication skills": Management communicates, and you listen, figure out what they want, and do it.

Dates & Places Used:

507

Pilots and Chopits

The chief of staff of the U.S. Air Force decided that he would personally intervene in the recruiting crisis affecting all our armed services. So he directed that a nearby air force base be opened and that all eligible young men and women be invited. As he and his staff were standing near a brand-new F-15 fighter, a pair of twin brothers who looked like they had just stepped off a marine corps recruiting poster walked up to them.

The chief of staff turned to them, stuck out his hand, and introduced himself. He looked at the first young man and asked, "Son, what skills can you bring to the air force?"

The young man looked at him and said, "I'm a pilot!"

The general got all excited, turned to his aide, and said, "Get him in today, all the paperwork done, everything, do it!" The aide hustled the young man off.

The general looked at the second young man and asked, "What skills to you bring to the air force?"

The young man said, "I chop wood!"

"Son," the general replied, "we don't need wood choppers in the air force. What do you know how to do?"

"I chop wood!"

"Young man," huffed the general, "you are not listening to me. We don't need wood choppers; this is the twentieth century!"

"Well," the young man said, "you enlisted my brother!"

"Of course we did," said the general. "He's a pilot!"

The young man rolled his eyes and said, "Well, think about it, man: I have to chop it before he can pile it!"

Dates & Places Used:

508

TOPIC: Jobs

Vice President of Peas

The new vice president was flaunting his title so much that one of his coworkers finally said to him, "These days vice presidents are a dime a dozen. In fact, the title is getting so ridiculous, my supermarket even has a vice president in charge of peas."

The new V.P. was insulted–and skeptical. So he phoned the store and asked for the vice president in charge of peas. The voice on the line asked, "Canned or frozen?"

Dates & Places Used:

TOPIC: Joy

A Joyful Old Heart

On October 16, 1995, Jeanne Calment of Paris was inducted into the *Guinness Book of World Records* by becoming the oldest human on record—over 120 years of age. She was born on February 21, 1875, a year before the telephone was invented by Alexander Graham Bell.

Jeanne remembered the construction of the Eiffel Tower and remembered selling colored pencils to the famed Vincent Van Gogh. She survived twenty-seven French presidents during the course of her long life. When asked, "What's the secret to your long life?" she responded, "Laughter!" No wonder the Bible tells us "a cheerful heart is good medicine" (Proverbs 17:22).

Dates & Places Used:

TOPIC: Joy

Promise to Smile

Frank Bettger was a major league ballplayer who turned to sales management after an injury. He later became famous for his inspirational speeches. He would ask people to make a promise to smile for thirty days. Here is what Frank said:

I have asked thousands of men and women in audiences all over the country for a pledge to smile, just for thirty days, their happiest smile at every living creature they see. Easily 75 percent of the people in each audience willingly raised their hands. What has been the result? I quote from one letter received from a Knoxville, Tennessee, man. It is typical of several letters that come to me.

> My wife and I had just about agreed to separate. Of course, I thought she was entirely at fault. Within a few days after I began to put this idea into action, happiness was restored in my home. I then came to realize that I had been losing out in business because of a sullen losing attitude. At the end of the day, I would go home and take it out on my wife and children. It was all my fault, not my

wife's at all. I am a totally different man from what I was a year ago. I'm happier because I've made others happy too. Now everybody greets me with a smile. In addition, my business has shown surprising improvement.

This man was so excited about the results he got from smiling that he kept writing me for years about it.

Dates & Places Used:

511

TOPIC: Justice

Riding Alone

A judge was horseback riding with a young lawyer when they came across an open stretch of country. They noticed a noose hanging from a tree. The judge turned to the lawyer and jokingly said, "If that gallows had its due, where do you suppose you would be right now?"

The young lawyer spurred his horse a few feet forward, then turned back to the judge and answered, "Riding alone."

Dates & Places Used:

512

TOPIC: Justice

All Cut the Same Size

A young man was helping his mother serve pie to his father and their guests at the dinner table. Each time the boy brought another piece of pie to the table, he would set it in front of his father, who would then pass it on to the others at the table.

After watching his father do this several times, the boy leaned toward his father and whispered, "It's no use, Dad. Mom cut all the pieces the same size."

Dates & Places Used:

513

Disarming Defense

A lawyer was defending his client who was accused of theft. The defense was not going well, so the lawyer attempted a different, more creative defense.

"All my client did was to insert his arm across the counter and into the cash register and remove a small sum of money. As a matter of fact, it was just his arm that committed this crime. My client's arm can hardly be seen as my client. I don't understand how you can punish the entire individual for a crime that was committed by a single limb."

The judge saw through the flimsy defense immediately and answered the lawyer accordingly: "You have stated the dilemma well. So by using your line of reasoning, I will sentence only the defendant's arm to one year of imprisonment. As a courtesy to the defendant, he may either accompany his arm or he may not, as he chooses." Upon completion of the sentencing, the judge sat back in his chair with a smug smile on his face. He had played along with the lawyer's defense but had still outsmarted him.

The defendant and lawyer smiled as well. With the assistance of his lawyer, the defendant detached his artificial limb, laid the criminal limb on the bench, and left the courtroom a free man.
Dates & Places Used:

514

Generous Big-City Lawyer

In a remote area out West, a rancher sued a railroad for the loss of his prize bull. The bull was missing from the section in which it had been grazing. The railroad called in a big-city lawyer to take the case against the rancher. The trial was scheduled to take place in the back room of the general store with the justice of the peace presiding. The big-city lawyer met with the rancher when he arrived and tried to get him to settle before going to court. He kept after the rancher with his best negotiating skills. The rancher kept telling the big-city lawyer that a settlement would not be right, it would not be appropriate, it would not be fair, and so on. But the big-city lawyer would not relent. Finally, the rancher gave up and agreed to settle with the railroad for half the amount he was asking to receive in damages. The big-city lawyer wrote out the check and handed it to the rancher. The rancher then signed the release statement for the railroad.

The big-city lawyer was immediately triumphant and could not contain his enthusiasm. He explained that the rancher would have won the case against the railroad. Case law would have favored the rancher, and even the justice of the peace would have known enough about the law to award the rancher with full damages. He put his arm around the rancher and said, "I hate to tell you this, old fellow, but I pulled a fast one on you. You could have won the case and received the entire amount you were asking for. That must make you feel a little disappointed."

The rancher was a bit embarrassed by all the fuss but said to the big-city lawyer as he stuffed the check into his back pocket, "To tell you the truth, I feel guilty enough about receiving any money from you at all. I was coming into court this morning to ask that we dismiss the case. But you kept on telling me to take your money, so I felt that I had better do it or you would never shut up. You see, that crazy bull showed up on the ranch late last night."

Dates & Places Used:

515

TOPIC: Kindness

Oil of Kindness

Kindness is the oil that takes friction out of life.
Dates & Places Used:

516

TOPIC: Knowledge

Reading Is Not Enough

A certain intellectual fellow loved to read. He read everything he could find about philosophy, and he became a philosopher. He read everything he could read about mathematics, and he became a mathematician. He read everything he could find about swimming, and he drowned. There are some subjects you just have to do more than read about.

Dates & Places Used:

517

TOPIC: Knowledge

Facts Are Misleading

The professor in Alfred Hitchcock's film *The Lady Vanishes,* upon being confronted with evidence that proves his theory wrong, replies, "Nonsense. My theory is perfectly correct. It is the facts that are misleading."

Dates & Places Used:

518

TOPIC: Knowledge

Count on Math

There are only three kinds of people: those who *can* count and those who *can't.*

Dates & Places Used:

519

TOPIC: Knowledge

Reading Lion

Two explorers were on a jungle safari when suddenly a ferocious lion jumped in front of them. "Keep calm," the first explorer whispered. "Remember what we read in the book on wild animals: If you stand perfectly still and look the lion in the eye, he will turn and run."

"Sure," replied his companion, "you've read the book, and I've read the book. But has the lion read the book?"

Dates & Places Used:

520

Say Something in French

It was the final day of a three-year French course. The teacher had worked hard to teach his students to communicate fluently in French.

The teacher excitedly asked one of his students, "What are the first words you will say when you get to France?"

The student thought for a moment and answered the teacher, *"Parlez-vous anglais?"*–which means, "Do you speak English?"

Dates & Places Used:

521

In an Emergency

A mother mouse felt that the time had come to introduce her baby mice to the larger world. So having cautioned them that they must pay strict attention to what she did, she proceeded to lead them out of their mouse hole. Upon leaving the hole and entering the living room, she suddenly saw a big cat sleeping a few yards away in the midst of her intended path. Frightened at what lay ahead but not wanting to appear cowardly to her children, the mouse led her family silently forward. Just as she was creeping past the cat, the cat's eyes popped open and she raised her paw. What was Mother Mouse to do to save her children from peril? As the paw began its downward descent, the mouse turned to the cat and barked like a dog. The cat was so frightened she turned and ran, whereupon the mother mouse turned to her baby mice and said, "In an emergency, it's always good to know a second language!"

It may be that the most important thing the church has to offer people in our world is the knowledge of a "second language"!

Dates & Places Used:

522

TOPIC: Laws

Lawyer Laws

Having lawyers create laws is like having doctors create diseases.
Dates & Places Used:

523

TOPIC: Laws

Decalogue-Bargaining

There is a cartoon in the *Hong Kong Tatler* that shows Moses as he comes down from the top of the mountain with the tablets in his hand. He's reporting to the children of Israel and says, "It was hard bargaining–we get the milk and honey, but the anti-adultery clause stays in."
Dates & Places Used:

524

TOPIC: Laws

Theater Etiquette

Movie theater rules that should not be broken:
Please take crying babies to the lobby. Pick them up immediately after the movie has ended.
Please refrain from talking to characters on the screen. Tests have shown they cannot hear you.
Dates & Places Used:

525

TOPIC: Laws

My Bible Doesn't Say That!

My boys were fighting again. If there hadn't been something called "sibling rivalry," Philip (age five) and David (age three) would have invented it. This time, however, the fighting had been going on most of the day. The yelling, the name calling, the tears, and the occasional punches had become almost intolerable.

My wife had tried every trick she knew. She threatened them, she reasoned with them, she tried to distract them, she sent them to bed, and she even applied an occasional swat to their bottoms, but nothing worked for long.

Late in the afternoon Philip initiated another skirmish. This time my wife took a desperate measure—she tried theology. "Philip," she said, "the Bible says, 'Be kind to one another.'" Philip stood up, put his hands on his hips, and said, "My Bible doesn't say that!"

Likewise, there are people in every church who will listen to exhortation, instruction, warnings, and challenges only to reply, by action and attitude, "My Bible doesn't say that."

Dates & Places Used:

526

TOPIC: Laws

Average Fugitive

I feel like a fugitive from the law of averages. *(William H. Mauldin)*

Dates & Places Used:

527

TOPIC: Laws

No Voodoo Curse

There's an old *Leave It to Beaver* rerun in which Wally, Eddie Haskell, and the Beaver are going to a movie. Mrs. Cleaver tells them to go see *Pinocchio*, not the other movie in town, *Voodoo Curse*.

As they approach the theater, Eddie suggests a way around the problem. He says, "Your mom told you not to take the Beaver to *Voodoo Curse*, but what if the Beaver took you?"

With that rationalization, they were convinced they had done nothing wrong. They obeyed the letter of the law but not the intent. Sometimes we do the same thing.

Dates & Places Used:

528

Some Rules Are Tougher Than Others

Four-year-old Jimmy was on a family vacation last summer, and he was given quarters for the video game machine by his older sister. Since Jimmy is not proficient in operating such games, the quarters went rapidly. Finally, he had to be told that there were no more quarters. He demanded, "But I want more."

His sister responded, "Jimmy, in life we don't always get what we want."

Jimmy paused and then shouted, "I hate that rule!"

Dates & Places Used:

529

TOPIC: Lawyers

Take Your Pick

A newspaper in the county seat ran an exposé on the unethical practices of some of the lawyers in that particular county. They ran the headline: "Half of the Lawyers in Our County Are Crooks!"

An association of the lawyers in the county threatened to sue the newspaper unless the "libelous" headline was retracted. The newspaper signed an agreement that did not admit that its story was inaccurate, but that they would indeed retract the headline. The following day the newspaper ran the new headline: "Half of the Lawyers in Our County Are Not Crooks!"

Dates & Places Used:

530

TOPIC: Lawyers

Jury of Lawyers

A defendant in a small county was brought before the judge. After listening to the man for several minutes, the judge could see that the man was clearly guilty. There were a couple of problems, though. The man demanded a jury trial, and it was getting late into the afternoon. The judge glanced at his watch and thought he might still get this case over with before the end of the day.

The judge called for a recess and walked out into the hallway of the court. He saw a group of lawyers there who were finished with their cases and were preparing to leave. He asked them if they would like to serve on a jury for a short case.

This was an opportunity for the lawyers to act in an entirely different way, so they all enthusiastically agreed to serve on the jury. In just a few minutes court was convened, the case was heard, and the lawyer jury was dismissed to consider the case.

After more than an hour, the judge was confused at the length of the jurors' deliberations. He sent his bailiff to see what was delaying the jury. The bailiff returned. The judge asked the bailiff what was taking the jury so long to reach a decision.

"Reach a decision?" the bailiff responded. "They haven't even finished their nominating speeches for foreman of the jury."

Dates & Places Used:

TOPIC: Lawyers

531

Research Lawyers

Did you know they are using lawyers now for medical research?

There are three reasons for this.

1.   There are more lawyers than white rats.
2.   Lawyers are slightly more humanoid than white rats.
3.   There are certain things you can't get a white rat to do.

Dates & Places Used:

TOPIC: Lawyers

532

Lawyer and a Thief

A man was charged with the theft of an expensive sports car. After a lengthy trial, the man was acquitted. Shortly after his trial, the acquitted man returned to see the judge and told him that he wanted to file a warrant against his lawyer. The judge wanted to know why the man wanted his lawyer arrested after his lawyer had won his case and his freedom for him.

The man explained, "Well, I didn't have enough money to pay my lawyer, so he took the car I stole as payment."
Dates & Places Used:

533

TOPIC: Lawyers

Father of Lawyers

A minister once asked a lawyer, "What do you do if you make a mistake on a case?"

The lawyer answered, "I try to fix it if it's big and ignore it if it's insignificant." The lawyer then asked, "What do you do?"

The minister told the lawyer, "I do more or less the same. Let me give you an example. The other day I meant to say, 'The devil is the father of liars,' but I said instead, 'The devil is the father of lawyers,' so I let it go."
Dates & Places Used:

534

TOPIC: Lawyers

In the Hands of a Lawyer

It is better to be a mouse in a cat's mouth than a man in a lawyer's hands.
Dates & Places Used:

535

TOPIC: Lawyers

The Unused Heart

An elderly patient needed a heart transplant and discussed his options with his doctor.

The doctor said, "We have three possible donors; you need to tell me which one you want to use.

"One is a young, healthy athlete who died in an automobile accident. The second is a young businessman who never drank or smoked and died in his private plane. The third is an attorney who just died after practicing law for forty years."

"I'll take the lawyer's heart," said the patient.

The doctor asked the patient why he wanted the heart of the lawyer.

"That's easy," the patient replied. "I want a heart that hasn't been used."

Dates & Places Used:

536

TOPIC: Lawyers

Marvelous Discovery

The story is going around that up in the Stanford Research Laboratories they have made an important change in procedure recently. Instead of using rats in their experiments, they are now using attorneys. When asked why this change was initiated, the head of the lab said, "Well, there are two reasons: there are more of them available, and we find that students don't get as emotionally attached to them."

Dates & Places Used:

537

TOPIC: Lawyers

Truth and Compliments

"You appear to be a man of intelligence," the opposing lawyer said during a trial as he cross-examined a witness.

The witness replied, "I would be glad to say the same of you, but I just swore to tell the truth."

Dates & Places Used:

538

TOPIC: Leadership

Baseball Managers

Billy Martin, former manager of the New York Yankees, once said, "The key to effective management is to keep the five guys who hate you from the five guys who are undecided."
Dates & Places Used:

539

TOPIC: Leadership

Anatomy of a Committee

A committee has six or more legs and no brain.
Dates & Places Used:

540

TOPIC: Leadership

Leaders and Followers

Why is the leader the last to know
where the followers want to go?
The leader looks to check the flock,
and finds that they are down the block.

Dates & Places Used:

541

TOPIC: Leadership

To Feed a Dog

A woman read that dogs were healthier when fed a tablespoon of cod liver oil each day. She wanted the healthiest dog possible, so she resolved to feed her dog a tablespoon of cod liver oil every day. But every day, it was the same routine–she would chase her dog around the house and force feed it a spoonful of cod liver oil.

One day while chasing down her dog, the woman knocked over the bottle of cod liver oil. Much to her surprise, her dog ran over to the puddle of oil and lapped it right up.

The dog loved cod liver oil—just not from the spoon. Perhaps there are times when our message is much more palatable than our method of presentation.

Dates & Places Used:

542

TOPIC: Leadership

Jack Benny on Scouting

A scout troop consists of twelve little kids dressed like shmucks following a big schmuck dressed like a kid. *(Jack Benny)*

Dates & Places Used:

543

TOPIC: Lies

Mark 17

A minister told his congregation, "Next week I plan to preach about the sin of lying. To help you understand my sermon, I want you all to read Mark chapter 17."

The following Sunday, as he prepared to deliver his sermon, the minister asked for a show of hands. He wanted to know how many had read Mark chapter 17. Every hand went up.

The minister smiled and said, "Mark has only sixteen chapters. I will now proceed with my sermon on the sin of lying."

Dates & Places Used:

544

TOPIC: Lies

Not Drunk

A man came home drunk after a night of carousing in a number of neighborhood bars. His wife helped him up to the bedroom and tucked him into bed. Then she kneeled at his bedside and whispered, "John, do you want me to pray for you?"

He agreed, and she began to pray, "Dear Lord, I pray for my husband who lies here before you drunk ..."

Before she could finish, he interrupted, "Don't tell him I'm drunk; just tell him I'm sick."

Dates & Places Used:

545

TOPIC: Lies

So Lost

A police car pulled up in front of Grandma Bessie's house, and Grandpa Morris got out. The polite policeman explained that this elderly gentleman said that he was lost in the park and couldn't find his way home.

"Oh, Morris," said Grandma, "you've been going to that park for over thirty years! How could you get lost?"

Leaning close to Grandma so that the policeman couldn't hear, Morris whispered, "I wasn't lost. I was just too tired to walk home."

Dates & Places Used:

546

TOPIC: Lightbulb Jokes

Lightbulb Jokes Keep Changing

How many Christians does it take to change a lightbulb?
Charismatics: Only one: hands already in the air.
Presbyterians: None: Lights will go on and off at predestined times.
Roman Catholics: None: candles only.
Baptists: At least fifteen: one to change the lightbulb and three committees to approve the change and decide who brings the potato salad.
Episcopalians: Eight: one to call the electrician and seven to say how much they liked the old one better.

Mormons: Five: one man to change the bulb and four wives to tell.

Unitarians: We choose not to make a statement either in favor of or against the need for a lightbulb. However, if in your own journey you have found that lightbulbs work for you, that is fine. You are invited to write a poem or compose a modern dance about your personal relationship with your lightbulb and present it next month at our annual lightbulb Sunday service, in which we will explore a number of lightbulb traditions, including incandescent, fluorescent, three-way, long-life, and tinted, all of which are equally valid paths to luminescence.

Methodists: Undetermined. Whether your light is bright, dull, or completely out, you are loved. You can be a lightbulb, turnip bulb, or tulip bulb. A church-wide lighting service is planned for Sunday, August 19. Bring bulb of your choice and a covered dish.

Nazarenes: Six: one woman to replace the bulb while five men review church lighting policy.

Lutherans: None: Lutherans don't believe in change.

Amish: What's a lightbulb?

Dates & Places Used:

TOPIC: Lightbulb Jokes

Lightbulb Changers—A Collection

Q: How many Calvinists does it take to change a lightbulb?

A: None: God has predestined when the lights will be on.

Q: How many Arminians does it take to change a lightbulb?

A: Just one, but it has to be changed again and again.

Q: How many Christian counselors does it take to change a lightbulb?

A: Only one, but the bulb has to be committed to long-term change.

Q: How many Presbyterians does it take to change a lightbulb?

A: They don't know, but they will appoint a commission to discuss it and report back at the next meeting, at which time it will be discussed and referred back for further work.

Q: How many Presbyterians does it take to change a lightbulb?

A: Are you kidding? They don't change burned out lightbulbs. After all, it was predestined to burn out. How can you fight predestination?

Q: How many liberals does it take to change a lightbulb?

A: Ten, as they need to hold a debate as to whether or not the lightbulb exists. Even if they can agree upon the existence of the lightbulb, they may not go ahead and change it for fear of alienating those who use fluorescent tubes.

Q: How many evangelicals does it take to change a lightbulb?

A: Evangelicals do not change lightbulbs. They simply read out the instructions and hope the lightbulb will decide to change itself.

Q: How many Brethren does it take to change a lightbulb?

A: Change?

Q: How many Amish does it take to change a lightbulb?

A: What's a lightbulb?

Q: How many campfire worship leaders does it take to change a lightbulb?

A: One: And soon all those around can warm up in its glowing.

Q: How many Baptists does it take to change a lightbulb?

A: A whole congregation. They need to vote on it!

Q: How many charismatics does it take to change a lightbulb?

A: Twenty-one: one to change it and twenty to share the experience!

Q: How many charismatics does it take to change a lightbulb?

A: Five: one to change the bulb and four to bind the spirit of darkness in the room.

Q: How many charismatics does it take to change a lightbulb?

A: Three: one to cast it out and two to catch it when it falls!

Q: How many Pentecostals does it take to change a lightbulb?

A: Ten: one to change it and nine others to pray against the spirit of darkness.

Q: How many missionaries does it take to change a lightbulb?

A: Ten: five to determine how many can be changed by the year 2005, four to raise the necessary funds, and one to go find a national to do the job!

Q: How many Southern Baptists does it take to change a lightbulb?

A: About 16 million: However, they are badly divided over whether changing the bulb is a fundamental need or not.

Q: How many televangelists does it take to change a lightbulb?

A: Honestly, we're not sure. But for the message of change to continue to go out, please keep those letters and checks coming.

Q: How many Episcopalians does it take to change a lightbulb?

A: Four: one to change the bulb, one to bless the elements, one to pour the sherry, and one to offer a toast to the old lightbulb.

Dates & Places Used:

548

TOPIC: Lightbulb Jokes

Marxist Lightbulbs

How many Marxists does it take to screw in a lightbulb?

None: The bulb contains within it the seeds of its own revolution.

Dates & Places Used:

549

TOPIC: Lightbulb Jokes

Lawyer Lightbulbs

How many lawyers does it take to change a lightbulb?

It takes just one lawyer to change your lightbulb into his lightbulb.

Dates & Places Used:

550

TOPIC: Lightbulb Jokes

Surreal Changes

How many surrealists does it take to change a lightbulb?

It takes two: one to hold the giraffe and the other one to fill the bathtub with brightly colored tools.

Dates & Places Used:

551

TOPIC: Lightbulb Jokes

Law Professors and Lightbulbs

How many law professors does it take to change a lightbulb? We don't know yet, but it took fifty of them to get the research grant.

Dates & Places Used:

552

TOPIC: Listening

Listen and Flatter

A good listener is a silent flatterer.

Dates & Places Used:

553

TOPIC: Listening

Good Listeners

Good listeners are not only popular everywhere, but after a while they know something.

Dates & Places Used:

554

TOPIC: Listening

Jumping the Gun

When my brother was about five years old, he wanted to answer the telephone, so he watched and listened very carefully. One day he got to the phone first. He picked up the receiver and knew just what to say: "Hello, nope, good-bye!" and immediately hung up the phone.

I think we sometimes make up our minds how to answer God without really listening to his message.

Dates & Places Used:

555

TOPIC: Logic

Let's Be Reasonable

A well-known preacher mentioned in a sermon that God came out of nowhere. After the message a fellow challenged him on that point. He said, "Preacher, let's be reasonable about this," to which the minister replied, "All right, if you want to be reasonable about it, the reason God came from nowhere was that there wasn't anywhere for him to come from, and coming from nowhere, he stood on nothing, for there was nowhere for him to stand. And standing on nothing, he reached out to where there was nowhere to reach and caught something when there was nothing to catch and hung something on nothing and told it to stay there, and nobody said a word. And the reason nobody said anything was that there wasn't anybody there to say anything, so God himself said, 'That's good!'"

Dates & Places Used:

556

TOPIC: Logic

Unending Logic

After giving a lecture on the solar system, philosopher William James was approached by a determined elderly woman with a theory.

"We don't live on a ball rotating around the sun," she said. "We live on a crust of earth on the back of a giant turtle."

James decided to be gentle. "If your theory is correct, madam, what does this turtle stand on?"

"The first turtle stands on the back of a second, far larger turtle, of course."

"But what does that turtle stand on?"

The old woman crowed triumphantly, "It's no use, Mr. James—it's turtles all the way down!"

Dates & Places Used:

557

TOPIC: Logic

Edison's Persistence

If Thomas Edison hadn't persisted, today we'd be watching TV by candlelight.
Dates & Places Used:

558

TOPIC: Logic

Economic Contradictions

Economics is the only discipline in which two people can share a Nobel Prize for holding to two contradictory theories.
Dates & Places Used:

559

TOPIC: Logic

Double-Duty Thermos

A little boy asked his mother what that thing was that his father took to work each day. His mother told him that it was a thermos. The boy asked what it was used for, and she told him that it was used to keep cold things cold and hot things hot. The boy asked his mother if she would buy him a thermos for school.

The boy was quite proud of his new thermos and wanted to fill it himself and take it to school. The first day he took his thermos to school, his teacher noticed it. "Where did you get the thermos?" the teacher asked.

The boy answered, "My mother bought it for me."

The teacher quizzed him, "What do you do with a thermos?"

The boy proudly answered, "You keep cold things cold and hot things hot."

The teacher continued, "So, what's inside your thermos?"

The boy told his teacher, "A cup of hot chocolate and two Popsicles!"
Dates & Places Used:

560

A Ticket to Ride

Three economists and three mathematicians were going for a trip by train. Before their journey the mathematicians bought three tickets (they could count to three) and the economists only one. The mathematicians were glad their stupid colleagues were going to pay a fine. When the conductor was approaching their compartment, however, all three economists went to the nearest restroom. The conductor, noticing that somebody was in the restroom, knocked on the door and in reply saw a hand with a ticket. He checked it, and the economists saved two-thirds of the ticket price.

The next day the mathematicians decided to use the same strategy. They bought only one ticket, and the economists did not buy tickets at all. When the mathematicians saw the conductor, they went to the restroom, and when they heard knocking, they handed in the ticket. They did not get it back. Why? The economists took it and went to the other restroom.

Dates & Places Used:

561

Spilled Milk Response

Instead of crying over spilled milk, go milk another cow.
Dates & Places Used:

562

Real Losses

A man was driving his brand-new BMW at a high rate of speed. He drove onto an overpass with a sharper curve than he had expected. His car spun out of control, and he realized that there was no hope of keeping the car from going over a steep embankment. At the very last moment, he opened his door and jumped. Unfortunately, he caught his arm on the door. His arm was torn from its socket as the car and his detached arm flew over the embankment and burst into flames below. The man ran to the side of the embankment and mourned his loss.

A trucker approached who had seen the tragic accident. He stopped his rig and ran up to the man. The trucker could hear the man lamenting the loss of his car: "Oh, my car, my car, my brand-new BMW!"

The trucker grabbed hold of the man and said, "Hey, mister, I've got to get you to the hospital right away. You've got more problems than the loss of your car; man, you lost your arm!"

The man snapped out of his shock and looked down at where his arm had been. He looked back up at the trucker in absolute terror and screamed, "Oh no, I've lost my Rolex!"

Dates & Places Used:

563

TOPIC: Loss

Did God Lose Someone?

A little girl was looking out the window during a lightning storm. She was clearly in awe. Her father walked over to her and asked her if everything was all right. The little girl looked up at her father with concern and asked, "Daddy, do you think God has lost somebody out there?"

Dates & Places Used:

564

TOPIC: Loss

Trail Lost

The tourist turned to his Native American guide and asked, "Are we lost?"

His guide paused and answered, "We not lost. We here. Trail lost."

Dates & Places Used:

565

TOPIC: Loss

Unbreakable Toys

Why are some toys unbreakable?
Those are the ones used to break the other toys.
Dates & Places Used:

566

TOPIC: Love

Child's View of Love

Some children were asked, "What is love?"
One little girl answered, "Love is when your mommy reads you a bedtime story. True love is when she doesn't skip any pages."
Dates & Places Used:

567

TOPIC: Love

Ocean of Emotion

Love is an ocean of emotion surrounded by an expanse of expense.
Dates & Places Used:

568

TOPIC: Loyalty

Loyalty to the End

What I call a good patient is one who, having found a good physician, sticks to him till he dies. *(Oliver Wendell Holmes)*
Dates & Places Used:

569

TOPIC: Loyalty

A Loyal Custodian

The following advertisement was extracted from the bulletin of a Presbyterian church in California.

Custodian/handyman–5 hours per day, 5 days per week (including Sundays). Must be able to make simple electrical, plumbing, and building repairs. Reverences required.

Dates & Places Used:

570

TOPIC: Marriage

Preferred Spouse

Marriage is the process of finding out what kind of person your spouse would have preferred.

Dates & Places Used:

571

TOPIC: Marriage

Wedding Ring Changes

The wedding ring is that small piece of jewelry placed on the finger that cuts off your circulation.

Dates & Places Used:

572

TOPIC: Marriage

Heavy Metal Rings

A teenage girl was examining her grandmother's wedding ring. The girl said, "Wow, what heavy and cumbersome rings those were fifty years ago."

The grandmother replied, "That's true, but don't forget that in my day they were made to last a lifetime."

Dates & Places Used:

573

TOPIC: Marriage

Happy Married Couple

A deaf husband and a blind wife are always a happy couple.
Dates & Places Used:

574

TOPIC: Marriage

A Charming Wife

An ideal wife is one who remains faithful to you but tries to be just as charming as if she weren't.
Dates & Places Used:

575

TOPIC: Marriage

Mysterious Marriage Decision

Marriage is the mysterious decision by a woman to give up the attention of many men for the inattention of one man.
Dates & Places Used:

576

TOPIC: Marriage

Complete or Finished?

A young man who was considering marriage spoke to his father about marriage: "Dad, why did you marry Mom?"

His father contemplated the question for a moment and said, "I guess I felt like I was incomplete."

The son continued, "Do you feel like you are complete now?"

The father paused for a longer time and finally said, "Usually, I feel I am complete; sometimes I feel like I'm finished!"
Dates & Places Used:

577

TOPIC: Maturity

Repetitive History

History repeats itself, which is good, because most people don't listen the first time.

Dates & Places Used:

578

TOPIC: Maturity

Fanatic Balance

A fanatic is an artist at taking a small piece of life and making it into the whole of life.

Dates & Places Used:

579

TOPIC: Maturity

Admitting and Acting

There are few women who will admit their age.
There are fewer men who will act theirs.

Dates & Places Used:

580

TOPIC: Memory

Focused Direction

Oliver Wendell Holmes, the eminent Supreme Court justice, was on a train reading his paper when the conductor came by punching tickets. The justice searched his coat pockets for his ticket. Then he searched his vest pocket. Each time he came up empty.

Finally, the conductor, who recognized him, said, "Justice Holmes, don't worry. I'm sure the great Pennsylvania Railroad won't mind if you send your ticket to us when you find it." With this the distinguished jurist looked up at the conductor and said, "My dear young man, the problem is not where is my ticket? The problem is, where am I going?"

Dates & Places Used:

TOPIC: Memory

Always Read Instructions

A man was at a banquet listening to a well-known and much-admired political leader making a speech. He was seated next to the speaker's wife. He had noticed that the speaker was immaculately attired; he even had fancy monograms on his socks. But when the man looked a little closer, he saw that the monogram was not your usual two or three letters–but rather four letters. And they didn't seem to have any relationship to his name's initials. Rather, on closer inspection he noticed that the monogram was TGIF. Puzzled by this familiar acronym being on the man's socks, he turned to the politician's wife and asked why he had TGIF on his socks, which everyone knows means "Thank Goodness It's Friday."

She nodded her head negatively and said, "Oh no, that's not what the letters are for. The monograms are there to help him get dressed. They stand for 'Toes Go In First'!"

Dates & Places Used:

TOPIC: Memory

Signs of Bad Memory

A clear conscience and forgiveness of others are usually signs of a bad memory.

Dates & Places Used:

583

TOPIC: Memory

Forgetful Conscience

It's easy enough to have a clear conscience—all it takes is a fuzzy memory.

Dates & Places Used:

584

TOPIC: Memory

Film for the Memory

Everyone has a photographic memory, but some don't have film!

Dates & Places Used:

585

TOPIC: Messages

Extra Arf

A dog walks into the telegraph office and tells the clerk to send a telegram. He tells the clerk to send the following message: "Arf-arf-arf- arf-arf- arf-arf- arf-arf."

The telegraph clerk tells the dog: "There's no additional charge for two more words. Do you want to add a couple more arfs?"

The dog thought for a moment and answered, "Wouldn't that sound a bit redundant?"

Dates & Places Used:

586

TOPIC: Messages

Clear the Ear

During a commercial airline flight, a woman complained of discomfort due to the changing air pressure, so the flight attendant gave her some gum, indicating that it would relieve the pressure on her ears during the descent.

But after landing, the woman complained it took an hour to get the gum out of her ears.

Dates & Places Used:

587

TOPIC: Messages

Untimely Disaster

A man got a call from his doctor, who said, "I have some bad news and some terrible news. Which would you rather hear first?"

The man said, "The bad news." The doctor said, "The lab messed up your tests, and when they redid them, they found out you only have forty-eight hours to live!"

The man exclaimed, "What could be more terrible than that?"

The doctor replied, "We tried all day yesterday to get hold of you, but your phone was busy!"

Dates & Places Used:

588

TOPIC: Messages

Reason for Voice Mail

Answering machine message: "Hello. I am home. The reason I am not answering the phone is because I am avoiding people I don't like. Please leave your name and number. If I call you back, you are not one of those people."

Dates & Places Used:

589

TOPIC: Miracles

Some Trick

A magician was booked on a cruise ship as the entertainment. In one part of his act, the magician had a parrot do some tricks, and the rest of the time the parrot was to sit on his perch and be quiet as the entertainer performed the rest of his show.

At one point the magician produced a bunch of flowers out of thin air, at which time the parrot said, "*Squawk!* They were up his coat sleeve."

This did not make the magician happy, but nevertheless he moved on to the next trick. The magician made his assistant vanish from under a cloak. Once again the parrot piped up and said, "*Squawk!* Trap door, trap door."

As one can guess, the show did not go over very well. And if this wasn't bad enough, during one of the magic shows, the ship's boiler blew up and sent most of the crew and passengers into the ocean.

As luck would have it, the magician found that he was holding on to a piece of driftwood. And who do you suppose was on the other end? That's right, the parrot. Three days went by, and the parrot never said a word.

On the fourth day, the parrot looked at the magician and said, "*Squawk!* Okay, I give up. What did you do with the boat?"

Dates & Places Used:

590

TOPIC: Miracles

Candid Prayer

A farmer had three sons: Jim, John, and Sam. No one in the family ever attended church or had time for God. The pastor and others in the church tried for years to interest the family in the things of God, but to no avail. Then one day Sam was bitten by a rattlesnake. The doctor was called, and he did all he could to help Sam, but the outlook for Sam's recovery was very dim. So the pastor was called and apprised of the situation.

The pastor arrived and began to pray as follows: "O wise and righteous Father, we thank thee that in thine wisdom thou didst send this rattlesnake to bite Sam. He has never been inside the church, and it is doubtful that he has, in all this time, ever prayed or even acknowledged thy existence. Now we trust that this experience will be a valuable lesson to him and will lead to his genuine repentance. And now, O Father, wilt thou send another rattlesnake to bite Jim, and another to bite John, and another really big one to bite the old man? For years we have done everything we know to get them to turn to thee but all in vain. It seems, therefore, that what all our combined efforts could not do, this rattlesnake has done. We thus conclude that the only thing that will do this family any real good is rattlesnakes; so, Lord, send us bigger and better rattlesnakes. Amen."

Dates & Places Used:

591

TOPIC: Miracles

Martini Miracle

An airline flight attendant was working her way down the aisle with drinks. She asked the man in an aisle seat if he wanted a cocktail. The man ordered a martini. She saw the man in the window seat reading the Bible. She asked him if he would like a tomato juice. He ordered the juice. What other book has the power to turn a martini into tomato juice?

Dates & Places Used:

592

TOPIC: Miracles

Special Walking Water

A mother was watching her four-year-old child playing outside in a small plastic pool half filled with water. He was happily walking back and forth across the pool, making big splashes. Suddenly he stopped, stepped out of the pool, and began to scoop water out of the pool with a pail.

"Why are you pouring the water out, Johnny?" the mother asked.

" 'Cause my teacher said Jesus walked on water, and this water won't work," the boy replied.

Dates & Places Used:

593

TOPIC: Mistakes

Tough Initiation

Two Texans were trying to impress each other with the size of their ranches. One asked the other, "What's the name of your ranch?"

He replied, "The Rocking R, ABC, Flying W, Circle C, Bar U, Staple Four, Box D, Rolling M, Rainbow's End, Silver Spur Ranch."

The questioner was much impressed and exclaimed, "Whew! That's sure some name! How many head of cattle do you run?"

The rancher answered, "Not many. Very few survive the branding."

Dates & Places Used:

594

TOPIC: Mistakes

Great Vision

Hindsight is an exact science.

Dates & Places Used:

595

TOPIC: Mistakes

Misplaced Space

A space can be a dangerous thing. One church secretary realized the "misplaced space" problem when she picked up her bulletin on Sunday morning–the one she had typed on Thursday morning. She read, "Refreshments after the sermon will be gin at 10:00 A.M."

Dates & Places Used:

TOPIC: Mistakes

Quick Stop at Victoria Station

A man who was traveling on a train asked the ticket collector what time the train would stop at Victoria Station.

"This train doesn't stop at Victoria; it's the express."

"You've got to be kidding! I have to get off at Victoria Station!"

"Sorry, sir, this train will not stop at Victoria."

"There must be something you can do."

"Well, there is one thing."

"What is it? I'll do anything. I have to get off at Victoria Station."

"I could get the engineer to slow down, and I could dangle you out the door and lower you onto the platform as we pass Victoria Station."

The man thought for a moment and asked, "Do you really think it will work?"

"I don't know, but if you want off at Victoria Station, then it's worth a try."

So when the train approached the platform at fifty miles per hour, the conductor held the man in midair at the door, and the man started running.

The man was running in midair as the conductor screamed, "Faster! Run faster!"

The conductor finally lowered the man down to the platform. As the man's feet touched the platform, smoke flew from his shoes and his heel came off. And the man was running for his life!

The conductor then let go of the man.

The man was able to keep from falling down and was steadily reducing his speed: forty miles per hour–thirty miles per hour–twenty miles per hour. . . . It looked like he was going to make it!

The other passengers watched in utter amazement.

As the last carriage passed the man, a hand reached out and grabbed the man by the shirt collar and lifted him back onto the train.

As the exhausted man was being pulled into the carriage, he heard a voice say, "You are so lucky I was here to help you! Didn't you know that this train does not stop at Victoria Station?"

Dates & Places Used:

597

The Right Verdict

Crime figure Joseph Galliono was on trial for first-degree murder. His lawyer was paid by Mr. Galliono to win this case or at least reduce the charges. It seemed clear that Mr. Galliono was guilty, but the lawyer was willing to do whatever it took to reduce the charges. The lawyer approached one of the jurors and was able to bribe him to hold out for the verdict of manslaughter; no other verdict would do. At the end of the trial, the jury deliberated for over a week. They finally returned a verdict of manslaughter.

When the lawyer met with the juror to pay the bribe, he asked, "How did you convince the other jurors to reduce the charge to manslaughter?"

"That's not exactly what happened," answered the juror. "You told me to get them to return a verdict of manslaughter or I wouldn't get paid. It took me a full week to convince them to vote with me on that verdict. They all wanted to acquit the man."

Dates & Places Used:

598

TOPIC: Mistakes

Mistakes and Laughs

If you learn to chuckle at your mistakes, you will seldom be short of laugh material.

Dates & Places Used:

599

TOPIC: Mistakes

What a Hot Dog!

A guy was walking along the beach in Malibu when he came across a salt-encrusted piece of metal. He worked for an hour or so to remove the salt. Lo and behold, it was a very old oil lamp.

The guy started to buff it to remove the verdigris when–*Poof!*–a genie appeared.

This genie, like all genies, was so happy to be freed from the lamp that he granted the guy three wishes.

"I wish to be a dollar richer than Bill Gates," said the guy.

The genie wasn't sure who Bill Gates was until the guy told him to check *Forbes* magazine. When the genie called up *Forbes* from inside the lamp, he learned that Bill Gates was indeed the richest man in the world.

"Guy," the genie said, "you will forever be a dollar richer than Bill Gates. What's your second wish?"

"Genie, I want the most expensive Porsche made: fire engine red, onboard GPS, and the finest audio system ever installed in an automobile."

"That's easy," said the genie. He waved his hand, and the best car anybody had ever seen popped out of the lamp. The genie then asked the guy for his third wish.

The guy mulled the question over and over. A girl–nah, with billions and billions of dollars he certainly had become a chick magnet.

World peace? Only wackos wanted that. The guy found a reason not to wish for anything that came to his mind.

"Genie," the guy said, "I can't think of anything now. May I save the third wish for later?"

"Gee, this is most unusual. But you hold the hammer. I can't escape from this lamp until you make a third wish. Call me when you're ready." *Woosh!* the genie disappeared into the lamp.

The guy carefully picked up the now ever-so-valuable lamp and placed it in the trunk of the Porsche. He turned the radio on and balanced the sound, making all the necessary adjustments to get his great audio system customized to his ears.

After that he pulled off the beach and headed south along the Pacific Coast Highway. Soon he was up to sixty, then seventy, then eighty miles per hour. The Porsche handled perfectly. The guy was so happy that he began to sing along with the radio.

"Oh, I wish I were an Oscar Meyer ..." *Poof!*

Dates & Places Used:

600

Fresh Evasion

A man had just totaled his car in a terrible one-car accident. Miraculously, he was able to get out of the wreckage. Within minutes a state trooper arrived on the scene. "This car is a total wreck. Are you okay?"

"Yes, Officer," the man answered. "I'm fine."

"How did the accident occur?" the officer asked as he carefully investigated the wrecked car.

"It was a terrible scare, Officer," the man replied. "I was driving along the road when about half a mile back a tree appeared right in front of me. I swerved to miss it, but then there was a tree on the other side of me. I swerved back to the right and then to the left and then to the right. It didn't matter–whichever way I turned there was a tree in front of me."

The state trooper continued to study the car. He then stepped away from the car and approached the man. "Sir," he said, "there is not a tree within five miles of this place. What you saw was not a tree; it was your air freshener swinging back and forth."

Dates & Places Used:

601

Grab a Skunk and Run

A funny thing happened in a small town in Maryland a few years ago. A mother of eight was coming home from a neighbor's house one afternoon. Things seemed too quiet as she walked across the front yard. Curious, she peered through the screen door and saw five of her youngest children huddled together, concentrating on something. As she crept closer to them, trying to discover the center of attention, she could not believe her eyes. Smack dab in the middle of the circle were five baby skunks.

The mother screamed at the top of her voice, "Quick, children, run!" Each kid grabbed a skunk and ran.

Dates & Places Used:

602

TOPIC: Money

Too Much Thrift

Some people carry thrift too far, like the man who took long steps to keep from wearing out his twenty-dollar shoes and split his forty-dollar pants.

Dates & Places Used:

603

TOPIC: Mothers

Mom Too Helpful

The Associated Press reported on August 5, 1995, about a mother who was just a little too concerned for her son's career. She apparently wanted to give him a boost, help him to make some extra money. You see, her son worked for the United States Forest Service as a firefighter. As a seasonal firefighter he received a base salary but was paid extra while fighting fires. So his mother saw to it that he got to fight fires. According to investigators, this sixty-year-old Mount Shasta woman had set five brush fires in the past year along a northern California highway. She could get twenty years in jail for her maternal attempt to advance her son's career. Oh, by the way, her son no longer works for the Forest Service.

Thanks, Mom!

Perhaps there is a limit to how much we can and should do for our children.

Dates & Places Used:

604

TOPIC: Mothers

Aspirin Instructions

If you are a mother with a lot of tension and you get a headache, do what it says on the aspirin bottle: "take two aspirin" and "keep away from children."

Dates & Places Used:

605

The Strategic Role of the Successful Mother

When all is said, it is the mother, and the mother only, who is a better citizen than the soldier who fights for his or her country. The successful mother, the mother who does her part in rearing and training aright the boys and girls who are to be the men and women of the next generation, is of greater use to the community and occupies, if she would only realize it, a more honorable as well as a more important position than any man in it. The mother is the one supreme asset of the national life. She is more important by far than the successful governmental leader, businessperson, artist, or scientist. *(Theodore Roosevelt)*
Dates & Places Used:

606

Tell Me about Your Mother

A small boy went to the lingerie department of a store to purchase a gift for his mother. He bashfully told the clerk that he wanted to buy a slip for his mom, but he didn't know her size. The woman explained that it would be helpful if he could describe her—was she fat, thin, short, tall? The youngster replied, "Well, she's just about perfect." So the clerk sent him home with a size 34. A few days later the mother came to exchange the gift, as it was too small. She needed a size 52! Just about perfect!
Dates & Places Used:

607

Mothers and Evolution

If progressive evolution is accurate, why do mothers still have only two hands?
Dates & Places Used:

608

Chance to Rest

An overworked mother of three active young boys was playing in the yard with her boys one afternoon when her neighbor came by to borrow a cup of sugar. One of her boys aimed his play pistol at his mother and yelled, "*Bang!* You're dead!"

The mother acted the part perfectly. She took the shot and fell to the ground. When she fell to the ground, she did not get up. Her neighbor waited for her to get up. But she did not get up, so the concerned neighbor rushed over to see if she was hurt from the fall. As the neighbor bent over, the mother opened one eye and whispered, "*Shhhhhh.* Please don't give me away. This is the only chance I ever get to rest."

Dates & Places Used:

609

TOPIC: Motivation

Employment Incentive

The interviewer explained the company policy to a job applicant: "Our company has a simple work-incentive plan. We call it unemployment."

Dates & Places Used:

610

TOPIC: Motivation

Misplaced Motivation

A wealthy businessman hosted a spectacular party for which he had filled his swimming pool with sharks, barracuda, and other assorted dangerous fish. He announced to his guests that he would like to challenge any of them to try swimming across the pool, and he would offer a first prize of either a new home in the mountains, a trip around the world for two, or a piece of his business.

No sooner had he made the announcement than there was a splash and a man swam rapidly across the infested waters and bounded up out on the other side. The millionaire said to the dripping man, "That was a stunning performance. What prize do you want?"

He answered tersely, "Right now I really don't care about the prize. I just want to get the name of the turkey who pushed me in."

Dates & Places Used:

611

TOPIC: Motivation

The Gift of Motivation

Richard Halverson tells a story about a frog who fell in a pothole and couldn't get out. Even his friends couldn't get him to muster enough strength to jump out of the deep pothole. They gave up and left him to his fate. But the next day they saw him bounding around just fine. Somehow he had made it out, so they asked him how he did it. They said to him, "We thought you couldn't get out."

The frog replied, "I couldn't–but a truck came along and I had to."

Dates & Places Used:

612

TOPIC: Motivation

Untimely Announcement

Thanksgiving is a time for family gatherings. At one such gathering a senior member of the family wanted to encourage the continuation of such gatherings. You see, his five children were in their late twenties or early thirties and were all married but had no children. The children were more concerned about furthering their careers than raising families. Therefore, this man had no grandchildren. And he was growing impatient!

Prior to the Thanksgiving Day meal, their father shared his heartfelt concern with his children and their spouses. "I have lived for sixty years and have made a great deal of money. And I have done so in the midst of a loving family and growing children. My life has been good. God has been gracious to our family. But I must say that I am concerned about you children. I think your values are misplaced, your fears are ungrounded. So, to encourage you to provide me with grandchildren, I have established a trust fund of fifty thousand dollars for my first grandchild. Now, let's pray."

After the man finished his heartfelt prayer, he lifted his face and discovered that all of his children and their spouses were gone!

Dates & Places Used:

613

TOPIC: Motivation

Excellent Explanation

Everybody but Sam had signed up for a new company pension plan that called for a small employee contribution. The company was paying the rest. Unfortunately, 100 percent employee participation was needed; otherwise the plan was off.

Sam's boss and his fellow workers pleaded and cajoled but to no avail. Sam said the plan would never pay off.

Finally, the company president called Sam into his office. "Sam," he said, "here's a copy of the new pension plan and here's a pen. I want you to sign the papers. I'm sorry, but if you don't sign, you're fired. As of right now."

Sam signed the papers immediately.

"Now," said the president, "would you mind telling me why you couldn't have signed earlier?"

"Well, sir," replied Sam, "nobody explained it to me quite so clearly before."

Dates & Places Used:

614

TOPIC: Music

Gifts—Assessing the Blame

A young man got up before the congregation and began to sing a hymn. He never hit one note correctly. After the service people really didn't know how to react or speak to the young man about the situation until one man walked up and said to him, "Son, your singing was to the best of your ability and it is no fault of yours how the song came out. However, the person who asked you to sing should be shot."

Dates & Places Used:

615

TOPIC: Music

Music and Spinach

It helps to think of rock music as youth's way of getting even for spinach. *(Robert Orben)*

Dates & Places Used:

616

TOPIC: Music

Vocational Hymns

In the spirit of "all things to all people," hymnals contain hymns for various vocations.

Builder's Hymn: "How Firm a Foundation."

Painter's Hymn: "Jacob's Ladder."

Meteorologist's Hymn: "There Shall Be Showers of Blessing."

Surveyor's Hymn: "When I Survey the Wondrous Cross."

Bread Maker's Hymn: "I Need Thee Every Hour."

Dispatcher's Hymn: "So Send I You."

Banker's Hymn: "On the Banks of the Jordan."

Veterinarian's Hymn: "All Creatures of Our God and King."

Hiker's Hymn: "Go Tell It on the Mountain."

Baker's Hymn: "When the Roll Is Called up Yonder."

Dentist's Hymn: "Crown Him with Many Crowns."

Railroad Worker's Hymn: "Blest Be the Tie That Binds."

Creditor's Hymn: "All to Thee I Owe."

Cheese Maker's Hymn: "Holy, Holy, Holy."

Consumer's Hymn: "In the Sweet By and By."

Dates & Places Used:

617

TOPIC: Music

Voicing Perspectives

A visiting cantor was invited to sing traditional Jewish songs at a Brooklyn synagogue. After the services he was bragging to members of the congregation that Lloyd's of London had insured his voice for $750,000.

Mrs. Siegel, an older woman, said, "So, cantor, what did you do with the money?"

Dates & Places Used:

618

TOPIC: Names

The Cob in the Cobweb

A little girl noticed a large cobweb on the ceiling and brought it to her mother's attention: "Look Mommy, there's a spider web with no spider in it!"

Her mother replied, "No, sweetie, that's a cobweb."

The skeptical child then asked, "Then where's the cob?"

Dates & Places Used:

619

TOPIC: Names

German Walter

At the summer Olympics, a man was carrying a long pole through the Olympic village. A reporter came up to him and asked, "Are you a pole vaulter?"

The man replied, "No, I'm a German, but how did you know my name was Walter?"

Dates & Places Used:

620

TOPIC: Names

Riding on Sunday

A marshal was tracking a cattle rustler and heard that the man had ridden into a small town up the trail. The marshal rode into town and asked around for information about him. Most of the folks suggested that the marshal talk to the man at the stable; the rustler had left his horse there.

The marshal rode to the stable and asked the man when he had last seen the rustler. The man answered, "I saw him when he rode in on Sunday and then three days later when he rode out of town on Sunday."

The marshal asked the man how a man could ride out of town three days later and it still be on Sunday.

The man explained, "Well, marshal, it's like this. I sold him a horse about a year ago, and its name is Sunday!"

Dates & Places Used:

621

TOPIC: Names

Burger King Pronounced

Two New Yorkers were driving through Louisiana. As they were approaching the town of Natchitoches (pronounced *nack-o-tish*), they started arguing about the pronunciation of the name. They argued back and forth until they stopped for lunch.

As they stood at the counter, one New Yorker asked the manager, "Before we order, could you please settle an argument for us? Would you please pronounce where we are ... very slowly?"

The manager leaned over the counter and said, "Burrrrrrrr-gerrrrrrr-Kiiiiing."

Dates & Places Used:

622

Chews a Name

A substitute teacher was teaching a certain class for the first time. She noticed a boy in the front of the room who was moving his jaws in a chewing fashion. So she asked the boy, "Are you chewing gum?"

The boy answered, "No, ma'am, I'm Bobby Jones."

Dates & Places Used:

623

Unliked Short Cummings

A large family by the name of Cummings belonged to a certain church. One Sunday the preacher really let loose a scorcher on sin. He talked about human failures, pride, and shortcomings. That day after church the youngest boy moped around the house. Mom and Dad finally asked him what was wrong. He said, "The preacher doesn't like me anymore."

Mom and Dad asked him where he had gotten such an idea. He said, "Well, he kept talking about how bad our short Cummings are, and I'm the only short Cummings in the church. So I suppose he doesn't like me anymore."

Dates & Places Used:

624

Bring Home the Bacon

A woman from West Texas went to see the governor to beg for her husband's release from prison. After a long wait she was ushered into the governor's office and proceeded to tell her story.

The governor asked, "What's he in for?"

"Stealing a dozen hams," said the woman. "Well that doesn't sound too bad," said the governor. "Was he a good husband?"

"As a matter of fact, he never said a kind word to me in all the years we've been married," said the woman.

"Was he a good worker?" the governor asked.

"No, I wouldn't say that. He's pretty lazy. I can't remember him ever having a steady job," she said.

"Well, was he a good father to the kids?" he asked.

"Well, the truth is, he's pretty mean to the kids. Never pays any attention to them until he's drunk. Then he's mean to them."

"Ma'am," said the governor, "I have to ask you, why do you want a man like that out of prison?"

"Well, governor," she said, "we're about outta ham."

Dates & Places Used:

625

TOPIC: Needs

When Junk Is Needed

Junk is something you throw away three weeks before you need it.

Dates & Places Used:

626

TOPIC: Nuisances

Things That Last

Nothing lasts as long as a new breakfast cereal you can't stand or wears as long as the ugly carpet whose bilious color you hate.

Dates & Places Used:

627

TOPIC: Nuisances

Alarming Clock

A young boy received an alarm clock from his grandparents for Christmas. He was quite proud of his gift and asked how the clock worked. His father showed him, and in no time the boy had mastered the settings on his new clock. The next morning the boy walked sleepily into the dining room as his parents were having breakfast. The boy's father was a bit surprised to see his son up so early. The father asked him, "How do you like your new clock?"

The boy answered, "Oh, I like my clock, except the crazy thing woke me up!"

Dates & Places Used:

628

TOPIC: Nuisances

A Questionable Muscular Solution

Remember, when someone annoys you, it takes forty-two muscles in your face to frown, but it takes only four muscles to extend your arm and smack that annoyance upside the head.

Dates & Places Used:

629

TOPIC: Obedience

Time to Go Home

The parsonage was next door to the church I was serving. One Sunday night after the evening service, our family ran home and got in the car to go to an appointment. As we drove up to the church where people were milling around talking and heading toward their cars, I saw my dog running after us, chasing the car. I stopped and yelled, "Go home!" at my dog. One of the elderly men with a hearing aid said, "Yes, sir, right away!"

Dates & Places Used:

630

TOPIC: Obedience

Not Oprah Winfrey

A Sunday school teacher was teaching her grade school class that we all need God's forgiveness. After the story she asked one of the girls, "When is a time you might need God's forgiveness?"

Noticeably perplexed, the girl was reassured by the teacher's son, who whispered, "It's okay, you don't have to tell her."

Then the boy looked his mother straight in the eye and sternly said, "We don't have to tell you our problems. This isn't *The Oprah Winfrey Show!*"

Dates & Places Used:

631

TOPIC: Obedience

Don't Forget the Water

A small boy is sent to bed by his father.
[Five minutes later]
"Da-ad ..."
"What?"
"I'm thirsty. Can you bring me a drink of water?"
"No. You had your chance. Lights out."
[Five minutes later]
"Da-aaaad ..."
"What?"
"I'm thirsty. Can I have a drink of water?"
"I told you no! If you ask again, I'll have to spank you!"
[Five minutes later]
"Daaaa-aaaAAAAD ..."
"WHAT?!"
"When you come in to spank me, can you bring me a drink of water?"

Dates & Places Used:

632

TOPIC: Obedience

Don't Mention It

A little boy said thank you to a man who had helped him. The man said, "Don't mention it."

The boy said, "But Mama told me to!"

Dates & Places Used:

633

TOPIC: Obedience

Stop First

As a driver's education instructor at Unionville-Sebewaing Area High School in Michigan, I've learned that even the brightest students can become flustered behind the wheel. One day I had three beginners in the car, each scheduled to drive for thirty minutes. When the first student had completed his time, I asked him to change places with one of the others. Gripping the wheel tightly and staring straight ahead, he asked in a shaky voice, "Should I stop the car?"

Dates & Places Used:

634

TOPIC: Offerings

Meditate on Heat

The pastor stood reverently at the pulpit, bowed his head, and spoke to his congregation. "Before we take our offering, let's all bow our heads and meditate on how much it costs to heat the church."

Dates & Places Used:

635

Offering Announcements

One pastor, thinking under the pressure of the moment that he was quoting Scripture, intoned to the congregation, "A fool and his money are soon parted. The ushers will now come forward to receive the offering."

Dates & Places Used:

636

Offerings Disperse Crowds

A young pastor fresh out of seminary thought it would help him in his career if he first took a job as a policeman for several months. He passed the physical examination and then took the oral examination to ascertain his alertness of mind and his ability to act quickly and wisely in an emergency. Among the other questions he was asked, "What would you do to disperse a frenzied crowd?"

He thought for a moment and then said, "I would take up an offering."

Dates & Places Used:

637

Offering for the Heathen

A young deacon with few manners was passing the collection plate one Sunday. After passing the plate by a rich woman, he noticed that she did not put anything in. So he passed the plate by again with the same result. Not to be undone, he passed it by a third time. This last time she tried to tell him that she wasn't going to put anything in the plate. Finally, the young deacon said, "If you aren't going to put anything in, take something out–it's for the heathen anyway."

Dates & Places Used:

638

TOPIC: Offerings

Ties and Offerings

One Sunday in church a little boy took off his tie and put it into the offering plate.

"What are you doing?" asked his mother.

"The preacher told us to give our ties and offerings."

Dates & Places Used:

639

TOPIC: Opinions

Marriage—How to Get Along

A lawyer and a psychologist were making small talk at a party. "You and your wife get along very well," said the lawyer. "Do you ever have differences of opinion?"

"Definitely," said the psychologist, "very often—but we get over them quickly."

"How do you do that?" asked the lawyer.

"Simple," said the psychologist, "I never tell her about them."

Dates & Places Used:

640

TOPIC: Opinions

Middle-Aged Changes

Middle age is when broadness of mind and narrowness of the waist change places.

Dates & Places Used:

641

Put Your Body Where Your Mouth Is

A Nova Scotia insurance salesman had been told by his boss that he and the other agents were not assertive enough. They were not as outgoing as they needed to be. The salesman wanted to prove his boss wrong, and he didn't have long to wait for an opportunity.

Outside his seventeenth-floor window he noticed a scaffold with some workmen on it. He wrote a note asking them if they'd be interested in life, accident, or disability insurance and held it up to the window.

They said they would listen to him if he would join them on the scaffold. He did, with the help of a cable from the roof, and he sold one of them fifty thousand dollars' worth of life insurance.

Dates & Places Used:

642

Open and Ready to Learn

The Roman scholar Cato started to study Greek when he was over eighty years old. Someone asked why he tackled such a difficult task at his age.

Cato said, "It's the earliest age I have left," and continued to study.

Dates & Places Used:

643

Assertive Fund Raising

A panhandler varied his usual pleas for money when he saw a prosperous-looking businessman coming down the street. He approached the man and said, "Look, I don't want to try to give you a snow job. I need a drink. Will you buy me one?"

The businessman, who was an admirer of truth and candor wherever he met it, decided to respond positively to this forthright approach. He said, "Come on into this bar, and I'll have a drink with you."

As he approached the bar the businessman said, "Bartender, two rye whiskeys." And the bum immediately added, "Make mine the same."

This may illustrate the truth "You have not, because you ask not." Maybe.

Dates & Places Used:

644

TOPIC: Opportunity

Sin of Wrong Perspective

Old Herb was the thriftiest farmer in the area. One day he stood on the bridge idly gazing down at the water. A canoeist coming down the river suddenly overturned. He came up gasping. Herb just looked on. Down the canoeist went again.

When he came up, Herb shouted to him, "If you don't come up the next time, can I have your canoe?"

Dates & Places Used:

645

TOPIC: Opportunity

Get Rich Quick

Wolves were destroying the sheep in a particular area. The ranchers were so outraged that local authorities established a bounty on wolves. Two men decided they could use the extra money. They hiked into the hill country to track the wolves. They would shoot the wolves and collect the bounty money.

The hunters had set up camp for the evening and had just fallen asleep under the stars. Suddenly, one of them awoke. From the reflected light of their fire, he saw a large circle of wolves with fangs gleaming! The man immediately woke up his friend and excitedly announced, "Wake up! Wake up! We're rich!"

Dates & Places Used:

646

No Better Time

A truck driver who was hauling clay for a landfill backed his dump truck too far over the grade. As a result, the weight in the back lifted up the front of the truck. His helper, alarmed, asked, "Now what do we do?" Glancing at the truck, the driver took some things out of the cab, slid under the truck, and said, "I guess I'll grease her. I'll never have a better chance."

Dates & Places Used:

647

An Optimistic Harvest

An optimist is a person who saves the pictures in the seed catalog to compare them with the flowers and vegetables he grows.

Dates & Places Used:

648

Locking Gas Cap

A man who fashioned himself an optimist filled his car at a self-service gas station. After he had paid and driven away, he realized that he had left the gas cap on top of his car. He stopped and looked. Sure enough, it was lost.

Being an optimist, he told himself that surely others had made the same mistake, so he began searching the side of the road for another gas cap to replace his. Sure enough, he hadn't been searching long when he found a gas cap. He tried it, and it went into place with a satisfying click.

"Things always work out," he thought. "I lost my gas cap, but I found another one that fits. In fact, this one's even better because it locks!"

Dates & Places Used:

649

TOPIC: Pain

Hurt All Over

A woman visited her doctor and told him that she hurt all over. The doctor asked her what she meant by "all over" and asked for a specific example.

The woman touched her knee and said, "Ouch, that hurts!"

The doctor asked the woman for another example.

She pointed to her shoulder and told him, "Oh, that hurts too!" Then she pointed to her ear. "That really hurts!"

The doctor stopped the woman before she touched any more body parts. "I know what your problem is," the doctor told her. "The reason you hurt all over is because you have a broken finger."

Dates & Places Used:

650

TOPIC: Pain

Severe Surgery

Two little boys were in beds in the same room at the hospital. The first one leaned over and asked, "What are you in here for?"

The second boy said, "I'm here to get my tonsils out, and I'm a little nervous."

The first boy said, "You have nothing to worry about; I had that done to me once. They put you to sleep, and when you wake up, they give you lots of Jell-O and ice cream. It's a piece of cake."

Then the second one asked, "What are you in here for?" to which the first responded, "Well, I'm here for a circumcision."

The second boy said, "Whoa! I had that done when I was born and I couldn't walk for a year."

Dates & Places Used:

651

TOPIC: Pain

Dental Diet

A dentist has discovered a new, effective diet. It is called the "Abscessed Tooth Diet."
Dates & Places Used:

652

TOPIC: Parents

Hereditary Parenting

Parenting is hereditary. If your parents didn't have any children, you're not likely to have any either.
Dates & Places Used:

653

TOPIC: Parents

Child Statistics

A statistician who had never taken care of his four small energetic children by himself reluctantly promised to look after them one Saturday afternoon while his wife went shopping. When she returned he gave her a note that read: "Dried tears–11 times. Tied shoelaces–15 times. Blew up toy balloons–5 per child. Average life of each balloon–10 seconds. Warned children not to run across street–26 times. Children insisted on running across street–26 times. Number of Saturdays I will go through this again–0!"
Dates & Places Used:

654

TOPIC: Parents

Grandparent's Reward

Grandchildren are God's reward for not killing your children.
Dates & Places Used:

655

TOPIC: Parents

Bowling Children

Having children is like having a bowling alley installed in your brain. *(Martin Mull)*
Dates & Places Used:

656

TOPIC: Parents

Testing—One, Two, Three

When my brother and his wife were considering adopting some children, they first took two little boys into their home as foster children to see how they would relate to one another before moving toward adoption. I was explaining this to my twelve-year-old daughter, who responded spontaneously, "Man, that's like test-driving a little kid."
Dates & Places Used:

657

TOPIC: Participation

Church and Poker

Church membership is like a poker game; you're either in or you're out. If you're in, then ante up.
Dates & Places Used:

658

TOPIC: Participation

Absent Creed

Each Sunday morning as they began class, the fifth graders would line up and recite their one section of the creed in the order that it was written. That teaching method worked well for about four months. Then one Sunday a problem arose. Class

began the same way. The first girl as usual recited her line flaw-lessly: "I believe in God the Father Almighty, maker of heaven and earth." The second, a boy, stood up and said his sentence: "I believe in Jesus Christ, his only Son, our Lord." But then silence descended over the class. Finally, one girl, who felt she had dis-covered the problem, stood up and loudly said, "I'm sorry, sir, but the boy who believes in the Holy Ghost is absent today!"
Dates & Places Used:

659

TOPIC: Patience

Backseat Scenery

A well-adjusted man is one who can enjoy the scenery even with kids in the backseat.
Dates & Places Used:

660

TOPIC: Patience

Reading Even the Begats

A learned old missionary woman was teaching a Bible class. One day she explained to her class that she had a system that enabled her to read the entire Bible during the course of a calen-dar year. One of the students confessed that though she had read the Bible through more than once, she tended to skip parts–like the genealogies. They were boring, and she told the teacher so. So she asked the teacher what her practice was when she came to the begats.

The teacher answered, "I read them, of course. They are a part of the Scripture, you know."

The pupil said, "But what on earth could I possibly learn by reading them over year after year?"

The teacher had a twinkle in her eyes when she answered, "Patience, my dear, patience."
Dates & Places Used:

661

Annals of Sheep

In the annals of sheep the wolves are always defeated and disgraced.
Dates & Places Used:

662

One-Seater Bathroom

A nurses' aide was helping a patient into the bathroom when the patient exclaimed, "You're not coming in here with me. This is only a one-seater!"
Dates & Places Used:

663

Loud New Rattle

The loudest sound known to humanity is the first rattle in a brand-new car. *(Earl Wilson)*
Dates & Places Used:

664

Twelve Thoughts on Accomplishment

I can please only one person per day. Today is not your day. Tomorrow isn't looking good either.

I don't have an attitude problem. You have a perception problem.

I love deadlines. I especially like the whooshing sound they make as they go flying by.

Two wrongs don't make a right, but three rights make a left.

If swimming is so good for your figure, how do you explain whales?

Am I getting smart with you? How would you know?

I'm not just a gardener; I'm a plant manager.

You're slower than a herd of turtles stampeding through chunky peanut butter.

I don't suffer from stress. I'm a carrier.

I'd explain it to you, but your brain would explode.

Tell me what you need, and I'll tell you how to get along without it.

Eagles may soar, but weasels don't get sucked into jet engines.

Dates & Places Used:

665

TOPIC: Perception

Sound in a Vacuum

A woman was playing a trivia game with friends one evening. She drew a card concerning science and nature. The question was: "If you are in a vacuum and someone calls your name, will you be able to hear it?"

The woman thought for a little while and asked her friends, "Do you think the vacuum is on or off?"

Dates & Places Used:

666

TOPIC: Persistence

The Snail Made It

By perseverance the snail reached the ark. *(Charles H. Spurgeon)*

Dates & Places Used:

667

TOPIC: Persistence

Other Bright Lights and Dim Bulbs

A father was trying to encourage his son who was talking about quitting school. He lectured him by saying, "Son, you've heard about Thomas Edison. He didn't quit. You've heard about Albert Einstein. He didn't quit. You've heard about Abraham Lincoln. He didn't quit. You've heard about Isador McPringle ..."

His son stopped him and said, "Dad, I've heard about those other guys, but who in the world is Isador McPringle?"

His father answered, "The reason you've never heard about him is because he quit!"

Dates & Places Used:

668

TOPIC: Perspective

Loyal Opposition

You see me as an atheist. God sees me as the loyal opposition.

Dates & Places Used:

669

TOPIC: Perspective

All in Your Point of View

A small boy and his sister, complete with ice cream cones, drifted away from their mother in a large department store. Pretty soon they made a game out of going up and down in the elevator. Suddenly the boy noticed his cone dripping, so he wiped it against the back of a woman's mink coat.

His sister said, "Watch yourself, Billy; you're getting fur in your ice cream."

Dates & Places Used:

670

Don't Forget the Coffee

A new flight attendant was making her first flight on a full plane out of Denver. The pilots made their routine announcements and forgot to turn off the intercom. One of the pilots began to muse about what heaven must be like. The other answered by saying that his idea of heaven was a cup of coffee in one hand and that pretty new flight attendant in the other.

The new flight attendant was in the back of the plane when she heard the pilots' conversation. Dutifully she rushed to the front of the plane to save the unsuspecting pilots from further embarrassment. As she ran past a little old lady, the woman jumped to her feet and cried out, "You forgot the coffee, honey!"

Dates & Places Used:

671

Submarine Tour

I happened upon a friend from high school after moving back to my hometown of Memphis, Tennessee. It was obvious from his appearance that he had joined the military.

I asked him, "How do you like life in the navy?"

"It's okay," was the less than enthusiastic reply. "When I enlisted they told me I would 'see the world'! I've been out of the United States for more than two years, but I haven't seen anything of the world."

"Really?" I asked, somewhat dismayed at his answer.

"Really," he said. "I've got to get off of that submarine!"

Dates & Places Used:

672

Political Alternatives

An aspiring politician gave his best shot at a campaign speech. He felt that it was a stirring, fact-filled speech. Then the candidate looked out on his audience and asked, "Are there any questions?"

Someone in the back row called out, "Who else is running?"

Dates & Places Used:

673

Inside or Out

The peace corps used a wonderful ad with a partially filled glass of water and asked the question, "Is this glass half empty or half full?" suggesting that a given perspective can help persuade people to see things differently and take a preferred course of action.

One mother did it this way. She left her four-year-old in the house while she ran to put something in the trash. When she returned to the house, her little boy had locked the door. She started to ask him to open the door, but she knew he was at the age where he was saying no to everything. She knew that she was in for a test of wills that might last for hours. Then inspiration hit. She said to him, "Oh, too bad. You just locked yourself in the house." The door came open immediately.

Dates & Places Used:

674

Almost Worldwide Flood

One hot day in western Texas a traveler stopped at a small store to buy a soft drink.

As he wiped the sweat from his face, he asked an old fellow sitting on the porch, "When's the last time you got any rain here?"

The old man thought for a little bit and then said, "Well, you remember in the Bible when we're told it rained for forty days and forty nights."

"Sure," the traveler replied, "I know the story of Noah."

"Well," the old man continued, "we got about an inch."

Dates & Places Used:

675

TOPIC: Pessimism

Getting It Done

Man who say it cannot be done should not interrupt man doing it!

Dates & Places Used:

676

TOPIC: Pessimism

Funeral Flowers

A cynic smells the flowers and then looks for the casket.

Dates & Places Used:

677

TOPIC: Pets

Parachuting Blind

A blind man was telling about how much he enjoyed the sport of parachuting. When he was asked how he could parachute, he explained that it was not that hard–others would help him. "They lead me to the plane, tell me when to jump, and place my hand on the release ring of the rip cord. When I get close to the ground, I can smell the soil, grass, and trees."

He was then asked by his listeners how he knew to lift his legs into a roll just before he landed. "Oh, that's easy," he explained. "My seeing-eye dog's leash goes slack."

Dates & Places Used:

678

TOPIC: Pets

Parakeet Pad

A carpet layer was exhausted after a hard day's work. His partner hadn't shown up, and he had finally finished laying carpet in a large home all by himself. Cleaning up his tools and preparing to leave, he patted his pocket and realized his cigarette pack was missing. Looking around, he suddenly noticed a small lump in the center of the carpeting he had just laid—just about the size of his cigarette pack. He thought for a minute and then laid a board over the lump and hammered the lump absolutely flat until it was virtually undetectable.

Sighing with relief that he didn't need to pull the carpet up again, he loaded his equipment into his truck, only to discover his cigarettes lying on the front seat. Just then the owner of the house ran out to his truck. "The carpeting looks great, thank you," she said. "By the way, have you seen my parakeet?"

Dates & Places Used:

679

TOPIC: Pets

Snake Tail

A kindergarten boy brought in a small black snake in a paper bag for show-and-tell. While he was waiting for his turn to speak, the snake escaped from the bag and was wiggling on the floor. Another little boy saw the snake and shouted, "Hey, look, everybody! There's a tail wagging without a dog attached!"

Dates & Places Used:

680

TOPIC: Pets

The Cat That Boiled

Four-year-old Noah was contentedly stroking his cat before the fire. The cat, also happy, began to purr loudly. Noah suddenly seized her by the tail and dragged her away from the hearth.

His mother said, "Noah, you must not hurt your kitty."

"I'm not," said Noah, "but I've got to get her away from the fire. She's beginning to boil."

Dates & Places Used:

TOPIC: Pets

681

Burial for Two

Little Tim was in the garden filling in a hole when his neighbor peered over the fence.

Interested in what the cheeky-faced youngster was up to, he politely asked, "What are you up to there, Tim?"

"My goldfish died," replied Tim tearfully without looking up, "and I've just buried him."

The neighbor was concerned. "That's an awfully big hole for a goldfish, isn't it?"

Tim patted down the last heap of earth, then replied, "That's because he's inside your stupid cat."

Dates & Places Used:

TOPIC: Pets

682

Meals on Wheels

A cat passed on, ending up in heaven. God greeted him and said, "You've been a very good cat, a true friend to your owner. Is there anything I can do to make your stay here more pleasurable?"

The cat replied, "I belonged to a very poor family and had to sleep on a hard floor every night. I'd love to have a soft bed."

God smiled and gave the cat a large fluffy pillow.

A few days went by, and a family of mice arrived in heaven. God greeted them and asked if there was anything he could do to make their stay more pleasurable.

One of the mice said, "We lived a hard life on a farm, always on the run from the farmer and his dog. Our feet are very tired. Could you give us some skates so we won't have to walk everywhere?"

God smiled and gave the family of mice several small pairs of roller skates.

A few days went by, and God came back to check up on the cat. "How are you doing?" God asked.

The cat replied, "Everything is wonderful. I love my new soft bed. And those meals on wheels you've been sending by are just terrific."

Dates & Places Used:

683

TOPIC: Pets

Wag a Dog's Tail

Money will buy a fine dog, but love will make him wag his tail.

Dates & Places Used:

684

TOPIC: Pets

Too Dark to Read

Outside of a dog, a book is man's best friend. Inside of a dog, it is too dark to read. *(Groucho Marx)*

Dates & Places Used:

685

TOPIC: Pets

Cat Experiences

Experience is valuable in most things we do. But the problem of getting a cat out of a tree is a new experience every time we do it.

Dates & Places Used:

686

Valued Pet

A minister preached a very short sermon. He explained, "My dog got into my office and chewed up some of my notes." At the close of the service a visitor said to him, "If your dog ever has pups, please let my pastor have one of them."
Dates & Places Used:

687

Both Parties Are Worse

The more you observe politics, the more you have to admit that each party is worse than the other. *(Will Rogers)*
Dates & Places Used:

688

Politics Minus Politics

An independent is a guy who wants to take the politics out of politics. *(Adlai Stevenson)*
Dates & Places Used:

689

Art of Politics

Politics is the art of looking for trouble, finding it everywhere, diagnosing it incorrectly, and applying the wrong remedies. *(Groucho Marx)*
Dates & Places Used:

690

TOPIC: Politics

The Money, Bible, or Whiskey?

A couple's twentysomething son was still living with them. The parents were a little worried, as the son had yet to decide on a career, so they decided to conduct a test.

They put a ten-dollar bill, a Bible, and a bottle of whiskey on the front hall table. Then they hid, pretending they were not at home.

The father said, "If our son takes the money, he will be a businessman; if he takes the Bible, he will be a priest; but if he takes the bottle of whiskey, I'm afraid our son will be a drunk."

So the parents stayed in the nearby closet and waited nervously. Peeping through the keyhole, they saw their son arrive. The son saw what they had left and took the ten-dollar bill, looked at it against the light, and slid it into his pocket.

After that, he took the Bible, flicked through it, and took it.

Finally, he grabbed the bottle, opened it, and took an appreciative whiff to be assured of the quality. Then he left for his room, carrying all three of the items.

The father slapped his forehead, and said, "Darn, it's even worse than I ever could have imagined – our son is going to be a politician!"

Dates & Places Used:

691

TOPIC: Politics

Stakes Are So Small

University politics are vicious precisely because the stakes are so small. *(Henry Kissinger)*
Dates & Places Used:

692

Quick Response

The well-known newspaper advice-giver Ann Landers was reported to be at an embassy reception when she was approached by a pompous, arrogant senator. He said to her, "So you're the famous Ann Landers. Say something funny."

Without missing a beat, she said, "Well, you're a politician. Tell me a lie."

Dates & Places Used:

693

TOPIC: Potential

Impossible Caution

I have learned to use the word *impossible* with great caution. *(Wernher von Braun)*
Dates & Places Used:

694

TOPIC: Poverty

Protected by Poverty

The sign on the fence gave all fair warning: "This property protected by poverty–there is nothing here worth stealing."
Dates & Places Used:

695

TOPIC: Power

Hawk, Lion, and Stinker

Three forest animals were arguing as to which animal was the most feared. The hawk claimed that he was the most feared, since he could fly and attack from above without being seen by his prey. The lion claimed that he was the most feared because of his great strength. The skunk told the other two animals that he was the most feared, for he did not need to fly or use his strength to frighten away other creatures. As the three animals continued their debate, a large bear came along and settled the argument by swallowing all three animals—hawk, lion, and stinker.

Dates & Places Used:

696

TOPIC: Power

Powerless Cape

A three-year-old boy received a Superman cape as a present. He excitedly put on his new costume and ran outside as fast as he could. After a few minutes of running and jumping in the backyard, the boy returned to the house and angrily tore the costume off and threw it on the floor. With disgust the boy complained, "It doesn't matter how hard I try; I can't get this stupid thing to work!"

Dates & Places Used:

697

TOPIC: Power

Strength in Wisdom

A strong young man at a construction site was bragging that he could outdo anyone in a feat of strength. He made a special case of making fun of one of the older workmen.

After several minutes, the older worker had had enough. "Why don't you put your money where your mouth is," he said. "I will bet a week's wages that I can haul something in a wheelbarrow over to that outbuilding that you won't be able to wheel back."

"You're on, old man," the braggart replied. "Let's see what you've got."

The old man reached out and grabbed the wheelbarrow by the handles. Then, nodding to the young man, he said, "All right. Get in."

Dates & Places Used:

TOPIC: Power

Name That Weapon

A little guy was sitting in a restaurant eating his meal and minding his own business when all of a sudden a great big man came in and–*whack!*–knocked him off his chair and said, "That was a karate chop from Korea."

The little guy thought, *Ouch!* but got back up on his chair and started eating and minding his own business again. Then all of a sudden–*whack!*–the big man knocked him down again and said, "That was a judo chop from Japan."

The little guy had had enough of that, so he left and was gone for about a half hour or so. When he came back–*whack!*–he knocked the big man down from his chair and out cold!

The little guy looked at the people around him and said, "When he comes to, tell him that was a crowbar from Sears."

Dates & Places Used:

TOPIC: Power

Get Your Own Dirt

One day a group of scientists got together and decided that man had come a long way and no longer needed God. So they picked one scientist to go and tell him that they were done with him.

The scientist walked up to God and said, "God, we've decided that we no longer need you. We're to the point that we can clone people and do many miraculous things, so why don't you just go on and get lost."

God listened very patiently and kindly to the man. After the scientist was done talking, God said, "Very well, how about this? Let's say we have a man-making contest."

The scientist replied, "Okay, great!"

But God added, "Now, we're going to do this just like I did back in the old days with Adam."

The scientist said, "Sure, no problem," and bent down and grabbed himself a handful of dirt.

God looked at him and said, "No, no, no. You go get your own dirt!"

Dates & Places Used:

700

TOPIC: Power

When Nobody but the Lord Will Do

A hurricane had struck, and people were huddled together listening to an old preacher praying with great oratorical effects in the midst of the violent storm. He cried out, "Send us the spirit of the children of Israel, the children of Moses, the children of the Promised Land."

At this an old man with less oratory skill but more directness prayed, "Lord, don't send nobody. Come yourself. This ain't no time for children."

Dates & Places Used:

701

TOPIC: Pragmatism

Live Dragons

It does not do to leave a live dragon out of your calculations if you live near him. *(J. R. R. Tolkien)*

Dates & Places Used:

702

TOPIC: Pragmatism

Job Sense

When you laugh at the boss's joke, it doesn't prove that you have a sense of humor; it proves that you have sense.

Dates & Places Used:

703

TOPIC: Praise

Praise Overcomes Fear

Try praising your wife even if it does frighten her at first.
(Billy Sunday)
Dates & Places Used:

704

TOPIC: Prayer

Prayer's Focus

A five-year-old girl was attending a formal wedding some years ago with her grandmother. She had been in Sunday school but had never attended a formal church service.

During the wedding, the minister said, "Let us pray." Each person bowed his or her head in prayer. The little girl looked around and saw all the heads bowed and eyes turned toward the floor, and she cried, "Grandmother, what are they all looking for?"

What are we all looking for when we pray?
Dates & Places Used:

705

TOPIC: Prayer

Old-Fashioned Prayer

A farmer was entertaining one of his sophisticated relatives from the city. Before the meal the farmer gave thanks for the food. When he finished, the visitor jeered, "This is old-fashioned; nobody with an education prays at the table anymore."

The farmer admitted that the practice was old and even allowed that there were some on his farm who did not pray before their meals.

Justified, the relative remarked, "So enlightenment is finally reaching the farm. Who are these wise ones?"

The farmer replied, "My pigs."
Dates & Places Used:

706

Instant Answers

My wife and I try to make prayer something we do for all our needs, concerns, and joys.

Our three-year-old daughter recently got an "ouchy." Jenny said, "Mommy, will you pray to Jesus to make it better?"

Mommy prayed a brief and simple prayer. As soon as she said, "Amen," Jenny asked, "Well, what'd he say?"

Oh, for the faith of a child to want and expect such clear and direct answers. Out of the mouth of babes . . .

Dates & Places Used:

707

TOPIC: Prayer

No Time to Pray

It's a frustrating thing to lose a soccer game. It's even more frustrating when the first goal is scored three seconds after the beginning of the game. But this is just what happened when two Brazilian teams faced each other. The Corinthian soccer team scored its first goal while the goalie for Rio Preto was still on one knee with head bowed praying for victory. There's a time to *pray*, and there's a time to *play*.

Dates & Places Used:

708

TOPIC: Prayer

Deli Bread: Lord's Prayer Mutilated

A little boy was with his father when he stopped at the delicatessen and purchased some cold cuts and some rye bread. The father told his son that there was no better bread in all the world.

When they returned home and the table was prepared for the meal, the son asked if he could pray. He emulated a portion of the Lord's Prayer to the best of his ability: "Give us this day our deli bread."

Dates & Places Used:

709

TOPIC: Prayer

Powerful Prayer

A legendary preacher named Brother Jackson was called to minister in the Ozarks of southwest Missouri some years ago. The church had been terrorized by a local thug who would get drunk and disturb services, harass the preacher, threaten the people, and beat up a few. In Brother Jackson's first sermon, he denounced the bully by name.

The two met on a road the next day, and the bully said he was going to beat up on this preacher as he had the others. Brother Jackson said he would likely accommodate him but asked first for a few moments to pray in preparation. The preacher began his prayer: "O Lord, thou knowest that when I was forced to kill Bill Hewett and John Brown and Jerry Smith and Levi Battles, I did it in pure self-defense. Thou knowest that when I cut the heart out of that young upstart Younger and strewed the ground with the brains of mean old Philip Yandy, it was forced upon me, and I did it only with great agony of soul. And now, O Lord, I am forced to put in his coffin this poor, miserable wretch of a bully, Sam Johnson. Have mercy on his soul and take care of his widow and his orphans. Amen."

Brother Jackson rose, took his knife from his pocket, and began to whet it on a stone. Then he started singing in a loud voice, "Nearer, my God, to thee, nearer to thee! E'en though it be a cross that raiseth me; still all my song shall be, nearer, my God, to thee . . ."

And when he looked around, the bully had disappeared!

Dates & Places Used:

TOPIC: Preferences

Moving the Farm South

The Michaels family owned a small farm in Canada just yards away from the North Dakota border. Their land had been the subject of a minor dispute between the United States and Canada for generations. Mrs. Michaels, who had just celebrated her ninetieth birthday, lived on the farm with her son and three grandchildren.

One day her son came into her room holding a letter. "I just got some news, Mom," he said. "The government has come to an agreement with the people in Washington. They've decided that our land is really part of the United States. We have the right to approve or disapprove of the agreement. What do you think?"

"What do I think?" his mother said. "Jump at it! Call them right now and tell them we accept! I don't think I could stand another one of those Canadian winters!"

Dates & Places Used:

TOPIC: Preferences

Bad Barney Movie

An older brother was telling his younger brother about the new Barney movie: "They're making a new movie about Barney, but the movie has a terrible, tragic ending: Barney survives."

Dates & Places Used:

TOPIC: Preferences

Daddy Has Standards

While I was shopping in the mall with my three children, a display in the window of a lingerie store caught my eye. "Do you think Daddy would like this?" I asked the kids, as I pointed to a lacy teddy with matching robe.

"No way," my horrified six-year-old son replied. "Daddy would *never* wear *that!*"

Dates & Places Used:

713

TOPIC: Prejudice

Local Perspectives

Two boys were playing football in New York City's Central Park when the smaller of the two boys was attacked by a rabid dog. Thinking quickly, the other boy ripped off a board from a nearby fence, wedged it inside the dog's collar, twisted the board, and broke the dog's neck.

A reporter from a New York newspaper saw the incident and ran over to interview the young hero. The reporter titled his article: "Young Giants Fan Saves Friend from Vicious Beast."

"But I'm not a Giants fan," the boy explained.

So the reporter tried again. "Little Jets Fan Rescues Friend from Rabid Dog Attack."

"I don't like the Jets either," the boy told him.

"But I figured that everyone in New York was either a fan of the Giants or Jets. So what team do you root for?" the reporter asked.

"I'm a Dallas Cowboys fan," the boy answered.

The reporter then headed his article: "Ruthless Child Destroys Beloved Family Pet."

Dates & Places Used:

714

TOPIC: Preparation

To Kill a Snake

The following is said to be from the U.S. Government Peace Corps Manual for its volunteers who work in the Amazon jungle. It tells what to do in case you are attacked by an anaconda.

An anaconda is the largest snake in the world. It's a relative of the boa constrictor, it grows to thirty-five feet in length, and it weighs between three hundred and four hundred pounds at the maximum.

1. If you are attacked by an anaconda, do not run. The snake is faster than you are.
2. Lie flat on the ground. Put your arms tight against your sides, your legs tight against one another.
3. Tuck your chin in.
4. The snake will come and begin to nudge and climb over your body.
5. Do not panic. [Think about that–Do not panic!]
6. After the snake has examined you, it will begin to swallow you from the feet end–always from the feet end. Permit the snake to swallow your feet and ankles. Do not panic.
7. The snake will now begin to suck your legs into its body. You must lie perfectly still. This will take a long time.
8. When the snake has reached your knees, slowly, and with as little movement as possible, reach down, take your knife, and very gently slide it into the side of the snake's mouth between the edge of its mouth and your leg. Then suddenly rip upwards, severing the snake's head.

[The last two suggestions were the ones that got me.]

9. Be sure you have your knife.
10. Be sure your knife is sharp.

Dates & Places Used:

715

TOPIC: Preparation

Politics and Thought

Politics is perhaps the only profession for which no preparation is thought necessary. *(Robert Louis Stevenson)*
Dates & Places Used:

716

TOPIC: Preparation

Carry the Car Door

Three men were walking in the desert. One was carrying a loaf of bread, another a bottle of wine, and the third a car door. They explained to each other:

"If I get hungry, I can eat the bread!"
"If I get thirsty, I can drink the wine!"
"If I get hot, I can roll down the window!"
Dates & Places Used:

717

TOPIC: Prices

Small Wonder

Two Irishmen who were traveling in the Holy Land came to the Sea of Galilee. They discovered that it would cost them fifty dollars each to cross the lake by boat. They cried out in protest. "The Lakes of Killarney are the most beautiful lakes in the world, and one can cross them for a few shillings."

The guide explained, "Oh, but this is the lake Jesus walked on!"

The Irishmen quickly retorted, "Small wonder, at the prices you charge for taking a boat."

Dates & Places Used:

718

TOPIC: Prices

Just Ribbing!

"I'm lonely," Adam told God in the Garden of Eden. "I need to have someone around for company."

"Okay," replied God, "I'm going to give you the perfect woman. Beautiful, intelligent, and gracious—she'll cook and clean for you and never say a cross word."

"Sounds good," Adam said, "but what's she going to cost me?"

"An arm and a leg."

"That's pretty steep," countered Adam. "What can I get for just a rib?"

Dates & Places Used:

719

Home Improvement Strategy

A good architect can improve the looks of an old house merely by discussing the cost of a new one.

Dates & Places Used:

720

Pay through the Nose

A little boy was getting examined by the family physician. As the doctor continued his examination, the boy asked him, "Are you going to look in my nose?"

The doctor asked the boy, "Why should I check your nose?"

The boy explained, "My dad said that we'll have to pay you through the nose."

Dates & Places Used:

721

Diamond Cut

A high-quality diamond will cut into anything–especially a man's bank account.

Dates & Places Used:

722

Tiny Turtle Ears

Did you ever wonder why Turtle Wax is expensive?
Perhaps it is because turtles have such tiny little ears.

Dates & Places Used:

723

Wet Plate Special

A man from Texas was dining at a fancy restaurant in New York City. The food server brought out bread and a plate. The man looked at the plate and asked the food server to return. He pointed to his plate and explained, "There must be some mistake; my plate is still wet."

"No mistake, sir," said the food server; "that's your soup."

Dates & Places Used:

724

TOPIC: Prices

Nothing Left Over

A man was going out of town and needed to board his horse for a couple of months. He asked a local farmer about it, and he said, "Sure, but I charge fifty dollars per week, and I keep the manure." Well, the fellow couldn't afford this, so the farmer referred him to ol' Jones down the road.

When approached with the request, Jones said, "Yup, I can do it for forty dollars a week, and I keep the manure." This was still too much, and Jones suggested that he try Mr. Brown.

When our desperate friend asked Mr. Brown, he was surprised to hear, "Sure, sonny. I'll be glad to for five dollars a month." With delight, the young man exclaimed, "Wow! I suppose for that price you'll want to keep the manure."

The old man looked at him with kind of a squint and said, "Feller, for five dollars a month, there ain't gonna be none!"

Dates & Places Used:

725

TOPIC: Pride

Too Much Improvement

A husband and wife met with a marriage counselor about their irreconcilable differences. The husband explained, "Ever

290

since we were married, my wife has set out to change me. She convinced me to stop smoking, drinking, and staying out all night at parties. She got me to dress well and to enjoy fine dining, classical music, and ballet. She even taught me to save money and to invest my savings."

The counselor considered all these sudden changes and then suggested, "It sounds like you may be experiencing latent bitterness toward your wife for so many behavioral changes at one time."

The husband disagreed with the counselor. "Oh no, not at all. I like the changes. It's just that I have improved in so many ways that now I think I am too good for this plain woman."

Dates & Places Used:

726

TOPIC: Pride

Related to King Kong

In an attempt to impress his date, a college student told her that he could trace his roots back to royalty. The young woman was already quite bored with his arrogance and agreed, "I'll bet your ancestor was King Kong."

Dates & Places Used:

727

TOPIC: Pride

Irreplaceable You

A preacher named Dick Jones lived as if everything in the whole community depended upon him. One morning he woke up early with a high fever, so his wife called a doctor friend. He diagnosed Dick with viral pneumonia and suggested that he stay in bed for several days, but Dick protested, "No! I've got a breakfast meeting at the school—I'm president of the PSTA Board. Then I've got crucial business at the office, a luncheon date, three very important appointments this afternoon, and a building committee meeting at church this evening. There's no way I can be sick today, doctor."

"I'm sorry," said his doctor friend. "But I don't know anyone who is indispensable, and I suggest that you stay in bed."

At that very moment, as the story goes, Dick's high fever sent him into a trance. And there in that trance he saw himself looking in on heaven. The angels were gathering around God's throne, but everything seemed to be in disarray. Some papers were being passed, and finally, after some discussion, the angels passed a significant-looking paper to God. He read it and was obviously upset. He got up off his throne and said, "Oh no! Oh no! What will I do today? What will I do?"

The angels in chorus said, "What is it, God? What is it?"

And God replied, "What will I do today? Dick Jones is sick!"

Dates & Places Used:

728

TOPIC: Priorities

Money or Your Life

"Your money or your life?" demanded the robber.

The overcautious victim replied, "Take my life. I'm saving my money for my old age."

Dates & Places Used:

729

TOPIC: Priorities

Wrong God

After church one Sunday I noticed my five-year-old son writing something in his take-home Sunday school paper.

"Dad," he said, "how do you spell *God?*"

I was pleased that he was obviously still thinking about his Sunday school lesson.

He wrote "God" and then asked, "Dad, how do you spell *Zilla?*"

Dates & Places Used:

TOPIC: Priorities

Wrong Purse

A teenage girl's purse had been stolen from her car. She returned home and made the necessary calls. She called the credit card companies and the bank. She had already filed a police report. It was now time to wake her mother up and tell her what happened. This would be the hardest part of all.

She stepped into her mother's bedroom. "Mom, are you still awake?"

"What's the matter?" her mother slowly answered.

"Someone broke into my car and stole my purse."

"Which purse, honey?" her mother asked.

"The green suede one," the girl answered.

The mother sat up in bed and turned on the light. "The green one," she exclaimed, "with that dress?"

Dates & Places Used:

TOPIC: Problems

Bad Time for a Jew

As a man was walking the streets of Belfast at night, he was grabbed from behind and a knife was forced to his throat. "Are you a Catholic or a Protestant?" his assailant asked.

The man carefully considered his dilemma. He did not know if his assailant was Catholic or Protestant. If he said the one his assailant was not, he may be killed. He played it safe: "I am a Jew!" he said.

His assailant jubilantly answered, "I must be the luckiest Arab terrorist in all the world!"

Dates & Places Used:

732

TOPIC: Problems

An Early Start

When the new patient was settled comfortably on the couch, the psychiatrist began his therapy session. "I'm not aware of your problem," the doctor said, "so perhaps you should start at the very beginning."

"Of course," replied the patient. "In the beginning, I created the heavens and the earth...."

Dates & Places Used:

733

TOPIC: Problems

No Refills

A man called his physician and asked about the blood pressure medication he had prescribed. "You did tell me I would have to take this medication for the rest of my life, right?"

"Yes," the doctor answered, "I'm afraid you will."

There was a moment of silence before the man hesitantly responded, "Then could you tell me exactly how serious this blood pressure thing is?"

The doctor was a bit confused by the man's question and the tone of the question and asked, "Why do you ask?"

"Because," the man explained, "the prescription on this bottle says, 'No Refills'!"

Dates & Places Used:

734

TOPIC: Problems

Clear Communication

The phone rang at three in the morning at the home of the local librarian. At the other end of the phone, a voice asked, "What time does the library open?"

Disgustedly, the librarian retorted, "It doesn't open until nine in the morning. Why in the world would you be calling at this hour to get in the library?"

"Get in?" said the little boy at the other end. "I don't want to get in; I want to get out!"
Dates & Places Used:

TOPIC: Problems

735

Two Red Ears

A common sense–challenged man with two red ears went to see the doctor. The doctor asked him what had happened to his ears; they looked like they were burnt.

The common sense–challenged man explained, "I was ironing a shirt, and the phone rang. Instead of picking up the phone, I accidentally picked up the iron and stuck it to my ear."

"Oh dear!" the doctor exclaimed in disbelief. "But what happened to your other ear?"

"The phone rang again!"
Dates & Places Used:

TOPIC: Procrastination

736

None of These Days

One of these days is none of these days.
Dates & Places Used:

TOPIC: Procrastination

737

Securely Behind

Behind an employee's cluttered desk was a sign:
"I have job security and cannot be fired; I'm too far behind in my work."
Dates & Places Used:

738

Keep Praying

During his many appearances in summer stock in the role of Tevye in *Fiddler on the Roof*, Robert Merrill had learned to expect the unexpected.

"One night on stage," he said, "as I implored God to give me a replacement for my horse, which had lost its shoe, suddenly a small spotted dog walked onto the stage."

"I looked up again and added fervently, 'Oh, God, please try again.'"

Dates & Places Used:

739

Did God Send the Pastor?

A young minister was being interviewed by a church board for the position of pastor. One old hardworking Irishman who was on the board looked at the young man sternly and asked, "Young man, did God send you here?"

He replied, "Well, I don't know if God sent me here. I am here trying to find the will of God and find out if you would like me for your next pastor."

The board member replied, "Young man, did God send you here?"

The young minister was somewhat at a loss for words and came back with, "Well, I just stopped by to talk with the board—"

The board member interrupted again and said, "Young man, did God send you here?"

Finally, he screwed up his courage and said, "Well, I guess God didn't send me here. I just stopped by to see about whether we could get together."

The old board member leaned back in his seat and said, "That's good. The last four said that God had sent them, and we have had nothing but trouble with all four of them!"

Dates & Places Used:

740

TOPIC: Punishment

Prayerful Revenge

A little boy was smarting after being punished by his father. Shortly afterward he knelt by his bed to say his prayers, which ended with the usual blessings for all the family but one. Then he turned to his father and said, "I suppose you noticed you weren't in it."

Dates & Places Used:

741

TOPIC: Puns

Roaming Catholics

What do you call a nun who walks in her sleep?
A Roaming Catholic.

Dates & Places Used:

742

TOPIC: Puns

Vulture Airlines

Two vultures boarded an airplane, each carrying two dead raccoons.

The flight attendant looked at them and said, "I'm sorry, gentlemen, only one carrion allowed per passenger."

Dates & Places Used:

743

TOPIC: Puns

Cereal Killer

Question: What do you call a man who kills Captain Crunch?
Answer: A serial (cereal) killer!

Dates & Places Used:

744

TOPIC: Puns

Uncollared

A priest went on vacation to a little resort town. A local fellow engaged him in conversation, and when he found out he was a priest, he said, "My lay church group is having a meeting tonight, and we'd love to have you speak to us."

The priest said he would but then remembered that he had not brought a clerical collar with him. So he went to the local priest, explained his situation, and asked if he might borrow a collar.

The other priest nodded and said, "I understand your situation: a *lay date* and a *collar short*."

Dates & Places Used:

745

TOPIC: Puns

Noah's Floodlights

Question: What kind of lights did Noah's ark have?
Answer: Floodlights!

Dates & Places Used:

746

TOPIC: Puns

Ears and Udders

A farmer was milking his cow when he happened to look up and see a fly buzz into one of the cow's ears. After he'd finished milking her, he noticed a fly in the milk pail. He said to himself, "Oh, well, in one ear and out the udder."

Dates & Places Used:

747

Solomon's Temple

Question: Where was Solomon's temple?
Answer: On his head.
Dates & Places Used:

748

Garbage Dump Guard

A man who had a job guarding a garbage dump site had to quit because a waste was a terrible thing to mind.
Dates & Places Used:

749

Little Rude Riding Hood

Question: Who is short, uses bad language, and is afraid of wolves?
Answer: Little Rude Riding Hood.
Dates & Places Used:

750

A Prophecy

Let's take a look into the future. It's 2020 and an American astronaut steps from his spaceship and creeps slowly across the surface of a strange planet. Suddenly a group of strange, furry creatures appears before him. "Take me to your leader," the astronaut says.

A furry creature leads him through a maze of tunnels, past hundreds of other furry creatures, until they reach a huge throne room. There he meets the leader, who looks just like the other creatures, except for the huge tube sticking out of the top of his head.

"What are you creatures?" the American asks.

"We're Furries," says one of the guides.

"Well, what do you call yourself?" he asks, looking at the leader.

The leader replies, "I'm the Furry with the Syringe on top."

Dates & Places Used:

751

TOPIC: Puns

Heat Your Kayak Too

Two Eskimos who were sitting in a kayak got chilly, but when they lit a fire in the craft, it sank. This proves that you can't have your kayak and heat it too.

Dates & Places Used:

752

TOPIC: Puns

Bacon Tree or Ham Bush?

Two men were shipwrecked on an island. After weeks without eating, one man said, "Why are we starving? Let's go over to that bacon tree and get some bacon."

The second said, "There's no such thing as a bacon tree."

"There is too a bacon tree," insisted the first man. He proceeded to march over to the other side of the island. After several hours he returned with his body full of arrows. "You were right," he gasped to his friend. "That wasn't a bacon tree. It was a ham bush."

Dates & Places Used:

753

TOPIC: Puns

Funny Tasting

A Christian comedy team was on its way to an international convention on comedy. On the way to their destination, their small plane had engine trouble and made an emergency landing in a remote jungle clearing. They were captured by a tribe of cannibals who wanted to eat them. But the cannibals decided against this and allowed them to leave when their plane was repaired.

As the plane lifted into the sky, one of the comedians asked the pilot why they were released. The pilot turned and answered the inquirer, "When I told them who we were, they were afraid we would taste funny."

Dates & Places Used:

754

TOPIC: Purpose

Knowing Your Limits

People are like thumbtacks. We can only go as far as our heads will let us.

Dates & Places Used:

755

TOPIC: Purpose

Contagious Joy

An insurance company sponsored a seminar for its sales-people. The title of the seminar was "Inspiration." The speaker was trying to inspire the agents to sell more policies, so he began telling them a success story about a man who was later identified as the president of their company. "I know a man who drove straight to his goal. He looked neither right nor left. He pressed forward at all costs and with only one destination in mind. Neither friend nor foe could delay or divert him from the road he had chosen. All who stood in his path did so at their own risk. He drove himself night and day. What would you call such a man, my friends?"

From the rear, from one of the obviously uninspired veteran salespeople, came the answer, "A truck driver!"

Dates & Places Used:

756

TOPIC: Purpose

How to Win a Race

Question: What is the best way to win a race?
Answer: Run faster than everyone else.
Dates & Places Used:

757

TOPIC: Questions

Practical Philosophy

The next time someone asks you what you are thinking, just tell that person you are wondering why banks put Braille dots on the keypads of their drive-up ATMs. Answers like that will reduce your number of questions quickly.
Dates & Places Used:

758

TOPIC: Questions

Dumb Questions

Don't be afraid to ask dumb questions; they're easier to handle than dumb mistakes.
Dates & Places Used:

759

TOPIC: Questions

Laughing Cows

The inquisitive little boy asked his mother, "When a cow laughs, does milk come out of its nose?"

Dates & Places Used:

760

TOPIC: Questions

Permanent Pressed Irons

If we have really advanced so much, why do our irons still have a setting for "permanent pressed" garments?

Dates & Places Used:

761

TOPIC: Questions

Drive-Up Question

A worker at a fast-food chain with a drive-up window was once asked about the strangest question he had ever been asked. His response was immediate. He said that the strangest question was one that was asked on a regular basis: "Can I get this order to go?"

Dates & Places Used:

762

TOPIC: Questions

That One Museum

I wonder where that museum is that has all the arms and legs from the statues from all the other museums.

Dates & Places Used:

763

TOPIC: Reasons

Why Poison Ivy?

At a Christian summer camp for children, one of the counselors was leading a discussion on the purpose God had for everything he created. They began to find good reasons for clouds and trees and rocks and rivers and animals and just about everything else in nature. Finally, one of the children said, "If God had a good purpose for everything, then why did God create poison ivy?"

The discussion leader gulped, and as he struggled with the question, one of the other children came to his rescue, saying, "The reason God made poison ivy is because God wanted us to know there are certain things we should keep our cotton-pickin' hands off of!"

Dates & Places Used:

764

TOPIC: Reasons

Cause of Baldness

Question: What causes baldness?
Answer: Lack of hair.
Dates & Places Used:

765

TOPIC: Reasons

Friend for Sale

A farmer was brought in for questioning concerning an election fraud scandal. "Did you sell your vote?" the attorney asked.

"No, sir, I did not," the farmer answered. "I voted for that fella 'cause I like him."

"Come on," the attorney replied, "I have evidence that the candidate gave you fifty dollars to vote for him."

The farmer explained, "I don't know about you, but when a fella gives me fifty dollars, I like him."

Dates & Places Used:

766

Season Pass to Dorms

During freshman orientation the college dean presented the rules to the new students.

"The male dormitory is off-limits to all female students, and the female dormitory is off-limits to the male students. Anyone caught breaking this rule will be fined $20 the first time." He continued, "Anyone caught breaking this rule the second time will be fined $60. Being caught a third time will cost you a fine of $180. Are there any questions?"

At this point, a male student in the crowd inquired, "How much is it for a season pass?"

Dates & Places Used:

767

Surefire Obedience

A mother had a particularly trying day with her young son. Finally, she flung up her hands and shouted, "All right, Billy. Do anything you please! Now let me see you disobey *that!*"

Dates & Places Used:

768

Grow Up to Be God

In January of 1993 my five-year-old grandson was in a kindergarten class near Sioux City, Iowa, when the teacher asked, "Who would you like to be when you grow up?"

Instinctively, my grandson blurted out, "I want to be God!"

He may have been simply acting smart, but did he not spontaneously speak the mind of humanity?

We want to be God, make our own rules, call the shots, and be top dog.

Dates & Places Used:

769

TOPIC: Rebellion

Quick Interest

The quickest way to get people interested in a project is to tell them it is none of their business.

Dates & Places Used:

770

TOPIC: Rebellion

Fickle Authorities

A police officer stopped a woman for speeding and politely asked her, "May I see your license?"

She replied in a huff, "I wish you guys could get your act together. Just yesterday you took my license away, and now today you expect me to show it to you."

Dates & Places Used:

771

TOPIC: Regret

Prior Proposals

Pangs of jealousy were in Miss Iceberg's heart when she heard that her former admirer had proposed to Miss Lovewell. She happened to run across Miss Lovewell in a bargain basement rush. She could not resist giving a dig. She gushed, "I hear that you've accepted Jack's proposal. I suppose he never told you he once proposed to me."

The fiancée responded, "No. But he did once tell me there were a lot of things in his life of which he was ashamed, but I didn't ask him what they were."

Dates & Places Used:

TOPIC: Relevance

Making It Personal

A young preacher had just begun serving his first congregation. This church was a small one and was composed entirely of
the population of a small logging town. Everyone in town
worked for the town's lumber mill, which was its only business
and was in fierce competition with the mill just upstream.

The preacher wasn't in town long before he had an experience that shook him up a bit. He was taking a walk through the
woods and chanced to see the workers at the town mill pulling
logs branded for the other mill out of the stream, cutting off the
branded ends, and running them through their own mill. Of
course, the preacher was very distressed and thus worked the
rest of the week on a powerful sermon. That Sunday he got up
and preached a sermon entitled "Thou Shalt Not Covet Thy
Neighbor's Property."

The sermon seemed to go over pretty well. Everyone told him,
as they went out the door, just how much they loved his preaching: "You really moved me preacher" and "Best sermon I ever
heard" were some of the remarks they made. But that next Monday morning it was business as usual at the mill. They were still
stealing logs. So the next Sunday the preacher delivered a real
"pulpit pounder" called "Thou Shalt Not Steal."

"Fantastic!" the people told him. "Wonderful!" they cried. But
on Monday morning the other company's logs were still being
swiped by the town mill.

Enough was enough! A man can take only so much, and then
he has to act. This time he wasn't going to hold anything back.
On Sunday he got up and preached a sermon he called "Thou
Shalt Not Cut Off the Branded Ends of Someone Else's Logs!"

They ran him out of town!

Dates & Places Used:

TOPIC: Relevance

Express Pulpits

Perhaps what many churches need is an express pulpit–for
preachers with six thoughts or less.

Dates & Places Used:

774

Obvious Ads

A man saw a sign over a plumbing supply store that read: "CAST IRON SINKS."

The man walked into the store and complained, "Listen, I don't know if you realize it or not, but everyone knows that cast iron sinks!"

Dates & Places Used:

775

Application Is Almost Everything

A soap manufacturer and a pastor were walking together down a street in a large city. The soap manufacturer casually said, "The gospel you preach hasn't done much good, has it? Just observe. There is still a lot of wickedness in the world and a lot of wicked people too!"

The pastor made no reply until they passed a dirty little child making mud pies in the gutter. Seizing the opportunity, the pastor said, "I see that soap hasn't done much good in the world, for there is much dirt and many dirty people around."

The soap manufacturer replied, "Oh, well, soap is only useful when it is applied."

And the pastor said, "Exactly—so it is with the gospel."

Dates & Places Used:

776

Communicating Truth through the Family Tree

A Sunday school teacher asked a group of children in her class, "Why do you believe in God?" In reporting some of the

answers the teacher confessed that the one she liked best came from a boy who said, "I don't know, unless it's something that runs in the family."
Dates & Places Used:

777

TOPIC: Religion

Joy in Religion

Let there be joy in religion. Too often it has had a dour countenance. Some men went to pick up a visiting minister, whom they had never met, from the airport. They approached one man getting off the plane and asked him if he was the guest minister. "No," he told them, "it's my ulcer that makes me look like this."
Dates & Places Used:

778

TOPIC: Religions

Cross-Bred Atheist

Question: What do you get when you cross an atheist with a Jehovah's Witness?

Answer: A person who knocks on your door for absolutely no reason at all.
Dates & Places Used:

779

TOPIC: Religions

Assembling Jehovah's Witnesses

A certain family kept getting unwanted visits from the Jehovah's Witnesses. It was an annoying inconvenience; the husband or wife would tell their unwelcome callers that they were not interested in the Jehovah's Witnesses. They would then explain to their two young children that Jehovah's Witnesses did not believe all the things that true Christians believed.

While on vacation in another city, this family drove by a Jehovah's Witness Assembly Hall. One of the young children carefully read the sign in front of the building and announced his discovery: "I found out where they make those Jehovah's Witnesses!"

Dates & Places Used:

780

TOPIC: Repentance

Acquitted But . . .

An uneducated old mountain man was arrested for stealing a horse. He wasn't too bright, but he was smart enough to hire a pretty good lawyer who managed to argue his case rather effectively. In fact, the attorney won the case for him. The judge told him he was acquitted. The mountain man scratched his head and said to the judge, "Does that mean I get to keep the horse?"

Dates & Places Used:

781

TOPIC: Repentance

Partly Sorry for Sins

I was driving down the road listening to a radio talk program, when the host became very sacrilegious in his clowning around about something. He facetiously said he needed to ask God for forgiveness. He asked the listening audience, "Does anyone out there remember the Act of Contrition?"

A few minutes later a woman called in saying she remembered something like "I am heartily sorry for my sins. . . ." But then she added, "But when I was a girl we learned to say it another way: 'I am partly sorry for my sins.'"

Isn't this the way of humankind? Isn't this why more don't come to God? They are only half-concerned with their sin.

Dates & Places Used:

782

Hearing Confessions

The new priest was nervous about hearing confessions, so he asked the older priest to sit in on his sessions. The new priest heard a couple of confessions; then the old priest asked him to step out of the confessional for a few suggestions.

The old priest suggested, "Cross your arms over your chest and rub your chin with one hand."

The new priest tried it.

The old priest then suggested, "Try saying things like, 'I see'; 'Yes, go on'; and 'I understand. How did you feel about that?'"

So the new priest said those things.

Then the old priest said, "Now don't you think that's a little better than slapping your knee and saying, 'No way! You're kidding! So what happened next?'"

Dates & Places Used:

783

TOPIC: Respect

Only to Old Ones

The messenger boy forgot to take his hat off when he got on the elevator. One fussy little woman complained, "Don't you take off your hat to ladies?"

"Only to old ones, ma'am," he replied.

Dates & Places Used:

784

TOPIC: Respect

Blind (but Cordial) Zeal

A young soldier on armed sentry duty for the first time had orders not to allow any car onto the military base unless it bore a special identification seal. The first car to pull up without the special seal was carrying a general. When the general testily told his driver to drive on through anyway, the sentry poked his

head in the window and said politely, "I'm new at this, sir. Whom do I shoot first, you or the driver?"
Dates & Places Used:

785

TOPIC: Respect

Presidents Are Winners

It's amazing how many people beat you at golf now that you're no longer president. *(George H. W. Bush)*
Dates & Places Used:

786

TOPIC: Responses

Clarifying the Message

From a father's letter to a son in college: "Am enclosing ten dollars as you requested in your letter. Incidentally, ten dollars is spelled with one zero and not two."
Dates & Places Used:

787

TOPIC: Responses

Facing the Electric Chair

A man on death row was about to be electrocuted. He phoned his lawyer shortly before the time of his execution and said, "It's almost time for me to go to the electric chair. You're my lawyer, so tell me what I should do now."

His lawyer thought for a moment and then answered, "Avoid sitting down."
Dates & Places Used:

788

Improving Response Time

A man was going up to bed when his wife told him he had left the light on in the garden shed; she could see it from the bedroom window. But he said that he hadn't been in the shed that day. He took a look, and there were people in the shed stealing things.

He called the police, but they told him that no one was in his area, so no one was available to catch the thieves. He said okay, hung up, counted to thirty, and called the police again.

"Hello. I just called you a few seconds ago because there were people in my shed. Well, you don't have to worry about them now; I just shot them all."

Within five minutes there were half a dozen police cars in the area, an armed response unit—the works. Of course, they caught the burglars red-handed. One of the policemen said to the home owner, "I thought you said you shot them!"

He replied, "I thought you said there were no cops available!"

Dates & Places Used:

789

Middle Age

Middle age is that difficult period between adolescence and retirement when you have to take care of yourself.

Dates & Places Used:

790

Who's in Charge?

Christian Herter, then governor of Massachusetts, was running hard for a second term. One day after a busy schedule of campaigning and no time for lunch, he arrived at a church barbecue famished. As he moved down the line, the governor held out his plate to the woman serving chicken. She put a piece on his plate and turned to the next person in line.

"Excuse me," Governor Herter said. "Do you mind if I have another piece of chicken?"

"Sorry," the woman replied, "I'm only supposed to give one piece to each person."

The governor was not a proud man, but he was hungry. So he decided to throw a little weight around. "Lady, do you know who I am? I'm the governor of this state."

"Do you know who I am?" the woman said. "I'm the lady in charge of the chicken!"

Dates & Places Used:

791

TOPIC: Results

Blind Hog Results

Even a blind hog occasionally turns up an acorn.
Dates & Places Used:

792

TOPIC: Results

One Love Letter a Day

A young man was determined to win the affection of a girl who refused to even see him. He decided that the way to her heart was through the mail, so he began writing her a love letter every day. When she didn't respond, he increased his output to three love letters a day.

In all, he wrote her more than seven hundred letters. And finally, after all those letters, she married the mail carrier.
Dates & Places Used:

793

Two Tied Losers

Did you hear about the two silkworms who had a race? It ended in a tie.

Dates & Places Used:

794

Fighting Fire with Fire

The former fireman was explaining to his wife why he was no longer working as a fireman. "Well, the fire on one end of the warehouse got so bad that I figured we would need to fight fire with fire. To make a long story short, the entire warehouse burned down."

Dates & Places Used:

795

Plant the Potatoes

A woman wrote to her husband who was serving time in prison for armed robbery. "When is the best time to plant the potatoes?" she wrote.

The husband wrote back, "Don't dig in the potato patch now. That is where I hid all of my guns."

The prison mail was monitored, of course, and soon the potato patch in question was being dug up by a whole squad of policemen. But there were no guns to be found.

Again, the wife wrote to her husband in prison. "They've dug up the whole potato patch," she complained.

Her imprisoned husband smugly wrote back, "The patch is now properly tilled. You may now plant the potatoes."

Dates & Places Used:

796

Percentage Prayers

Three Native Americans—a Navajo, a Hopi, and an Apache—were speaking about how powerful their prayers were.

The Navajo said, "You know, we Navajos pray for healing, and the patients get well about half the time."

The Hopi said, "Well, we Hopis pray for rain, and it happens about 70 percent of the time."

Finally, the Apache spoke up: "Yes, but we Apaches have the sunrise dance, and it works every time."

Dates & Places Used:

797

Active Prayer Life

A pious but cranky old woman was put out because her neighbors had not invited her to a picnic. On the morning of the picnic one of the neighbors finally called to ask her to go along. "It's too late," snapped the woman at the caller; "I've already prayed for rain."

Dates & Places Used:

798

Living Revenge

Bumper sticker wisdom: GET REVENGE: LIVE LONG ENOUGH TO BE A PROBLEM TO YOUR CHILDREN.

Dates & Places Used:

799

TOPIC: Revenge

Hit Him with a Bat

Never hit a man with glasses. Hit him with a baseball bat.
Dates & Places Used:

800

TOPIC: Revenge

The Other Person's Candle

Blowing out the other person's candle won't make your candle shine any brighter.
Dates & Places Used:

801

TOPIC: Risk

Remember the Averages

The race is not always to the swift nor the battle to the strong; but that's the way to bet. *(Damon Runyon)*
Dates & Places Used:

802

TOPIC: Risk

Safe Fall

The best way to fall off a thirty-foot ladder and not get hurt is to fall off the first rung.
Dates & Places Used:

803

TOPIC: Risk

Sistine Risk

If no one ever took risks, Michelangelo would have painted the Sistine floor. *(Neil Simon)*

Dates & Places Used:

804

TOPIC: Romance

When Love Is Gone

How do you know love is gone? If you said that you would be there at seven and you get there by nine, and he or she hasn't called the police yet–it's gone. *(Marlene Dietrich)*

Dates & Places Used:

805

TOPIC: Sacrifice

You Be Jesus

Kevin and Ryan, ages five and three, were waiting for breakfast one Saturday morning. As their mother was preparing some pancakes, the boys began to argue loudly over who would get the first one from the griddle. Their mother saw the opportunity for a moral lesson and said, "If Jesus were sitting here, he would say, 'Let my brother have the first pancake–I can wait.'"

Kevin immediately turned to his younger brother and said, "Okay, Ryan, you be Jesus."

Dates & Places Used:

806

TOPIC: Sales

Just Start Selling

A true account is told of a man who was looking for a job. He went to a furniture store to interview for a sales position. Upon arriving at the store, he had to wait for several other interviewees. While he waited, he began talking to customers about the furniture. By the time the company was ready to interview him, he had assisted several customers, and these customers had purchased nearly three thousand dollars' worth of furniture. His interview was short. The company was in a big hurry to get him back out on the floor to sell furniture.

Dates & Places Used:

807

TOPIC: Sales

Bad Advertising

Mixing bowl set for sale: designed to please a cook with round bottom for efficient beating.

Dates & Places Used:

808

TOPIC: Sales

Dual Purpose Obituary

A woman from the deepest, most southern part of Alabama went into the local newspaper office to see that the obituary for her recently deceased husband was written. The obit editor informed her that the fee for the obituary was fifty cents a word.

She paused, reflected, and then said, "Well, then, let it read: 'Billy Bob died.'"

Amused at the woman's thrift, the editor said, "Sorry, ma'am. There is a seven-word minimum on all obituaries."

Only a little flustered, she thought things over and in a few seconds said, "In that case, let it read: 'Billy Bob died–1983 pickup for sale.'"

Dates & Places Used:

TOPIC: Sales

The Math That Counts

On the occasion of the twentieth anniversary of their graduation, some college alumni were gathered for a class reunion.
They were scattered about in little groups reminiscing about
college days. In one group the conversation turned to a classmate they all remembered named Harvey. And the thing they
remembered most about Harvey was that whenever he was
asked what he was going to do after graduation, he always
replied, "I'm going to be a millionaire." Harvey always expected
he would make his millions. But another thing they remembered about Harvey was that he was one of the intellectually
slowest students in their class. And he was especially poor in
mathematics. Here was a man who expected to make millions,
but he could hardly add up a column of figures.

As the members of the group were exchanging "Harvey" stories, up pulled a brand-new, chauffeur-driven Rolls-Royce, and
out stepped Harvey wearing an expensive, tailor-made, three-
piece suit and everything that went with it. His classmates quickly
gathered around him and began throwing questions at him.

"Hey, Harvey, where did you get that car?"

"Harvey! Wow! What happened? How did you do it?"

Harvey said, "Well, you see, I came upon an invention that
costs me only five dollars to manufacture and I sell it for one
hundred dollars. And you'd be surprised how fast that 10 percent profit adds up!"

Dates & Places Used:

TOPIC: Salvation

Teamwork with God

The deacons were interviewing a little boy for membership in
their church. They asked, "How did you get saved?"

The boy answered, "God did his part, and I did my part."

The deacons were not so sure what the boy meant by that
answer, so they questioned further.

The boy explained what he meant by his answer: "God did
the part of saving, and I did the part of sinning. I ran from God

as fast as I could, and God took out after me until he finally ran me down."

Bible teacher J. Vernon McGee says, "My friend, that is the way I got saved also."

Dates & Places Used:

811

TOPIC: School

Count the Cost of Higher Education

A first grader came home from school one day and said to his little brother who was in kindergarten, "Don't ever let anyone teach you to spell 'cat.'"

The little brother asked, "Why?"

"Because," he said, "the words get harder after you learn to spell 'cat.'"

Dates & Places Used:

812

TOPIC: School

Both Sides of the Slides

Two teachers from different school systems were comparing how cheap their school systems were. One teacher finally won the contest with this statement: "My school system is so cheap they make us write on both sides of our transparency slides."

Dates & Places Used:

813

TOPIC: School

Teacher and Parent Pact

A wise schoolteacher sends this note to all parents on the first day of school: "If you promise not to believe everything your child says happens at school, I'll promise not to believe everything he says happens at home."

Dates & Places Used:

814

TOPIC: School

Geography or Spelling

A third-grade teacher told her class they were going to learn the capitals of all fifty states. A boy in the class raised his hand and told his teacher that he already knew all the state capitals. The teacher was impressed with the lad's confidence but thought she would confirm his claim. She asked the young man, "Then what is the capital of Wisconsin?"

The boy answered, "That's an easy one. It's *W*."

Dates & Places Used:

815

TOPIC: School

Soliloquy to Finals

To sleep or not to sleep—that is the question;
Whether 'tis nobler for the grade to suffer
The slings and arrows of outrageous teachers,
Or to take arms against a sea of courses
And by opposing flunk them. To lie: to sleep.
To sleep: perchance to dream. Aye, there's the rub.
For in that restless sleep what dreams may come
When we have shuffled off these passing grades
Must give us nightmares.

(With a nod to Shakespeare's *Hamlet*, Act III, Scene 1)

Dates & Places Used:

816

TOPIC: Secrets

Feeling Important

The secret of making another person feel important is to tell him a secret. He will feel important when he shares it with someone else.

Dates & Places Used:

817

TOPIC: Self

Quoting Self

I often quote myself! It adds wit to the conversation. *(George Bernard Shaw)*

Dates & Places Used:

818

TOPIC: Self

Ego Focus

An egotist is a person who is more interested in himself than in me.

Dates & Places Used:

819

TOPIC: Self

Wrong Hero

When we're self-centered we think the whole world revolves around us. Unfortunately, we're sadly mistaken, and often we wind up terribly embarrassed.

One morning on the *Today* show, Willard Scott was talking about this very thing. He said he had occasion to fly into a small community airport that only had one runway and one small hangar. As he was getting off the plane, he noticed a group of about seventy-five people all cheering and clapping, so he made a sweeping bow and waved. And that was when he noticed that the people weren't watching him; they were watching an air show.

Pride or self-importance makes yourself your focal point. Pretty soon you begin to think that God and everybody else owe you something.

Dates & Places Used:

820

Child-O-Centric Music

Our daughter has been teaching our two-year-old grandson Stephen the children's song "God Made Me." So far his rendition begins: "Me, me, me!"

Isn't that so characteristic of human nature?

Dates & Places Used:

821

Cuss Words Come Back

A young man regularly cut a pastor's lawn. One day the boy announced to the pastor that he would no longer be able to mow his yard because he was leaving for college. The pastor asked the young man if he knew anyone who would be interested in taking over the job. The young man said that he did not but offered to sell his lawn mower to the pastor.

The pastor thought about the offer and concluded that buying the mower may be the best solution, so he purchased the mower from the young man.

The next day the young man was walking by the pastor's house and saw him pulling the mower's starter rope. The pastor called him over and asked, "How do you get this thing started?"

The young man apologized. "Oh, I'm sorry. I forgot to tell you that you have to cuss at the mower before it will start. There are times that you have to cuss at it a lot."

The minister said, "Well, I don't think I can do that. It's been a long time since I've used any cuss words. I wouldn't even know where to start."

The young man encouraged him, "I'll tell you what; you just keep pulling that rope long enough, and those cuss words will come right back to you!"

Dates & Places Used:

822

TOPIC: Self-Control

Self-Controlled Beggar

A beggar walked up to a well-dressed woman shopping on Rodeo Drive in Hollywood and said, "I haven't eaten anything in four days."

The woman looked at the beggar with admiration and said, "I sure wish I had your willpower."

Dates & Places Used:

823

TOPIC: Self-Control

Prayer or Swear

A nun was stranded on the side of the road trying to change her flat tire with a jack that did not fit the car correctly. A motorist saw her distress and decided that he would stop and help. He tried to position the jack, but as he tried to lift the car, it slipped—and he swore. The nun was appreciative of his efforts on her behalf but was concerned about his loss of self-control and his subsequent swearing, and she told him so.

The man apologized and tried again. The jack slipped again, and the man swore once more. The nun told the man that if he had to swear, it would be better for him not to help her. She suggested that he turn his swearing into prayer; that is, the next time he felt like swearing, he should say something like, "Please, dear God, help me lift this heavy load."

The man thanked the sister for the advice and tried to lift the car for the third time. The same thing happened, and he started to swear. But he caught himself this time and prayed, "Please, dear God, help me lift this heavy load."

No sooner had he prayed than the entire car miraculously rose ten inches off the ground. The nun looked at the car as it floated in the air—and *she* swore!

Dates & Places Used:

824

Look at Something Bigger

A wealthy socialite went to see a famous psychotherapist. He said at the first interview, "Now tell me all about yourself."

She needed no second invitation. At the end of the hour the doctor said, "That will do for now. I'll see you again tomorrow."

The same pattern was repeated several times a week for several weeks. Finally, in exasperation the doctor said to the woman, "I advise you to take the first train to Niagara Falls, and there take a long, lingering look at something bigger than yourself."

Dates & Places Used:

825

Importance Is Relative

George had a friend with an inflated opinion of himself. As a friend should, George decided to help his friend lose this quirk. Subtly, George mentioned that he knew Johnny Carson.

The friend said, "Oh yeah? Prove it."

In a few minutes they were in front of a large house near the beach. They knocked, and out came Johnny Carson saying, "Come on in, George, and bring your friend."

On the way home the friend grudgingly said, "Okay, so you know Johnny Carson."

Obviously, this was not enough, so George said offhandedly, "Yes, he and I and the president are well acquainted."

The friend looked incredulous and cried out, "That's too much! I'll pay the costs—let's go to D.C. and see."

They arrived at the White House, and out came the president to greet them, saying, "Come on in, George, and bring your friend."

Later George's friend looked around sheepishly and admitted, "Well, yeah, you do know the president."

George sensed his friend needed further deflation. So casually he remarked, "Yeah, but you know, the pope has a nicer office."

"What!" yelled his wide-eyed friend, "You know the pope! I'll bet you ten thousand dollars you can't even get in to see the pope."

In a few days they were in Rome, with George knocking on a door to the Vatican. A cardinal came out extending his hand to George but saying, "Your friend will have to stay outside!"

About an hour went by when out came the pope onto the balcony, waving at the crowd with one arm around George. Later, outside, George looked around for his friend and found him out cold in the courtyard. George rushed over and helped his friend up and apologized for shocking him so.

But his friend simply shook his head and mumbled, "It's not that you knew the pope. It was the crowd. They kept asking each other, "Who's the guy with George?"

Dates & Places Used:

826

TOPIC: Sermons

Sermonic Threat

A church bulletin ran this notice: "Someone has taken the paper cutter from the church office, and we are in dire need of it. Please bear in mind that without the paper cutter the sermons will get longer and longer."

Dates & Places Used:

827

TOPIC: Sermons

On Sermonizing

Public speaking is like a vacation. It helps to know where to stop.

Dates & Places Used:

828

TOPIC: Sermons

Preaching Just Seems Long

A sign hung over a saloon piano in the Old West: DON'T SHOOT THE PIANIST. HE'S DOING THE BEST HE CAN. Maybe a sign like that ought to hang over a few pulpits.

A young pastor made the mistake of apologizing for preaching so long. "Oh, it really wasn't that long," said a woman trying to encourage him. "It only seemed that way."

Dates & Places Used:

829

TOPIC: Sermons

Church of Ostriches

Ostriches do everything together. They all yawn as a group before they go to sleep. And they repeat the group yawn when they awaken. Come to think of it, my congregation does that too!

Dates & Places Used:

830

TOPIC: Sermons

Just a Poor Preacher

The new minister's car broke down just after the morning service, so on Monday he had it towed to the local garage for repairs.

"I hope you'll go a little easy on the price," he told the mechanic. "After all, I'm just a poor preacher."

"I know," came the reply; "I've heard you."

Dates & Places Used:

831

TOPIC: Sermons

Real Fire and Brimstone

Dr. Stephen Power, a surgeon in England, tells of the embarrassed parson whose breath caught fire every time he blew or attempted to blow out the altar candles. According to our good doctor, the cause was an internal buildup of an inflammable gas due to the parson's duodenal ulcer. An operation took the fire out of the parson's mouth!

Dates & Places Used:

832

TOPIC: Service

Back in Ten

An old storekeeper, who was also the community's postmaster, was a real go-getter. He had no helper, and when he had to leave his store to meet the mail train, he was tormented by thoughts of tourists stopping for gas and soft drinks and finding him gone and his store closed. Finally, he hit upon a shrewd solution. He printed a sign in bold letters that explained everything during his enforced absences:

BACK IN FIFTEEN MINUTES
ALREADY BEEN GONE TEN

Dates & Places Used:

833

TOPIC: Sexuality

Babies and Turning

A man was complaining to his wife, "It seems that every time I turn around, we are having another baby!"

His wife answered, "Then stop turning around."

Dates & Places Used:

834

Thumb Sucking and Pregnancy

A boy had reached four without giving up the habit of sucking his thumb, though his mother had tried everything from bribery to reasoning to painting it with lemon juice in her efforts to discourage his habit. Finally, she tried threats, warning her son, "If you don't stop sucking your thumb, your stomach is going to blow up like a balloon."

Later that day, walking in the park, mother and son saw a pregnant woman sitting on a bench. The four-year-old considered her gravely for a minute, then said to her, "Uh-oh, I know what you've been doing."

Dates & Places Used:

835

TOPIC: Sharing

Everything Is Fifty-Fifty

A young man saw an elderly couple sitting down to lunch at McDonald's. He noticed that they had ordered one meal and an extra drink cup. As he watched, the gentleman carefully divided the hamburger in half, then counted out the fries, one for him, one for her, until each had half of them.

Then he poured half of the soft drink into the extra cup and set that in front of his wife. The old man then began to eat, and his wife sat watching with her hands folded in her lap.

The young man decided to ask if they would allow him to purchase another meal for them so that they didn't have to split theirs. The old gentleman said, "Oh no. We've been married fifty years, and everything always has been and always will be shared 50/50."

The young man then asked the wife if she was going to eat. She replied, "Not yet. It's his turn with the teeth."

Dates & Places Used:

836

For the Sick

Right in the middle of the church service, little Bobby whispered to his mother that he felt sick and thought he was going to throw up. His mother told him to quickly go to the back of the church and then go to the boys' room. Moments later little Bobby returned and was wiping his mouth with his hand. His mother was concerned that he was not gone long enough to get to the boys' room. She asked her son, "How did you do that so quickly?"

Bobby explained, "When I got to the back of the church, I saw a box with a sign on it that was there for me."

Mom continued, "What do you mean? What did the sign say?"

Bobby answered, "The sign said, 'FOR THE SICK.'"

Dates & Places Used:

837

TOPIC: Signs

Amish Carriage

While driving on a country road, a family came up behind an Amish carriage.

The owner of the carriage obviously had a sense of humor, because attached to the back of the carriage was a hand-printed sign:

ENERGY EFFICIENT VEHICLE
RUNS ON OATS AND GRASS
CAUTION: DO NOT STEP ON EXHAUST

Dates & Places Used:

838

TOPIC: Signs

Preacher Parking Only

An effective sign in front of the pastor's parking place was as follows:

PREACHER'S PARKING ONLY
YOU PARK, YOU PREACH

Dates & Places Used:

839

Roadkill Possum

A sign in a restaurant in a remote town in the southeastern United States read:

DON'T EVEN ASK IF WE SERVE ROAD KILL POSSUM.

WE ONLY SERVE RANCH-RAISED POSSUM!

Dates & Places Used:

840

More Power for Light

A student took his car over to Chick's Garage and told the mechanic, "Something's wrong. I don't have any lights."

The mechanic suggested, "The battery is probably dead."

"No," the student explained, "My horn still blows; it can't be the battery."

The mechanic replied, "It still might be the battery, because it takes more power to give light than it does to blow a horn."

An interesting point, isn't it? It's easier to toot than to shine. It's easier to say than to do.

Dates & Places Used:

841

Keep Your Mouth Shut

Have you heard the story about the mountain climber who fell and slid into a deep crevice? His friends lowered a rope to him and said, "Grab hold of the rope!"

"I can't," came the reply; "my arms are broken."

"Then wrap your legs around it!"

"I can't," he said; "I've broken my legs too."

"Then grip it with your teeth and we'll haul you up carefully."

So he did. And they began to pull.

After a few moments someone shouted from above, "How are you doing?"

All they heard was, "Okay–uh-oh."

Dates & Places Used:

842

TOPIC: Silence

In Too Deep

When you are in over your head, there is no better time to keep your mouth shut.

Dates & Places Used:

843

TOPIC: Sin

Preaching against Sin

President Calvin Coolidge returned home from attending church early one Sunday afternoon. He was asked by his wife what the minister spoke on.

"Sin," Coolidge replied.

Wanting to know more, she pressed him for some words of explanation.

Being a man of few words (as only you wives can appreciate), Coolidge responded, "I think he was against it."

Dates & Places Used:

844

TOPIC: Sin

Raw Deal for the Devil

He had been in politics for too long a time. He was jaded. His sensitivity was gone. And into his office walked the devil himself. Satan conversed with him for a few moments–cordial conversation–that's all. And then he presented his offer. The devil told the politician that he would brighten his political future

with greater power, prestige, and possessions. All the man
needed to do was to trade his soul for these demonic blessings.
The politician never hesitated. He immediately signed the
papers to consummate the deal.

As Satan was walking out of the office, the politician stopped
him and asked, "Now that we have closed our deal, please tell
me: I get all these wonderful things from you and all you get is
my soul; what's the catch?"

Dates & Places Used:

845

TOPIC: Sin

Prodigal Son in the Key of F

Here's one you can memorize and then recite at the church
social. It is a lighter version of the familiar parable. I guess you
could say it is in the "key of F."

Feeling footloose and frisky, a featherbrained fellow forced
his fond father to fork over the farthings and flew to foreign
fields and frittered his fortune, feasting fabulously with faithless
friends. Fleeced by his fellows in folly, and facing famine, he
found himself a feed flinger in a filthy farmyard. Fairly famish-
ing, he fain would have filled his frame with foraged food from
fodder fragments.

"Fooey! My father's flunkies fare far finer," the frazzled fugitive forlornly fumbled, frankly facing facts. Frustrated by failure
and filled with foreboding, he fled forthwith to his family.
Falling at his father's feet, he forlornly fumbled, "Father, I've
flunked and fruitlessly forfeited family favor."

The farsighted father, forestalling further flinching, frantically
flagged the flunkies to fetch a fatling from the flock and fix a
feast. The fugitive's fault-finding brother frowned on fickle forgiveness of former folderol. But the faithful father figured, "Filial
fidelity is fine, but the fugitive is found! What forbids fervent fes-
tivity? Let flags be unfurled. Let fanfares flare." And the father's
forgiveness formed the foundation for the former fugitive's
future fortitude.

Dates & Places Used:

846

TOPIC: Sin

Betrayed by the Light

The entire University of Michigan football team checked into their hotel rooms the night before the big game with Ohio State University. The Michigan coach had given clear instructions that his players were to get a good night's sleep. They were not to leave their rooms.

One rebellious lineman, however, wanted to get out and see the city of Columbus by night. The lineman deceptively put a floor lamp on the bed and put covers around it so it looked like he was already asleep in bed. Then he left his room to go out on the town. Late that night the coach went around to all his players' rooms and did a bed check. He opened each door and hit the light switch.

Arriving at the lineman's room, he turned on the light. The covers were still covering the floor lamp, but the player had not unplugged the lamp. So when the coach hit the switch, the lamp shed light on the lineman's deception.

Light does that. Light reveals darkness.

Dates & Places Used:

847

TOPIC: Sin

You Can't Hide the Evidence

A little girl cut her own hair while her mommy was gone. To be sure, it was a terrible patchwork job. When her mommy got home she was horrified to see her child. The little girl said, "But, Mommy, how did you know? I hid all the hair very carefully in the wastebasket."

Dates & Places Used:

848

TOPIC: Size

A Fitting Fish

It was the first day of the season, and a fisherman had just caught a huge bass. He tossed it back and caught another fish, medium sized. He tossed it back too. Finally, he caught and kept two smaller bass. A curious boy who had seen the entire episode asked him why he hadn't kept the bigger fish. The reply: "Small pan."

Dates & Places Used:

849

TOPIC: Size

Fat Goalies

Here is a great idea for the National Hockey League. Why don't they recruit the fattest man in the world to become the goalie?

Dates & Places Used:

850

TOPIC: Size

Short Bible Men

The three shortest men in the Bible were Knee-High-My-A (Nehemiah), Bildad the Shoe Height (Bildad the Shuhite), and the centurion who slept on his watch.

Dates & Places Used:

851

TOPIC: Size

Conquering Spirit

A few years back at a Congress on Biblical Exposition meeting in Anaheim, California, it was reported that a man weighing

between 350 and 400 pounds was seen on the street wearing a
T-shirt that read: I OVERCAME ANOREXIA.
Dates & Places Used:

852

TOPIC: Sleep

Bean Counter Tries Counting Sheep

An accountant was having a hard time sleeping, so he went to
see his doctor. "Doctor, I just can't get to sleep at night."

"Have you tried counting sheep?" the doctor asked.

"Yes, I think that's part of the problem. I make a mistake, and
then I spend the next three hours trying to find it."

Dates & Places Used:

853

TOPIC: Sleep

Sleeping like Babies

People who say they sleep like a baby usually don't have one.

Dates & Places Used:

854

TOPIC: Sleep

Stop the Snoring like Spiders

The reason female black widow spiders kill the males after
mating is to stop the snoring before it starts.

Dates & Places Used:

855

TOPIC: Sleep

Comforting Sermons

If all who have gone to sleep during my sermons were put end to end, they would be more comfortable!

Dates & Places Used:

856

TOPIC: Sleep

Concerted Alarm

A man was dragged to a concert by his wife. In the middle of the concert, his wife nudged him and said, "Look over there. So-and-so is sleeping."

The man replied, "You had to wake me for that?"

Dates & Places Used:

857

TOPIC: Sleep

How It All Began

In the Old Testament, kings believed that God gave them direction in dreams. If they wanted to know what they were supposed to do in their administration, they would try to dream and receive a direct word from God. And if they weren't getting any messages in their dreams while lying in their own beds, they would sleep in the temple. They believed that it would work better there. This is the origin of the time-honored tradition of sleeping in church.

Dates & Places Used:

858

TOPIC: Sleep

Sleep Talk

A psychiatrist was with his client, who happened to be a pastor with a low self-image. One of the questions he asked was if the pastor ever talked in his sleep.

"Oh no," answered the pastor, "but I do talk while others sleep."

Dates & Places Used:

859

TOPIC: Society

Progress?

It only took the movies fifty years to go from silent to unspeakable.

Dates & Places Used:

860

TOPIC: Solutions

Deflating Solution

A truck driver had miscalculated while passing under a bridge, and his truck had become wedged between the road and the bridge. He at first attempted to back up the truck but to no avail. Finally, he and the others who were trying to assist him concluded that there were only two alternatives: to cut off the top of the truck or to chop into the bridge. A little boy looking on asked, "Why don't you just let the air out of the tires?"

Dates & Places Used:

861

TOPIC: Solutions

Love Your Neighbor

A man was bothered by his neighbor's chickens' invading his yard, sidewalk, drive, and porch. They left quite a mess. So one night he planted a dozen eggs in and around his bushes when the neighbor wasn't looking. Then when the neighbor was looking, he went out with a basket and gathered the eggs. He never had any more trouble with the neighbor's chickens.

Dates & Places Used:

862

TOPIC: Solutions

Creative Solution

A young clerk's responsibilities included bringing the judge a hot cup of coffee at the start of every day. Each morning the judge was enraged that the coffee cup arrived two-thirds full. The clerk explained that he had to rush to get the coffee delivered while it was still hot, which caused him to spill much of it along the way. None of the judge's yelling and insults produced a full cup of coffee, until he finally threatened to cut the clerk's pay by one-third if he continued to produce one-third less than the judge wanted.

The next morning he was greeted with a cup of coffee that was full to the brim, and the next morning, and the morning after that. The judge couldn't resist gloating over his success and smugly complimented the clerk on his new technique.

"Oh, there's not much to it," admitted the clerk happily. "I take some coffee in my mouth right outside the coffee room and spit it back in when I get outside your office."

Dates & Places Used:

863

TOPIC: Speech

Having and Speaking Less

Have more than thou showest;
Speak less than thou knowest.

Dates & Places Used:

TOPIC: Speech

Try It on Her Mother

Eight-year-old Molly brought her report card home from school.

Her marks were good, but her teacher had written across the bottom: "Molly is a smart little girl, but she has one fault. She talks too much in school. I have an idea I am going to try, which I think may break her of the habit."

Molly's dad signed her report card, putting a note on the back: "Please let me know if your idea works on Molly. If it does work, I would like to try it out on her mother."

Dates & Places Used:

TOPIC: Speeches

Nothing like a Good Rain

"Well," the candidate asked, "how did you like my speech on the agricultural problem?"

"It wasn't too bad," the farmer replied, "but a good rain would do a lot more good."

Dates & Places Used:

TOPIC: Speeches

One Faithful Listener

A young pastor was invited to speak at a conference at which there were multiple speakers. He was honored at the opportunity to speak and felt that this would be his first real break for recognition outside the confines of his own congregation. He was told by the conference planners that he was the sixth speaker.

At the beginning of the conference the auditorium was packed. During the course of the event, the crowds dwindled, and when it was his turn to speak, the auditorium was almost empty. There was only one man left! Nonetheless, the preacher had come to preach, and preach he did. At the conclusion of his sermon, he walked down and thanked the man for staying throughout his sermon and for coming to listen in the first place.

The man replied, "Oh, I didn't come to hear you speak; I'm the final speaker."

Dates & Places Used:

867 TOPIC: Speeches

Dangerous Tricks

Two Presbyterian denominational executives were on the road together, speaking night after night at a great variety of churches, rural and metropolitan, small and large. One of the men gave the same talk night after night. The other man gave a different presentation every night. After a while he got tired of hearing the other man's repetitious presentation, so he asked his colleague if he could go first that night. The other gladly acceded.

The executive then proceeded to give the other man's talk, which he had heard so many times that he had memorized it, and sat down. Totally unabashed, his friend got up and gave a brand-new talk that he had not used before. When the service was over neither man mentioned to the other what had taken place. In fact, several days went by until finally the first man couldn't stand it any longer and asked, "Didn't it bother you that I got up and gave your talk a few days ago?"

His friend replied, "No, it didn't bother me at all. Actually, I had given that talk at that church a few months ago."

Dates & Places Used:

868 TOPIC: Speeches

If the Shoe Fits

In the middle of a service and just before the sermon, one woman in the congregation remembered she had forgotten to turn off the oven at home. Hurriedly she scribbled a note and passed it to the usher to give to her husband who was in the

choir. Unfortunately, the usher misunderstood her intention and took it to the pulpit. Unfolding the note, the pastor read aloud, "Please go home and turn off the gas."
Dates & Places Used:

869

TOPIC: Speeches

Nice Guys Finish Fast

A basic rule for all preachers and public speakers is this: Nice guys finish fast!
Dates & Places Used:

870

TOPIC: Speeches

Speeches Are like Babies

Giving speeches is like having babies; they are easy to conceive, but they are hard to deliver.
Dates & Places Used:

871

TOPIC: Sports

Competitive to the End

Two "not-so-bright" friends had grown up together. They were best of friends, but they were as competitive as any two people have ever been with each other. All their lives they had competed with each other, always trying to prove that one or the other was better. The competition never ended. On one occasion they thought it would be fun to skydive. This was one sport in which the fun and thrill was apt to replace their need to compete. The first friend jumped from the plane. Then the other. The first fellow pulled his rip cord, but the parachute did not release. He then pulled the cord for the emergency chute. Nothing happened.

About this time, his friend was falling alongside of him. His friend called out, "I don't believe it! Okay, if that's the way you want it. Let's race!"
Dates & Places Used:

872

TOPIC: Sports

Skiing Downhill

Old skiers never die; they just go downhill.
Dates & Places Used:

873

TOPIC: Sports

Psycho-Coach

When the psychology professor had finished her lecture on mental health, she asked her class some review questions. "So how would you diagnose a patient who walks back and forth screaming at the top of his lungs one minute, then sits in a chair weeping uncontrollably the next?"

A tall young man in the rear of the room raised his hand and answered, "My basketball coach?"
Dates & Places Used:

874

TOPIC: Sports

Self-Disciplined Sports Fans

Football builds self-discipline. What else would induce a spectator to sit out in the open in freezing weather?
Dates & Places Used:

875

Home of the Cardinals

When the pope announced that he wanted to go to the United States, he was asked where in the United States he would like to visit. He said that he just wanted to go to St. Louis.

When asked why he just wanted to go to St. Louis, he answered, "Because I hear that's the home of the Cardinals."

Dates & Places Used:

876

Dog Football

I volunteered to chaperone my son's third-grade field trip. On the bus I was seated beside a talkative eight-year-old boy. He wanted me to know all about him, especially his fondness for dogs and football.

"My uncle played for the Green Bay Packers!" he boasted.

"Wow," I said. "What position?"

"I'm not sure," he replied thoughtfully. "I think he was a golden retriever."

Dates & Places Used:

877

Faint Saints

A man in Louisiana invited his friends over to watch a football game at his house. While his friends were watching the game, the man brought in his dog to show his friends what the dog could do.

The dog came into the room and sat down by the couch. After about a half hour the New Orleans Saints moved the ball toward the end zone but were unable to score a touchdown. The Saints prepared to kick a field goal.

The dog began to crawl slowly toward the television as he watched the screen intently. The moment the football went through the crossbars, the dog began to yelp and do flips in front of the television.

Needless to say, the man's friends were impressed. Every time the Saints kicked a field goal, the dog would begin his routine of yelping and flipping. Again and again his friends exclaimed, "Hey, that's a great dog you have there!" And then they asked, "What does this dog do when the Saints score a touchdown?"

The man replied, "I don't know yet. I've only had this dog for six years!"

Dates & Places Used:

878

TOPIC: Sports

Watching for Landry's Smile

Coach Tom Landry was known as the unemotional coach who for years paced the sidelines of the Dallas Cowboys football team. Walt Garrison, former Dallas Cowboys running back, was once asked if Landry ever smiled.

Garrison replied, "I don't know. I only played nine years."

Dates & Places Used:

879

TOPIC: Sports

World Series

The Minnesota Twins' 1980 program explains the game of baseball: You have two sides, one out in the field and one in. Each man who's on the side that's in goes out, and when he's out he comes in and the next man goes in until he's out.

When three men are out, the side that's out comes in and the side that's been in goes out and tries to get those coming in out.

Sometimes you get men still in and not out.

When both sides have been in and out nine times including the not outs, that's the end of the game.

Dates & Places Used:

880

TOPIC: Statistics

Meaningless Statistics

People have always been strangely fascinated with statistics. For example, David Letterman once announced that three out of four people make up 75 percent of the entire population.

Dates & Places Used:

881

TOPIC: Stewardship

Let the Church Walk, Pastor, Let Her Walk!

One Sunday morning the pastor encouraged his congregation to consider the potential of the church. He told them, "With God's help we can see the day when this church will go from crawling to walking."

And the people responded, "Let the church walk, pastor; let the church walk."

He continued, "And when the church begins to walk, next the church can begin to run."

And the people shouted, "Let the church run, pastor; let the church run!"

The pastor continued, "And finally the church can move from running to flying. Oh, the church can fly! But of course it's going to take a lot of money for that to happen!"

The congregation grew quiet, and from the back someone mumbled, "Let the church walk, pastor; let the church walk."

Dates & Places Used:

882

TOPIC: Stewardship

Safe Investment

One July day a farmer sat in front of his shack smoking his corncob pipe. Along came a stranger who asked, "How's your cotton coming?"

"Ain't got none," was the answer. "Didn't plant none. 'Fraid of the boll weevil."

"Well, how's your corn?"

"Didn't plant none. 'Fraid o' drought."

"How about your potatoes?"

"Ain't got none. Scairt o' tater bugs."

"Well," finally asked the stranger, "what did you plant?"

"Nothin'," answered the farmer. "I just played it safe."

Likewise, some churches are not doing much planting. They are not winning the lost in the community and are giving little, if any, to missions. They are not seeking to enlist members in the work of the church or to lead them to grow in stewardship. For one reason or another, they do not have a financial plan for the church and do not ask the members to make a pledge or to tithe. They just "play it safe."

Dates & Places Used:

883

TOPIC: Stress

Verbal Stress

Stress is what happens when your gut says no and your mouth says, "Yes, I'll be glad to do that!"

Dates & Places Used:

884

TOPIC: Stress

Sleeping like a Baby

The stock market was experiencing a great deal of fluctuation, so investors had good cause for concern. One investor went to his stockbroker to gain some reassurance. He asked his broker if he was worried.

The stockbroker told his client that he was sleeping like a baby.

The investor was amazed at his broker's ability to take all of these fluctuations with so much confidence. "Really?" the investor responded. "Even with all these fluctuations?"

The stockbroker answered, "Yes, just like a baby! I sleep for a couple of hours, then I wake up and cry for a couple of hours."
Dates & Places Used:

885
TOPIC: Success

Mark of Real Success

You are not really successful until someone claims he sat beside you in school.
Dates & Places Used:

886
TOPIC: Success

Serious Subjects

To be successful at the game of life, take everyone seriously except yourself.
Dates & Places Used:

887
TOPIC: Success

Reason for Success

Thomas Wheeler, while he was chief executive officer of the Massachusetts Mutual Life Insurance Company, told a good story on himself.

He said that while he and his wife were out driving, he noticed they were low on gas, so he pulled off at the first exit and came to a dumpy little gas station with one pump.

There was only one man working the place, so he asked the man to fill it up while he checked the oil. He added a quart of oil and closed the hood, and he saw his wife talking and smiling at the gas station attendant. When they saw Wheeler looking at them, the station attendant walked away and pretended as if nothing had happened. Wheeler paid the man, and he and his wife pulled out of that seedy little station.

As they drove down the road, he asked his wife if she knew the attendant. Well, she admitted she did know him. In fact, she had known him very well. Not only had they gone to high school together, but they had dated seriously for about a year.

Wheeler couldn't help bragging a little and said, "Boy, were you lucky I came along. Because if you'd married him, you'd be the wife of a gas station attendant instead of the wife of a CEO."

His wife replied, "My dear, if I had married him, he'd be the CEO and you'd be the gas station attendant."

Dates & Places Used:

888

TOPIC: Success

Success Hangs On

Success is the ability to hang on after all others have let go.
Dates & Places Used:

889

TOPIC: Success

Secret of Success

Sam Findley decided it was time to retire from the garment business, so he called in his son Mervyn and gave him the news and a bit of advice: "Son, it's all yours. I've made a success of this business because of two principles—reliability and wisdom. First, take reliability. If you promise goods by the tenth of the month, you must deliver by the tenth even if it costs you overtime, double time, golden time. You deliver what you promise."

Mervyn thought about this for a few moments and then asked, "But what about wisdom?" His father shot back, "Wisdom is never making such a stupid promise."

Dates & Places Used:

TOPIC: Success

Still a Winner

Ninety-two years after the flamboyant nineteenth-century writer Oscar Wilde died penniless in Paris, a notice was sent to him at his former address to tell him that he may have won a fortune in a publisher's sweepstakes. The mailing said, "You may never have been closer to winning a fortune than you are at this moment!"

"I'm just rather amused," said the owner of the home formerly owned by Wilde in Chelsea, England. He said it was the first time in seventeen years of living at the house that he had received a letter addressed to Wilde. Wilde had reached the third stage in the "Strike It Rich" draw and could win the three-hundred-thousand-dollar top prize, a trip for two to Tahiti, or a sports utility vehicle.

Dates & Places Used:

TOPIC: Tax

Depreciating Wife

An IRS auditor once asked a man about one of his deductions. "We have some questions about your tax return, Mr. Jones."

"Like what?" Mr. Jones asked.

"Well, let's begin with where you claim depreciation on your wife."

Dates & Places Used:

TOPIC: Tax

Audited by the IRS

Robert Perlman of Intel says, "Playing host to the IRS is a delightful experience. It's like being head-down in a hot tub."

Dates & Places Used:

893

Taxation Power

The Internal Revenue Service has what it takes to take what you've got!
Dates & Places Used:

894

Taxing the Whole World

A Sunday school teacher began the lesson with a review of what the class had learned last week. The teacher asked, "Who decreed that the whole world would be taxed?"

With all the disdain that one of the little boys in her class could muster, he answered, "The Democrats!"
Dates & Places Used:

895

Computer Crashes and Car Crashes

If the car industry behaved like the computer industry has over the last thirty years, a Rolls-Royce would cost five dollars, get three hundred miles per gallon, and blow up once a year killing all the passengers inside.
Dates & Places Used:

896

Before Remotes

Son to his father as they watch television: "Dad, tell me again how when you were a kid you had to walk all the way across the room to change the channel."
Dates & Places Used:

897

Capital Idea

A teacher asked her students to name the capital of the United States. One student answered, "Washington D.C."

The teacher then asked the student what D.C. stood for. The student again answered with confidence: "Dot Com."
Dates & Places Used:

898

Abort, Retry, Ignore?

(To the meter of "The Raven" by Edgar Allan Poe)
Once upon a midnight dreary, fingers cramped and vision
* bleary,*
System manuals piled high and wasted paper on the floor,
Longing for the warmth of bed sheets, still I sat there doing
* spreadsheets.*
Having reached the bottom line I took a floppy from the
* drawer,*
I then invoked the SAVE command and waited for the disk to
* store,*
Only this and nothing more.

Deep into the monitor peering, long I sat there wond'ring,
* fearing,*
Doubting, while the disk kept churning, turning yet to churn
* some more.*

353

But the silence was unbroken, and the stillness gave no token.
"Save!" I said, "You cursed monster! Save my data from before!"
One thing did the phosphors answer, only this and nothing
    more,
Just "Abort, Retry, Ignore?"

Was this some occult illusion, some maniacal intrusion?
These were choices undesired, ones I'd never faced before.
Carefully I weighed the choices as the disk made impish noises.
The cursor flashed, insistent, waiting, baiting me to type some
    more.
Clearly I must press a key, choosing one and nothing more,
From "Abort, Retry, Ignore?"

With fingers pale and trembling, slowly toward the keyboard
    bending,
Longing for a happy ending, hoping all would be restored,
Praying for some guarantee, timidly I pressed a key.
But on the screen there still persisted words appearing as before.
Ghastly grim they blinked and taunted, haunted, as my
    patience wore,
Saying, "Abort, Retry, Ignore?"

I tried to catch the chips off guard, and pressed again but
    twice as hard.
I pleaded with the cursed machine: I begged and cried and
    then I swore.
Now in mighty desperation, trying random combinations,
Still there came the incantation, just as senseless as before.
Cursor blinking, angrily winking, blinking nonsense as before.
Reading, "Abort, Retry, Ignore?"

There I sat, distraught, exhausted, by my own machine
    accosted.
Getting up I turned away and paced across the office floor.
And then I saw a dreadful sight: a lightning bolt cut through
    the night.
A gasp of horror overtook me, shook me to my very core.
The lightning zapped my previous data, lost and gone
    forevermore.
Not even "Abort, Retry, Ignore?"

To this day I do not know the place to which lost data go.
What demonic netherworld us wrought where lost data will be
    stored,

Beyond the reach of mortal souls, beyond the ether, into black
  holes?
But sure as there's C, Pascal, Lotus, Ashton-Tate, and more,
You will be one day left to wander, lost on some Plutonian
  shore,
Pleading, "Abort, Retry, Ignore?"

Dates & Places Used:

899

TOPIC: Technology

Technology Not So New

There is nothing new about some of our high-tech inventions.
For example, teleconferencing and answering machines existed
prior to their high-tech counterparts in the form of a party line.

Dates & Places Used:

900

TOPIC: Technology

Light Speed Travel Troubles

Technology is not all that it is cracked up to be. For example,
what happens when we all travel in spaceships at the speed of
light? When it gets dark in outer space, we will turn the lights
on, and nothing will happen. We will be traveling too fast for the
lights to work.

Dates & Places Used:

901

TOPIC: Technology

God Supplies the RAM

Abraham bought himself a fancy new computer and was
showing it to Isaac one day. "Look at all the wonderful pro-
grams it has on it. And look at all the neat things it can do."

Isaac was impressed but a little concerned. "But, Dad, I don't think your computer has enough memory."

Abraham said, "Don't worry, Son; the Lord will provide the RAM."

Dates & Places Used:

902

TOPIC: Teens

Teen Wisdom

The best substitute for being wise is being sixteen.

Dates & Places Used:

903

TOPIC: Teens

Teen Tele-Monopoly

Teenagers were put on earth to keep adults from wasting time on the telephone.

Dates & Places Used:

904

TOPIC: Teens

Motivating Teenagers

A community club was discussing the proposed establishment of a youth center. A youthful member of the club spoke out in favor of having a young person oversee the center—someone young enough, she said, to know what teenagers really like to do.

"Yes," agreed an older member, "but also old enough to see that they don't."

Dates & Places Used:

905

TOPIC: Teens

Chickens or Owls

A teenage son told his father that when he finished college he wanted to settle down and raise chickens.

His father responded, "Son, take my advice. Forget the chickens and raise owls. Their hours will suit you better."

Dates & Places Used:

906

TOPIC: Teens

Teen Sacrifice

A Sunday school teacher asked her grade-school class how old they thought Isaac was when God told Abraham to sacrifice his son. One boy raised his hand and said that Isaac could not have been over twelve years old.

The teacher asked him how he knew this.

The boy explained, "I have a brother and sister who are in their teens. I'm not sure it would have been that much of a sacrifice if Isaac had been older than twelve."

Dates & Places Used:

907

TOPIC: Teens

Free Radio

A man asked his son what he wanted for his birthday. The boy answered, "I'd like a free radio, Dad."

"What kind of radio do you want?"

"The kind of free radio," the boy answered, "that comes inside a new sports car."

Dates & Places Used:

908

TOPIC: Teens

Sound Advice

Sound travels slowly. Sometimes the things you say when your kids are teenagers don't reach them till they're in their forties.

Dates & Places Used:

909

TOPIC: Teens

Short Bulletin

We try to make our church bulletin relevant to all ages. One day I asked one of the high school students, in a "picking-his-brain" tone of voice, if he read the bulletin each week.

"Yeah," he said with a grin, "in church!" Then he added with a broader grin, "During the sermon." Then he added again, "Short bulletin!"

Dates & Places Used:

910

TOPIC: Temptation

An Open Reason

A father was called to come into the principal's office at his son's school. Apparently his son had shoved a chalkboard eraser into the mouth of one of his classmates. The father was furious and demanded an answer from his son: "What reason could you possibly have had to put a chalkboard eraser in that girl's mouth?"

The boy meekly answered, "Because her mouth was open."

Dates & Places Used:

911

TOPIC: Temptation

Wine, Women, and Song

While attending a church in a small town just outside of the military base, I was asked by the pastor's wife, "How do you maintain your moral character and integrity around the other soldiers? From what I've seen, all soldiers care about is wine, women, and song."

"That's not entirely true," I responded. "Most of them don't care that much about song."

Dates & Places Used:

912

TOPIC: Temptation

Untried Evil

If you must choose between two evils, pick the one you've never tried.

Dates & Places Used:

913

TOPIC: Temptation

Dealing with Temptation

There are several good protections against temptation, but the surest is a cowardly response to the fact that you might get caught.

Dates & Places Used:

914

TOPIC: Temptation

In Two Places

On the TV show *Hee Haw*, Doc Campbell was confronted by a patient who said he broke his arm in two places. The doc replied, "Well, then stay out of them places." He may have something there. We cannot regularly put ourselves in the face of temptation and not be affected.

Dates & Places Used:

915

TOPIC: Tests

Contingent Answer

A college student was taking his first examination in a philosophy class. On the paper there was a single line that simply said, "Is this a question?–Discuss."

After a short time he wrote, "If that is a question, then this is an answer."

The student received an A on the exam.

Dates & Places Used:

916

TOPIC: Tests

Grandma's Colors

I didn't know if my granddaughter had learned her colors yet, so I decided to test her. I would point out something and ask what color it was. She would tell me, and always she was correct. But it was fun for me, so I continued.

At last she headed for the door, saying sagely, "Grandma, I think you should try to figure out some of these yourself!"

Dates & Places Used:

917

TOPIC: Tests

Same Questions, Different Answers

An economist returned to visit his old school and was interested in the current exam questions. He asked his old professor to show him some current exams. To his surprise they were exactly the same ones he had taken ten years earlier! When he asked the professor about this, the professor answered, "The questions are always the same; only the answers change!"

Dates & Places Used:

918

TOPIC: Tests

Three Times Three

Three old men were at the doctor's office for a memory test. The doctor said to the first old man, "What is three times three?"

"Two hundred seventy-four," he replied.

The doctor said to the second man, "It's your turn. What is three times three?"

"Tuesday," replied the second man.

The doctor said to the third man, "Okay, your turn. What's three times three?"

"Nine," said the third man.

"That's great," said the doctor. "How did you get that?"

"Simple! I subtracted 274 from Tuesday."

Dates & Places Used:

919

TOPIC: Tests

Animal Tests

Animal testing is a terrible idea; they get all nervous and give the wrong answers.

Dates & Places Used:

920

TOPIC: Thanksgiving

Gobble Prophecy

Gobble, gobble, gobble!

"Ain't it odd," you say,
"The only word the turkey knows
Precurses his fate on the tray."
Dates & Places Used:

921

TOPIC: Thanksgiving

Thanksgiving as a Family

Thanksgiving is the time of the year when we remember and enact the traditions of our ancestors. They had one particularly unusual tradition. They would sit down as a family to eat a meal and finish it without having the phone ring.
Dates & Places Used:

922

TOPIC: Thanksgiving

Mom Knows

Before Thanksgiving a teacher was describing to her second graders the hardships of the Pilgrims during their first winter. She especially emphasized the shortage of food and clothing.

In the midst of her story a little boy raised his hand and exclaimed, "Too bad my mommy wasn't there. She always knows what to do!"

Moms always seem to know what to do to manage even in difficult situations.
Dates & Places Used:

923

TOPIC: Thanksgiving

What's for Lunch?

An optimist is anyone who has a twenty-eight-pound turkey for Thanksgiving and the next day asks, "What's for lunch?"
Dates & Places Used:

924

TOPIC: Thanksgiving

Be Thankful

It was Thanksgiving Day and the town grouch was grumbling as usual. "Don't you have anything to be thankful for?" a neighbor asked.

"Nope," he said.

"Have you considered thanking God for turning your nose right side up? He could have put it on you upside down. Then when it rained you would have drowned and when you sneezed you would have blown your thankless head off."

Dates & Places Used:

925

TOPIC: Thanksgiving

In the Eye of the Beholder

There are all kinds of things to be thankful for, because thankfulness is in the eye of the beholder. One evening I asked the members of a confirmation class (eighth grade) to give a one-sentence prayer of thanks for something good that happened during the previous week. Most gave typical responses: "Thanks that we're here together"; "Thanks for the hunting trip"; and so on. Then one boy said, "Thank you that I was sick Friday so I didn't have to go to school."

Dates & Places Used:

926

TOPIC: Thanksgiving

Sleep Counts

The easiest way to get some sleep is to count your blessings instead of your problems.

Dates & Places Used:

927

TOPIC: Thanksgiving

Most Valuable Word Is *Thanks*

In his heyday, it is said that every word Rudyard Kipling wrote was worth twenty-five shillings. Hearing this, a group of college students got together and wrote him a letter that said, "We understand that every word you write is worth twenty-five shillings. Enclosed is twenty-five shillings; send us your best word."

A couple of days later, these college students received a telegram from Mr. Kipling. The telegram consisted of one word. That one word, his best word, was "Thanks!"

That may very well be the best word there is in English or any other language. Gratitude and thankfulness are the most precious gifts we can have.

Dates & Places Used:

928

TOPIC: Time

Living Longer Lives

A young single woman just learned from her doctor that she only had one year to live. "Isn't there anything I can do to extend my life?" she asked her doctor.

The doctor reflected on her question, hesitated, and then said, "Well, you might try marrying a boring man. Perhaps your last year of life will seem like more."

Dates & Places Used:

929

TOPIC: Time

Time's Timing

Time is what keeps everything from happening at once.

Dates & Places Used:

930

TOPIC: Time

Value of Tomorrow

Tomorrow is the most important thing in life. It comes to us at midnight very clean. It's perfect when it arrives and it puts itself in our hands. It hopes we've learned something from yesterday. *(John Wayne)*
Dates & Places Used:

931

TOPIC: Time

24-Hour Banks

You have seen the signs that say: 24-HOUR BANKING. But who has that long to stand in line at the bank?
Dates & Places Used:

932

TOPIC: Time

Time in Life

There comes a time in every man's life, and I've had plenty of 'em! *(Casey Stengel)*
Dates & Places Used:

933

TOPIC: Time

Truth: The Irreducible Minimum

Ian Pitt-Watson said, "I heard a silly story about an elderly Scottish couple who had never flown before, but who decided they were going to visit their children in New York and see their grandchildren for the first time. They were on a charter flight in a Lockheed TriStar (three engines). They were about halfway out over the Atlantic when their pilot's voice came over the intercom: 'This is your captain speaking. Ladies and gentlemen, I feel I ought to let you know that one of our three engines has failed. There is, of course, no need for alarm. This plane is entirely airworthy flying on two engines, but I regret to say we will be one hour late in arriving in New York.'

"Half an hour later, inevitably, with that desperate calm that is reserved by air pilots and astronauts for conditions of extreme emergency, the pilot of the TriStar spoke again: 'This is your captain speaking. I regret that we have lost the second of our engines. But I would like to reassure you that we have every expectation of making a normal and safe landing at JFK airport. We shall, however, be three hours late in arriving.'

"At this, Grandma turned to Grandpa with a hint of irritation in her voice and said, 'My dear, if that third engine goes, we shall be up here all night.'"

Dates & Places Used:

934

TOPIC: Time

Do-It-Over Time

If you don't have time to do it right, you must have time to do it over.

Dates & Places Used:

935

TOPIC: Time

An A.M. Radio

Bill's mother bought him a radio for his birthday. She called a few days later to see how Bill liked his new radio. "Oh, I like it a lot," Bill answered. "But I think I will buy another one to play at night."

"Why is that?" his mother asked.

"I can only play this one during the day," Bill explained, "because it is an A.M. radio."

Dates & Places Used:

936

TOPIC: Time

Trouble with the Future

The trouble with our times is that the future is not what it used to be.
Dates & Places Used:

937

TOPIC: Travel

Airport Locations

If God had meant for humans to fly, he would have made airports closer to town.
Dates & Places Used:

938

TOPIC: Travel

The Only Planet Visited

A fourth-grade class was studying the solar system, and the teacher had assigned each student to choose a topic to investigate and report on to the rest of the class. One boy took Venus, another chose Mars, but young Walter selected Earth.

His reason seemed very logical. He said, "It's the only planet I have visited."
Dates & Places Used:

939

TOPIC: Travel

Wish You Were Here

A friend of mine once sent me a postcard with a picture of the entire planet Earth taken from space. On the back it said, "Wish you were here."
Dates & Places Used:

940

TOPIC: Travel

TOPIC: Travel

Rough Landing

A commercial airline pilot encountered a particularly bad landing on a windy day. Just as he was about to touch down, the wind forced his plane against the runway with an impact that far exceeded any landing he had ever made. It was an embarrassing landing!

As the embarrassed pilot stood at the exit door and thanked his passengers for flying his airline, one elderly man took hold of his arm and asked, "Son, perhaps you can tell me what happened–did you land the plane or did we get shot down?"

Dates & Places Used:

941

TOPIC: Travel

Stop Buying Hotels

The new travel manager was trying to trim the travel budget for the sales department without much success. He called one of the salespeople into his office to go over some of the travel receipts. "And what's this item on your report?" the travel manager asked.

"Oh," answered the salesperson, "that's for my hotel."

"Well, I have a cost-saving suggestion for you," replied the travel manager. "From now on, how about *not buying* the hotel?"

Dates & Places Used:

942

TOPIC: Trials

Things Can Get Worse

A middle-aged woman was sitting in her den when all of a sudden a small black snake crawled across the floor and under the couch. Being deathly afraid of snakes, she promptly ran to the bathroom to get her husband, who was taking a shower. The man of the house came running from the shower to the den with only a towel around his waist. He took an old broom handle and began poking under the couch to retrieve the snake. At that point the family dog, who had been sleeping, awoke and became excited. In the dog's frenzy over the actions of the husband, the little terrier touched his cold nose to the back of the man's heel. Not realizing what had happened, the man surmised that the snake had out-maneuvered him and bitten him on the heel. He fainted dead away. The wife sprang into action. She concluded that her husband, because of the physical exertion over trying to kill the snake, had had a heart attack. She ran from the house to a hospital emergency room that was one block away. The ambulance drivers arrived promptly and placed the man, who was now semiconscious, on a stretcher. As the attendants were carrying the man out of the den, the snake reappeared from beneath the couch. At this point one of the drivers became so excited that he dropped his end of the stretcher and broke the patient's leg.

Dates & Places Used:

943

TOPIC: Trials

Impossible Challenge

The next time somebody tells you nothing is impossible, ask him to put his skis over his shoulder and go through a revolving door.

Dates & Places Used:

944

TOPIC: Trials

Talking Back to God

At times when we've been in trouble, we may have felt that God was against us. St. Theresa, a sixteenth-century reformer, stood mired in mud on one of her journeys and cried out to God, "If this is the way you treat your friends, no wonder you don't have many!"

Dates & Places Used:

945

Things Are Going Wrong When ...

You call your wife and tell her you would like to eat out tonight and she says there will be a sandwich on the front porch.

The gypsy fortune teller looks at your palm, shakes her head, and offers to refund your money.

Everyone avoids you the morning after the company office party.

The worst player on the golf course wants to play you for money.

Dates & Places Used:

946

A Worst-Case Scenario

We were climbing a hill on our moped at the end of a beautiful day in Bermuda when we were suddenly slammed into by a car. The driver was going to pass us but was confronted by another car approaching over the crest of the hill.

My wife and I were transported by ambulance to the hospital, where we were treated for injuries. My leg was broken in two places and the ligaments were ruptured. A full leg cast was put on and crutches were provided.

We got back to New York in time for me to preach on Sunday. As people came to church I was there to greet them as always. They asked me what had happened, and when I told them how I had broken my leg, several of them told me of their own experiences in which they had broken their legs.

One woman told me, "It could have been worse"–a comment I have never found very helpful.

"How could it have been worse?" I wanted to know. "My leg is fractured in two places, the ligaments are torn apart. I have to have this cast on for three months and sit on a bar stool to preach. How could it have been worse?"

With a twinkle in her eye she said, just before I went to speak, "You could have broken your jaw."

Dates & Places Used:

947

TOPIC: Trouble

Partial Coverage

You know it's going to be a bad day when you wake up in a hospital in traction and your insurance agent tells you that your accident policy covers falling off the roof, but it doesn't cover hitting the ground.

Dates & Places Used:

948

TOPIC: Trouble

Through the Rough Spots

A husband and wife were discussing old times when the husband said, "My dear, I have taken you safely over all the rough spots of life."

"Yes, dear," said the wife, "and I don't think you missed a one of them."

Dates & Places Used:

949

TOPIC: Trust

Counting Ribs

Some things you just can't learn from the Bible. Word has it that Eve would get so jealous of Adam that she would count his ribs every night when he got home.

Dates & Places Used:

950

TOPIC: Trust

Hold the Bigger Hand

A father and his son were hiking along a steep mountain trail. At the beginning of the climb, the way was easy. They were walking along throwing rocks through the trees and talking with each other. Then the path became steep and hiking became difficult. Finally, they reached a narrow passageway. One slip and they would fall down a deep canyon.

The father said, "Son, you'd better hold my hand."

Looking up at his father, the son replied, "No, Daddy, you hold my hand. You're bigger than I am."

Dates & Places Used:

951

TOPIC: Truth

Power of the Scales

Two curious little boys were looking at the bathroom scales. "How does this thing work?" asked one of the boys.

The other boy answered, "I'm not sure exactly, but I do know that when you stand on it, it either makes you mad or it makes you cry."

Dates & Places Used:

952

TOPIC: Truth

Truth Will Set You Free

Tell the boss what you really think, and the truth will set you free.

Dates & Places Used:

953

TOPIC: Truth

Precious Truth

Most writers regard the truth as their most valuable possession and therefore are most economical in its use. *(Mark Twain)*

Dates & Places Used:

TOPIC: Understanding

Understanding Christianity

I don't understand Christianity. I don't understand electricity either, but I don't intend to sit in the dark until I do.
Dates & Places Used:

TOPIC: Understanding

Something to Do with Russia

Bill was telling his girlfriend, Janice, about the speed-reading course he had just taken. "I was able to read *War and Peace* in just twenty minutes."

Janice was impressed. "Twenty minutes! Bill, that's a big book! What was it about?"

Bill answered, "I'm pretty sure it had something to do with Russia."
Dates & Places Used:

TOPIC: Understanding

Brightening Their Day

The United States Postal Service was changing its rates for first-class postage. The day before the change was to take effect, a long line of people wanted to buy first-class postage stamps at a small-town post office. The post office was running low on stamps because of the high demand and was selling only a limited supply to each person so as to help as many people as possible. This news of the post office's rationing was greeted with anger and frustration as the customers wanted to purchase more than the post office was willing to sell. The solitary postal clerk was taking verbal and emotional beatings one after another. She looked ragged from the ordeal and was about done in.

One of the customers was waiting patiently in line. When it was this customer's turn, she purchased her allotted quota of stamps and decided to help the clerk out. She said in a loud voice for all in the line to hear, "What do you mean you're running out of stamps? After all, I've only known about this for three or four weeks. I have put it off and put it off, and now I come in here at the last minute with all the rest of these people and you tell me that you're running out of stamps! Well, I never!" She gave the postal clerk a big wink, paid for her stamps, and left. The postal clerk had brightened considerably, and you could have heard a pin drop among the people waiting in line.

Dates & Places Used:

957

TOPIC: Unity

Vultures Will Win

One hot day in the middle of summer a lion and a boar went to a spring to drink. "Step aside," the boar said. "I was here first."

"I showed you where to find the spring," the lion replied angrily. "I will be the first to drink." Quickly the disagreement escalated from a verbal confrontation and they began to attack each other with great ferocity.

A few minutes later, stopping to catch their breath, they both saw some vultures seated on a rock above, waiting for one of them to be killed. The sight so sobered them that they quickly made peace, saying, "If we continue to fight, the only winner will be the vultures."

Dates & Places Used:

958

TOPIC: Unity

If We All Think Alike

General George Patton once said to his staff, "If we are all thinking alike, somebody isn't thinking."

Dates & Places Used:

TOPIC: Unity

Island Churches

The following is a "generic" story in which you can fill in the denomination.

Six men were marooned on a desert island. Two were Jewish, two were Catholic, and two were Baptist. The two Jews founded "Temple Immanuel." The two Catholics organized "The Church of the Holy Name." The two Baptists broke ground for the "First Baptist Church" and the "Second Baptist Church."

Dates & Places Used:

TOPIC: Unity

One with Everything

What did the Zen master say to the hot dog vendor?
Make me one with everything.

Dates & Places Used:

TOPIC: Unity

Digging the English Channel

A Frenchman was saying how wonderful it was that the English were going to such trouble to be united to the mainland of Europe by building the English Channel tunnel.

"Oh, that's nothing," says the Englishman. "You should have seen the trouble we had digging the channel in the first place!"

Dates & Places Used:

962

Picture of Happiness

Happiness is when your neighbor takes six hundred slides of his trip to Europe and discovers that his lens cap was down.

Dates & Places Used:

963

In Tough Times

While prime minister of Great Britain, David Lloyd George had many problems to contend with, including World War I, the economic crisis, and the Sinn Fein movement for Irish liberation to name a few. When he was asked how he retained his good spirits, he replied, "Well, I find that a change of nuisances is as good as a vacation."

Dates & Places Used:

964

Our Wimp Culture

The company had a new president, and he gathered the employees together to give them a pep talk and to announce some important changes. He told them about new advances in high-tech automation and how they were soon going to have a number of robotic machines that would eliminate much of the boring work many of them had to do.

But he also tried to reassure his employees that though the company was moving into a more automated future, they shouldn't worry; no one was going to be laid off. Natural attrition, retirements, and so on would take care of some of the reduction in workforce. And they would actually profit from this automation. Since there would be less need for their work, they would increasingly be given additional time off without a cut in pay. In fact, in time they would only have to work one day a week. And when they came to that place, they would only have to come in on Wednesdays.

At this a hand went up in the back of the room. One of the employees had a question. He said, "Will we have to come in every Wednesday?"

Dates & Places Used:

965 TOPIC: Values

Don't Forget the Penny

A Scottish lad and his lassie were sitting next to each other in the Scottish Highlands. They sat in silence for a while gazing over the glen.

The lass turned to the lad and said, "A penny ferr your thoughts."

The lad was taken aback, and then he answered, "I was just a-thinkin' how nice it'd be if ye'd give me a wee bit of a kiss."

The flattered lass kissed the lad. But then the lad slipped into a pensive mood again.

His lass once more asked, "What arrre yuh thinkin' now?"

The lad answered, "I was just a-hopin' yuh hadn't forgotten the penny!"

Dates & Places Used:

966 TOPIC: Values

Alligators and Oysters

Admiring a Native American's necklace, a woman tourist finally asked, "What are those things?"

"Alligator teeth, ma'am," came the reply.

"Oh, I see. I suppose they have the same value for your people that pearls have for us?"

"Not quite," he replied. "Anyone can open an oyster."

Dates & Places Used:

967

TOPIC: Violence

Violent Mood Ring

My husband bought me a mood ring the other day. When I'm in a good mood, it turns green.

When I'm in a bad mood, it leaves a red mark on his forehead.

Dates & Places Used:

968

TOPIC: Violence

Works That Follow Faith

A little girl had a problem. She was worried because her brother had built some traps to catch rabbits. She loved rabbits and didn't want any of them to be hurt or killed in her brother's traps. She tearfully begged her brother not to use the traps, but he refused to change his plans.

The little girl chose another course of action and was able to sleep that night with a quiet confidence that God would protect the rabbits from her evil brother. Later she explained, "I prayed that God wouldn't let those cute little rabbits get caught in those cruel traps. And then I went outside and broke the traps into a million pieces!"

Dates & Places Used:

969

TOPIC: Violence

Ways to Skin a Cat

There's more than one way to skin a cat. In fact, when I was a kid, my friend down the street knew sixteen ways to do it.

Dates & Places Used:

TOPIC: Vision

Blind Luck

One day at a busy airport the passengers on a commercial airliner were seated, waiting for the cockpit crew to show up so they could take off. The pilot and copilot finally appeared in the rear of the plane and began walking up to the cockpit through the center aisle.

Both appeared to be blind. The pilot was using a white cane, bumping into passengers right and left as he stumbled down the aisle, and the copilot was using a guide dog. Both had their eyes covered with huge sunglasses. At first the passengers did not react, thinking that it must be some sort of practical joke. After a few minutes, however, the engines fired and the airplane started moving down the runway.

The passengers looked at each other with some uneasiness, whispering among themselves and looking desperately to the flight attendants for reassurance. Then the airplane started accelerating rapidly and people began panicking. Some passengers were praying, and as the plane got closer and closer to the end of the runway, the voices were becoming more and more hysterical. Finally, when the airplane had less than twenty feet of runway left, there was a sudden change in the pitch of the shouts as everyone screamed at once. And at the very last moment the airplane lifted off and was airborne.

Up in the cockpit, the copilot breathed a sigh of relief and said to the captain, "You know, one of these days the passengers aren't going to scream, and we're gonna get killed!"

Dates & Places Used:

TOPIC: Vision

The Eye of Faith

One of Gutzon Borglum's great works as a sculptor is the head of Lincoln in the nation's Capitol. He had cut it from a large square block of stone in his studio. One day, when the face of Lincoln was just becoming recognizable in the stone, a young girl was visiting the studio with her parents. She looked at the half-done face of Lincoln, her eyes registering wonder and astonishment. She stared at the piece for a moment and then ran to the sculptor and asked, "Is that Abraham Lincoln?"

"Yes," he replied.

The little girl said, "Well, how in the world did you know that he was in that block of stone?"

Dates & Places Used:

972

TOPIC: Vision

Irish Vision

May you have the hindsight to know where you've been,
the foresight to know where you're going,
and the insight to know when you're going too far.

Dates & Places Used:

973

TOPIC: Wages

Oops—Too Late

The employees of a company that paid salaries in cash found the following message printed on their pay envelopes: "If the amount of cash in this envelope does not agree with the amount printed on your pay slip, please return the envelope unopened to the cashier."

Dates & Places Used:

974

TOPIC: Wages

Inspired to Pay

As a conscientious objector eager to learn more about the peace testimony of my denomination, I enrolled at the Earlham School of Religion, a Quaker seminary in Richmond, Indiana.

With my family to support, it was not long before I found myself filling a student pastorate at a small Friends church in rural Indiana. As a "silent meeting" Quaker, accustomed to unprogrammed worship, I had an idea of vocal ministry quite different from that of these rural Friends, who expected a well-prepared, evangelical sermon every First Day.

After one such meeting, during which the congregation had sat in restless silence for the entire hour because I had not felt moved by the Spirit to speak and no one else in the meeting house had been moved to lead worship, a church elder offered me this counsel: "Friend John, if you wish us to feel moved by the Spirit to pay you next week, you should come prepared to be inspired to preach."

Dates & Places Used:

975

TOPIC: War

Nuclear War Sameness

Bumper Sticker: NUCLEAR WAR—WHEN YOU'VE SEEN ONE, YOU'VE SEEN THEM ALL.

Dates & Places Used:

976

TOPIC: War

Pick Your Kind of War

Television news and newspapers continually remind us that all the major governments throughout the world are trying to eliminate the threat of nuclear war. But the same countries seem to participate in warfare. Therefore, it seems safe to conclude that these governments are not so much opposed to war as they are interested in choosing which kind of war they get to fight—they like the long, drawn-out ones.

Dates & Places Used:

TOPIC: Wealth

Everything Has Its Price

The jetliner had just taken off and all the passengers had settled down. In the first-class section, a man sat next to a well-dressed matronly woman who was wearing a stunning diamond pendant. He said to her, "Excuse me, but I couldn't help noticing that beautiful necklace. It's the most exquisite stone I've ever seen."

She responded, "Well, thank you. It's the Klopman diamond, you know."

He looked puzzled, and said, "I'm sorry, but I don't think I have ever heard of it."

Her response was, "Well, it's a lot like the Hope diamond. It's not as large, of course, but the clarity and beauty of the Klopman are the absolute equal. And, just like the Hope diamond, it comes with a curse for the person wearing it."

"That's positively amazing! What kind of curse?"

"Mr. Klopman!"

Dates & Places Used:

TOPIC: Weddings

Enough Said

A young country fellow was walking with his girl on a moonlit night. He was overcome with the romance of the moment, and he blurted out, "Honey, I love you so much. Will you marry me?"

She did not hesitate. "Of course, I will marry you," she said joyfully.

They walked along for a little while longer in silence, and she said, "Dearest, why don't you say something?"

He looked at the ground and said, "I think I've said too much as it is."

Dates & Places Used:

979

TOPIC: Weddings

Not Losing a Daughter

Said the mother of the bride, "I'm not losing a daughter. I'm gaining a bathroom and a telephone."
Dates & Places Used:

980

TOPIC: Weddings

First and Last Marriage

A young couple filled out a marriage license. Beside a blank on the license was the word "Marriage." The prospective groom wrote the word, "First." The prospective bride wrote, "Last."
Dates & Places Used:

981

TOPIC: Wisdom

Collected Wisdom

Don't sweat the petty things; and don't pet the sweaty things.
One tequila, two tequila, three tequila, floor.
I doubt, therefore, I might be.
Procrastination is the art of keeping up with yesterday.
Men are from earth. Women are from earth. Deal with it.
Give a man a fish and he will eat it for a day. Teach him how to fish, and he will sit in a boat and drink beer all day.
Before they invented drawing boards, what did they go back to?
If you try to fail, and succeed, which have you done?
The tongue weighs practically nothing, but so few people can hold it.
If it weren't for electricity, we'd be watching television by candlelight.
Misery doesn't love company. Misery doesn't love anything.
Sometimes the fool who rushes in gets the job done.
It's true that you can't take it with you, but you ought to remember that how you got it may determine where you go.
Dates & Places Used:

982

Why One Wife?

A thirteen-year-old girl in Kansas City asked her pastor-father, "Why can't a man have more than one wife?"

Her daddy, the Reverend Parker Dailey, told her to open her Bible to Matthew 6:24, where she read, "No one can serve two masters."

Dates & Places Used:

983

Too Willing to Help

A man placed a classified ad that read, "Wife wanted."

A few days later he received several letters that all said the same thing: "You can have mine."

Dates & Places Used:

984

Baby or Moose?

At a wedding rehearsal dinner Grandpa and his grandson Kyle were working one of those find-and-circle-the-word puzzles for children. Kyle was a prereader, but Grandpa was trying to help Kyle spell and pronounce the words. Grandpa wasn't having much luck. He asked, "Okay, now what sound does *b* make. What sound does *a* make? And what sound does *y* make? Okay, now put them all together and what does *b-a-b-y* spell?" Kyle smiled real big and said, "Moose!"

Dates & Places Used:

TOPIC: Words

Fewer Words Better

The most valuable of all talents is that of never using two words when one will do.

Dates & Places Used:

TOPIC: Words

Daffynitions

Adult: A person who has stopped growing at both ends and is now growing in the middle.

Beauty parlor: A place where women curl up and dye.

Cannibal: Someone who is fed up with people.

Chickens: The only animals you eat before they are born and after they are dead.

Committee: A body that keeps minutes and wastes hours.

Dust: Mud with the juice squeezed out.

Gossip: A person who will never tell a lie if the truth will do more damage.

Handkerchief: Cold storage.

Inflation: Cutting money in half without damaging the paper.

Myth: A female moth.

Mosquito: An insect that makes you like flies better.

Raisin: Grape with a sunburn.

Secret: Something you tell to one person at a time.

Toothache: The pain that drives you to extraction.

Tomorrow: One of the greatest labor-saving devices of today.

Yawn: An honest opinion openly expressed.

Dates & Places Used:

987

Three Wives

A district attorney in a rural court appeared before the judge with accusations against the prisoner: "Your Honor, I intend to show that this man is guilty of bigotry."

"Why do you say that?" the judge asked.

"You see," answered the district attorney, "this man has three wives."

"Three wives!" scoffed the judge. "What kind of lawyer are you? Don't you realize that's not bigotry? That's trigonometry!"

Dates & Places Used:

988

Ideas and Work

The problem with ideas is that they do not work until we do.

Dates & Places Used:

989

Sad Commentary

At a tiny general store in the country the proprietor had a clerk who may have been the laziest man who ever lived. One day a customer noticed that this clerk was nowhere to be found.

The customer asked the proprietor where the clerk was.

The proprietor answered, "Oh, he retired."

The customer inquired, "Retired? Then what are you doing to fill the vacancy?"

The owner replied, "Jake didn't leave no vacancy!"

Dates & Places Used:

990

Lucky Boss

"You know," said Olle, "I got a real good reference from de boss at my last yob."

"Really?" said Sven.

"Ya, he wrote, 'If you get Olle to verk for you, you'll be lucky!'"

Dates & Places Used:

991

Disadvantage of Doing Nothing

One disadvantage of having nothing to do is you can't stop and rest.

Dates & Places Used:

992

The Long and Winding Work

A retired fellow felt like he had been tricked by his employer. For his retirement he had been given a beautiful gold watch that winded automatically whenever he would move his hand. The problem was that he had to continue to work to keep his watch from stopping.

Dates & Places Used:

993

Footprints That Work

He who would leave footprints in the sands of time will have to wear work shoes.
Dates & Places Used:

994

TOPIC: Work

Working Dog

A salesman dropped in to see a business customer. Not a soul was in the office except a big dog who was emptying wastebaskets. The salesman stared at the animal, wondering if his imagination could be playing tricks on him.

The dog looked up and said, "Don't be surprised. This is just part of my job."

"Incredible!" exclaimed the man. "I can't believe it. Does your boss know what a prize he has in you? An animal that can talk!"

"No, no," pleaded the dog. "Please don't tell him! If that man finds out I can talk, he'll make me answer the phone too."
Dates & Places Used:

995

TOPIC: Worry

Time of Worry

Today is the yesterday you worried about tomorrow.
Dates & Places Used:

996

Swallowed a Horse

A man who told his doctor he had swallowed a horse was referred to an associate who was a psychiatrist. The psychiatrist was familiar with this malady and told the man that his problem could easily be fixed. All the man had to do was undergo a simple surgery to remove the horse from his stomach. The man enthusiastically agreed, so the psychiatrist and the surgeon prepared for their performance. The two doctors arranged to bring a horse into the operating room after the man was asleep. When the man awoke, he saw the horse, and the doctors triumphantly announced, "The operation was a complete success. We were able to get the horse out."

The man looked at the horse, looked at his stomach, and protested, "I'm sorry, but that's not the horse I swallowed; the horse I swallowed was white, and this one is brown!"

Too much worry and not enough reality. It's really more common than we would like to admit. Care for some surgery?

Dates & Places Used:

997

Worry or Work

Studies show that more people die from worry than from work. This should come as no surprise, however, for the law of averages is in the worriers' favor. At any given moment there are more people worrying than working.

Dates & Places Used:

998

Heave Quietly

Found in a Magnolia, North Carolina, church bulletin: "If you choose to heave during the postlude, please do so quietly so as not to interrupt those remaining for worship and meditation."

Dates & Places Used:

389

999

Playing with Anticipation

Four-year-old Jimmy was thrilled when the family got a piano. Immediately he was up on the piano bench pounding on the keys.

After a while he climbed down in frustration.

"It's no use!" he anguished. "'Jesus Loves Me' just isn't there!"

Moral of the story: You get out (of worship, discipleship, etc.) what you put into it!

Dates & Places Used:

1000

Too Old to Know It All

I am not young enough to know everything. *(James M. Barrie)*

Dates & Places Used:

1001

Forever Young

When police arrested a street hustler for selling eternal youth pills, they discovered he was a repeat offender. He'd been arrested on the same charge in 1265, 1845, and 1902.

Dates & Places Used:

1002

Why Are We Here?

A mother and baby camel are talking one day when the baby camel asks, "Mom, why have I got these huge three-toed feet?"

The mother replies, "Well, son, when we trek across the desert, your toes will help you to stay on top of the soft sand."

A few minutes later the young camel asks, "Mom, why have I got these long eyelashes?"

"They are there to keep the sand out of your eyes on the trips through the desert."

"Mom, why have I got these great big humps on my back?"

"They are there to help us store water for our long treks across the desert, so we can go without drinking for long periods."

"Let's see, we have huge feet to stop us from sinking, long eyelashes to keep the sand out of our eyes and these humps to store water."

"Yes, dear."

"So why are we in the San Diego Zoo?"

Dates & Places Used:

Index of Subtopics

Each illustration number is cross-referenced from two to five times. Numbers indicate entry number, not page.

Consensus: 189
Consequences: 9, 20, 64, 109, 112, 157, 168, 226, 337, 390, 408, 492, 505, 513, 514, 576, 597, 609, 624, 780, 793, 845, 847, 913, 975, 977
Consideration: 804, 956
Consistency: 458, 460, 1001
Construction: 339
Consultants: 202, 288
Content: 848
Contentment: 148, 347, 398, 528, 570, 694, 719, 983
Contests: 890
Contracts: 256
Contradictions: 558
Contrition: 781
Convenience(s): 761, 896, 931
Conversation(s): 12, 326, 361, 552, 639, 817, 818, 985
Conversion: 103, 104, 196, 590, 810
Cooking: 225, 807
Cooperation: 7, 224, 507, 540, 624, 658, 835, 871, 957, 958
Copyrights: 113
Cost: 720
Coughing: 421
Counseling: 26
Counterfeiting: 497
Counting: 518
Courage: 675, 714, 913
Court: 207, 780
Courtesy: 380
Courting: 792
Courtship: 400
Covenant: 346
Covetousness: 148
Cows: 759
Crashes: 895
Creation: 50, 69, 494, 556, 699, 718, 763, 949
Creationism: 60, 699

Creativity: 89, 100, 232, 280, 521, 539, 557, 795, 803, 988
Credibility: 418, 889, 890
Creeds: 658
Crime: 407, 603
Criticism: 214, 366, 439
Crucifix: 255
Cults: 779
Culture: 859
Cultures: 839
Cunning: 560
Cures: 171, 428, 442
Curiosity: 48, 769
Curious: 66
Curses: 977
Cussing: 821
Customs: 524
Cynicism: 676
Damage: 565
Danger: 97, 99, 402, 455, 478, 534
Daniel: 496
Darkness: 846
Dates: 351
Dating: 78, 106, 276, 314, 575, 792
Deaf: 36
Death: 5, 15, 19, 98, 157, 180, 239, 240, 252, 274, 351, 422, 568, 587, 676, 681, 733, 808, 872, 890, 997
Debt: 11, 258, 473
Debtor: 203
Debts: 720
Decalogue: 523
Deceit: 16, 251, 274, 321
Deception: 81, 111, 174, 188, 209, 240, 245, 276, 279, 319, 324, 348, 355, 410, 481, 497, 514, 532, 543, 544, 545, 549, 560, 846, 847, 861, 968
Decisions: 180, 530, 575, 751, 775, 883
Dedication: 755
Deductions: 158
Defeat: 877
Defense: 698

Defiance: 630
Definitions: 333, 452, 986
Delegation: 446
Delight: 416
Deliverance: 680, 700, 753
Delusions: 732
Demands: 286
Democrats: 688, 894
Denial: 297, 544
Denominations: 546, 547, 959
Dentists: 423, 436
Dependency: 429
Depravity: 471, 844
Desire(s): 329, 911
Despair: 212
Destinations: 434
Destruction: 11, 975, 976
Details: 221, 256, 323, 947
Determination: 75, 631, 792
Devil: 533
Diagnosis: 873
Diet(s): 283, 328, 329, 334, 409, 422, 440, 442, 651, 822, 849, 851, 951
Differences: 358, 526
Difficulty: 6, 966
Diplomacy: 529, 783
Direction: 323, 404, 580, 596, 857, 972
Directions: 101, 223, 243, 286, 322, 604
Disabilities: 650
Disability: 419
Disadvantages: 627
Disappointment: 671
Disciples: 779
Discipleship: 704
Discipline: 67, 114, 342, 631, 740, 874, 944
Discovery: 181, 226
Discretion: 142, 731, 782
Disease(s): 171, 522
Dishonesty: 34

395

396

Alphabetical Index of Titles

Several titles have been abbreviated for your convenience.
Numbers indicate entry number, not page number.

407

Numerical Index of Titles

420

List of Sources

Brackets contain dates of use in Saratoga Press Publications:
[PEJun01] indicates *Parables, Etc.*, June 2001
[SFFeb99] indicates *The Pastor's Story File*, February 1999

#1: Adapted [PEJun01]
#2: [PEJun01]
#3: Dicky Love [PESep96]
#4: [PEJan02]
#5: Clyde Murdock, submitted by Robert Strand [PEAug86]
#6: Ronnie Milsap, submitted by Dicky Love [PEJul97]
#7: Submitted by James Dyke [PESep97]
#8: [PENov99]
#9: Submitted by Micheal Kelley [PESep02]
#10: [PEOct02]
#11: Told by Rick Cato, submitted by Sandy Wylie [PEMay91]
#12: [PEJul01]
#13: [PEDec91]
#14: Ernest Hemingway, submitted by Gene Sikkink [PEJul90]
#15: Source unknown [PEJan83]
#16: Submitted by James Dyke [PENov97]
#17: [PEMar81]
#18: Submitted by Micheal Kelley [PEJan02]
#19: [PEMay99]
#20: [PEMar85]
#21: [PEOct81]
#22: James Hewett [PENov82]
#23: Submitted by Steve Hodgin [PEDec97]
#24: [PENov00]
#25: [PEOct00]
#26: Chinese proverb, submitted by David Rushton [PESep97]
#27: Submitted by Charles F. Krieg [PENov96]
#28: [PEMar01]
#29: [SFJun89]
#30: Submitted by Robert J. Strand [PEMay96]

#31: Submitted by J. Danny Doss [PEJun96]
#32: M. Maureen Killoran [PEAug91]
#33: Benjamin Disraeli, submitted by Dicky Love [SFAug97]
#34: Adapted from a submission by Robert Strand [PEOct97]
#35: [PEJul01]
#36: Charles Ashman, submitted by Don Julian [PEFeb01]
#37: [PEApr00]
#38: Jim Smith [PEMar83]
#39: Submitted by Jim Petty [PEJan00]
#40: [PEJun91]
#41: [PEAug98]
#42: Adapted [PESep94]
#43: [PEFeb98]
#44: Submitted by C. Richard Stone [PEMay95]
#45: [PEAug02]
#46: Submitted by Ray William Smith [PEOct82]
#47: Submitted by Steve Coles [PEOct82]
#48: [PESep83]
#49: Submitted by Norman Porath [PEAug86]
#50: Submitted by C. Richard Stone [PEOct99]
#51: Adapted from a submission by Mary Spitzer [PESep93]
#52: Submitted by Jim Schibsted [PEDec85]
#53: [PEMar89]
#54: [PEJul00]
#55: [PEApr83]
#56: Submitted by Jim Petty [PEApr00]
#57: [PEMay00]
#58: Submitted by Martin R. Bartel [PEJan00]

#59: [PEMar02]
#60: Submitted by Dave Werner [PEAug99]
#61: Submitted by Don Maddox [PENov89]
#62: [PEMar01]
#63: [PESep89]
#64: Submitted by Philip Hines [PEApr85]
#65: [PEJul84]
#66: Submitted by Don Maddox [PEJul91]
#67: Submitted by George Price [PEMay90]
#68: Submitted by Micheal Kelley [PEAug01]
#69: Submitted by Ralph Holt [PEOct98]
#70: Joey Adams, submitted by John Fitts [SFNov91]
#71: James Hewett [PESep81]
#72: Norm Howe [PEApr89]
#73: [PEApr98]
#74: Submitted by John Lefever [PENov00]
#75: Charles Hodge, submitted by Eugene Barron [SFAug89]
#76: [PEAug89]
#77: Submitted by Billy D. Strayhorn [PEAug99]
#78: Submitted by Keith Knauf [PEMay94]
#79: Dolly Parton, submitted by Michael Malone [PESep97]
#80: [PEJun00]
#81: [PEJun02]
#82: [PEJul82]
#83: Submitted by Micheal Kelley [PEJul02]
#84: Submitted by Robert Strand [SFJun91]
#85: [PEJan02]
#86: Submitted by C. Richard Stone [PEAug02]
#87: Submitted by C. Richard Stone [PEMay98]
#88: Adapted from a submission by John J. Sempa [PEJul99]
#89: Submitted by Jim Petty [PEFeb01]

#90: Submitted by George Price [PEMay90]
#91: Submitted by John Lefever [PEJun00]
#92: Doug Larson [PEApr92]
#93: [SFJul97]
#94: [PENov82]
#95: [PEMar98]
#96: [PEMay93]
#97: Malayan proverb [PEOct96]
#98: [PEMar02]
#99: [PESep96]
#100: Henri Bergson [PEJan82]
#101: Adapted [PEFeb82]
#102: Will Rogers [PEJun94]
#103: [PESep98]
#104: Ben Haden, submitted by Don Cheadle [PEJul85]
#105: Submitted by Robert Strand [PEJan86]
#106: Submitted by Paul Wharton [PEFeb86]
#107: Submitted by Tim McLemore [PEDec85]
#108: [PEFeb89]
#109: [PENov82]
#110: Submitted by Deb Somer [PEApr00]
#111: Submitted by Jim Petty [PEFeb99]
#112: [PENov00]
#113: Bishop Fulton J. Sheen, submitted by Milton Weisshaar [PEFeb97]
#114: As told by Vernon Janzen, submitted by Dennis Fast [PEAug92]
#115: Submitted by Billy D. Strayhorn [SFJun91]
#116: [SFJan93]
#117: [PEJul00]
#118: [SFDec97]
#119: [PEAug83]
#120: As told by Tom Borchert, submitted by Steve Hodgin [SFDec97]
#121: Submitted by Don Maddox [SFDec92]
#122: Submitted by Charles F. Krieg [SFDec88]

#123: Submitted by G. Patrick White [SFDec85]
#124: Submitted by Charles F. Krieg [SFDec87]
#125: Billy D. Strayhorn [SFDec92]
#126: Gloria Pitzer, submitted by Milton Weisshaar [PEMar95]
#127: [SFAug93]
#128: Submitted by William T. McConnell [PEJun83]
#129: O. A. Newlin, submitted by Myers P. Kimmel [PEMar84]
#130: Submitted by Jack Lee [PENov85]
#131: Adapted from a submission by John Fitts [PEFeb97]
#132: [PEJan01]
#133: Submitted by James Paul [PEJul85]
#134: [PESep92]
#135: Adapted [PESep94]
#136: An actual account as told by Dr. Robert Tuttle Jr., submitted by Ron Watts [PEJun96]
#137: [PEJul98]
#138: [PEAug81]
#139: Adapted from a cartoon, submitted by Micheal Kelley [PEMay97]
#140: Submitted by James Dyke [SFMar97]
#141: Submitted by William Hardman [PEJul83]
#142: Submitted by Bruce Rowlison [PEJul86]
#143: Submitted by Bill Flanders [SFAug92]
#144: Submitted by James Dyke [PEMay97]
#145: Submitted by Rich Thomson [PEDec96]
#146: Submitted by Billy D. Strayhorn [PENov91]
#147: Submitted by Kenneth Dodge [PEFeb85]
#148: [PEMay93]
#149: [PEMay97]
#150: An old Irish toast [PEMar99]
#151: Submitted by John Lefever [PEMar01]

#152: Adapted from *Sunshine Magazine*, August 1973 [PEOct90]
#153: Submitted by Diane M. Sickler [PEJan96]
#154: [PEFeb00]
#155: Mark Twain, submitted by Michael W. Malone [PENov96]
#156: Submitted by Jon H. Allen [PEMay83]
#157: Submitted by James Dyke [PESep97]
#158: Submitted by Brett Kays [PEDec98]
#159: Submitted by C. Scott Venable [SFJan86]
#160: Submitted by Brett Kays [PEOct99]
#161: [PEJan01]
#162: Submitted by Steve Morrison [PESep00]
#163: Gerald Barzan [PEApr89]
#164: Debbie Adams, submitted by Nick Boeke [PEOct91]
#165: [PEMar01]
#166: [PEJun02]
#167: Submitted by Billy D. Strayhorn [PEJun91]
#168: Submitted by Norma Hewett [PEJan85]
#169: [SFOct96]
#170: [PEAug96]
#171: [PENov83]
#172: Adapted from a submission by Don Maddox [PESep95]
#173: Submitted by C. Richard Stone [PEJul01]
#174: Submitted by Lynn Jost [SFNov84]
#175: Adapted from a submission by Carey Barnett [PEJan98]
#176: Adapted from a submission by Mary Spitzer [PEOct93]
#177: [PENov97]
#178: Adapted [PEJan85]
#179: [PEJun97]
#180: Erma Bombeck [SFJan86]
#181: [PEFeb01]
#182: [PEFeb94]
#183: Submitted by Richard L. Bersett [PEDec97]

#184: Submitted by Milton Weisshaar [SFMar86]
#185: [SFApr94]
#186: Submitted by Billy D. Strayhorn [SFApr94]
#187: Submitted by Billy D. Strayhorn [PEOct93]
#188: [PEMar83]
#189: Arabian proverb, submitted by Michael Smith [PEJul86]
#190: [PEJun97]
#191: [PEDec99]
#192: [SFMay96]
#193: Submitted by Dick Underdahl-Peirce [SFMay88]
#194: Submitted by John Fitts [SFMay88]
#195: Submitted by Jack Lee [PEApr84]
#196: Submitted by Charles F. Krieg [SFJul88]
#197: Adapted from a submission by Mary Spitzer [PEJan95]
#198: Alaskan Shepherd [PEJul85]
#199: [PEJul00]
#200: [PEJun02]
#201: Adapted from a submission by Doug Sabin [PEDec96]
#202: [PENov97]
#203: Submitted by Roger Kleinheksel [PEApr91]
#204: Submitted by J. Danny Doss [PEJul96]
#205: Mark Twain [PEApr81]
#206: [PEMay00]
#207: [PEJun98]
#208: [PEJan98]
#209: Submitted by John Lefever [PEAug01]
#210: Submitted by Billy D. Strayhorn [PEJul02]
#211: Submitted by Micheal Kelley [PEMay97]
#212: A slightly mangled quote from Woody Allen at the Yale Commencement [PENov81]
#213: Submitted by C. Richard Stone [PEOct99]
#214: [PENov82]
#215: Submitted by James Dyke [PEFeb97]

#216: [PEJan01]
#217: Submitted by James Dyke [PEJul97]
#218: Adapted from a submission by John Sempa [PENov98]
#219: [PEDec93]
#220: [SFSep85]
#221: [PEJul84]
#222: [PEFeb01]
#223: Submitted by C. Richard Stone [PEJun99]
#224: Peter W. Hamill, submitted by Al Reutter [PEAug92]
#225: Submitted by Martin R. Bartel [PEOct96]
#226: [PEMay97]
#227: [PEJan98]
#228: [PEJan98]
#229: [PEJul00]
#230: Martin Vanbee [PEDec85]
#231: A true account by Michael Hodgin [SFMay96]
#232: Submitted by Micheal Kelley [PESep02]
#233: [PEFeb01]
#234: A. A. Milne [PEFeb83]
#235: [PEJan00]
#236: [PEJun91]
#237: Adapted from a submission by Brett Kays [PEApr99]
#238: Zsa Zsa Gabor, submitted by Steve Morrison [PESep00]
#239: Submitted by Milton Weisshaar [PEDec98]
#240: Walter Matthau, submitted by Dicky Love [PESep97]
#241: [PESep00]
#242: [PEMay99]
#243: [PEJan02]
#244: Submitted by Robert Strand [SFSep91]
#245: [PEAug98]
#246: [PEJul01]
#247: [PEMar01]
#248: [PEFeb98]
#249: Adapted from a submission by Len Woods [PENov03]
#250: Submitted by Benjamin D. Hodgin [PEFeb00]
#251: [PEMay93]
#252: [SFJul97]

#253: An actual account witnessed by Earl T. Wheatley Jr. [SFJan97]
#254: Submitted by Gene Sikkink [PEApr89]
#255: [PEJul83]
#256: [PEFeb83]
#257: [PESep93]
#258: Submitted by Gene Sikkink [SFMay91]
#259: Adapted from a submission by Milton Weisshaar [PEApr98]
#260: Submitted by James Dyke [PESep01]
#261: Submitted by David Spencer [PEFeb02]
#262: [PEJul84]
#263: Adapted from a submission by James Dyke [SFAug92]
#264: Submitted by Calvin Habig [PEMar97]
#265: Submitted by Frank King [PEMar01]
#266: Submitted by Don and Barb Julian [PEJul98]
#267: Submitted by James Dyke [SFFeb97]
#268: Submitted by Micheal Kelley [PEMay98]
#269: [PEMay02]
#270: Submitted by Micheal E. Kelley [PEOct91]
#271: Submitted by Martin R. Bartel [PEFeb97]
#272: Submitted by Steve Hodgin [PEOct93]
#273: Submitted by Jim Petty [PEAug00]
#274: [PEFeb85]
#275: [PEFeb83]
#276: [PEJul84]
#277: Adapted from a submission by Steve Hodgin [PEFeb98]
#278: Howard Pierce [PEMay84]
#279: [PEMay99]
#280: Submitted by Earl Thornton [PEJun89]
#281: [SFApr92]
#282: Submitted by Mac Fulcher [PEMar94]

#283: Submitted by John Fitts [PEFeb97]
#284: [PEJul00]
#285: [PEJul00]
#286: Submitted by Jim Pearring [PEFeb98]
#287: [PENov00]
#288: Submitted by James Dyke [PENov97]
#289: [PEJun88]
#290: Submitted by Daniel R. Koehler [PEMay98]
#291: Submitted by Ryan Hodgin [PEJun99]
#292: [PEMay99]
#293: [PEDec00]
#294: Submitted by Don Elmore [SFJun92]
#295: [PEMay01]
#296: Submitted by C. Richard Stone [PEOct00]
#297: Adapted, submitted by Wayne Rouse [PEAug94]
#298: [SFApr92]
#299: Submitted by Michael J. Brooks [PEFeb83]
#300: J. Vernon McGee, submitted by Robert Smith [PEMar89]
#301: Submitted by Dick Ford [PEMar00]
#302: Adapted from a submission by C. Richard Stone [PEJan96]
#303: Submitted by Jim Petty [PENov99]
#304: Dick Underdahl-Peirce [PEOct84]
#305: [PEJun82]
#306: Submitted by Samuel M. Silver [PEDec90]
#307: [PEJun82]
#308: Bill Cosby [PEMay02]
#309: Submitted by Earl T. Wheatley Jr. [PEOct96]
#310: [PEJun02]
#311: Submitted by Jim Petty [PEAug00]
#312: [PEMay82]
#313: Submitted by Charles F. Krieg [PESep97]
#314: [PEJun85]
#315: Ernest Haskins [PENov97]

#316: Will Rogers [PENov85]
#317: [PEMay98]
#318: Submitted by Larry and Ann Menschel [PEAug91]
#319: [PEJun02]
#320: [PEJan02]
#321: Submitted by William Ehlers [PEApr85]
#322: [PEMay00]
#323: [PEJun02]
#324: [PEJun01]
#325: [PEJan01]
#326: Winston Churchill [PEJun86]
#327: Submitted by Billy D. Strayhorn [PEOct99]
#328: [SFApr97]
#329: Michael Hodgin [PESep00]
#330: Submitted by Norm Wilson [PEDec99]
#331: [PESep00]
#332: [PEMar97]
#333: [SFApr97]
#334: Submitted by Micheal Kelley [PEJul02]
#335: [PEAug01]
#336: [PESep97]
#337: [PESep02]
#338: [PEDec88]
#339: Submitted by Thomas Davitt [PEJun96]
#340: [PENov97]
#341: [PEFeb01]
#342: Submitted by Dick Underdahl-Peirce [SFApr86]
#343: Submitted by Kathleen Brandt [PEFeb97]
#344: Jim Vorsas [PEAug82]
#345: [PEAug92]
#346: Submitted by Jack Haberer [PEJul86]
#347: Submitted by Frank King [PESep97]
#348: Submitted by Bernard Brunsting [PEMar89]
#349: [PEMar89]
#350: Submitted by Steve Morrison [PESep00]
#351: Adapted from a submission by Mike Dominick [PEMay97]
#352: [PEMar97]

#353: Submitted by Billy D. Strayhorn [SFJan94]
#354: As told by Jay Leno, submitted by Ralph Rebandt [PEJul89]
#355: [PEJan01]
#356: Adapted [PESep94]
#357: [PEJun82]
#358: [PEJan02]
#359: Submitted by Babs Eggleston [PEMar00]
#360: Submitted by Jim Petty [PEJan00]
#361: Conan O'Brien, submitted by C. Richard Stone [PESep01]
#362: [PEMar00]
#363: Submitted by Jay Martin [PENov99]
#364: [PESep00]
#365: Adapted from a submission by Jim Pearring [PEFeb98]
#366: [PEJan02]
#367: Submitted by Phil Hines [PEDec85]
#368: Submitted by G. W. McNeese [SFAug95]
#369: [PEDec91]
#370: [PEJun84]
#371: [PEMar91]
#372: Submitted by Billy D. Strayhorn [PEApr94]
#373: Submitted by Dicky Love [PESep96]
#374: [PEAug01]
#375: Buddy Hackett, submitted by Randall Mundt [SFApr92]
#376: [PEJan02]
#377: Gerald Ford, submitted by Randall Mundt [SFApr92]
#378: [PEJun02]
#379: [PEMay00]
#380: [PEFeb02]
#381: [PEJan02]
#382: Mark Twain, submitted by Dicky Love [PEJun98]
#383: Submitted by Carl Ericson [PEJul91]
#384: Submitted by Deb Somer [PEJul01]
#385: Submitted by Steve Morrison [PEJul98]
#386: [PEJul00]

#387: [PEApr01]
#388: [PESep81]
#389: [PEFeb02]
#390: [PEJun91]
#391: Adapted [PEJun84]
#392: [PEApr89]
#393: Javier Pascual Salcedo, submitted by Dicky Love [PEMay96]
#394: William Graham Sumner [PESep91]
#395: Submitted by Steve Hodgin [PEOct93]
#396: Submitted by Micheal Kelley [PEAug01]
#397: Submitted by Deb Somer [PEJul01]
#398: Submitted by Charles F. Krieg [PEApr89]
#399: Adapted from an actual account as submitted by Jim Pearring [PEDec97]
#400: [PEMar98]
#401: [PEApr01]
#402: Submitted by J. J. Jackson [PESep93]
#403: Submitted by Don Maddox [PEMar85]
#404: [PEAug89]
#405: [PEApr02]
#406: [PEFeb01]
#407: [PEJul89]
#408: William R. Inge [PEMay81]
#409: Submitted by Don Maddox [PEOct01]
#410: Submitted by Jim Pearring [PEAug95]
#411: Submitted by Brett Kays [PEOct99]
#412: Henry Ward Beecher [PEAug82]
#413: [SFJan87]
#414: Submitted by Jim Pearring [PEDec95]
#415: [PEApr83]
#416: Submitted by T. Parker [PEJun97]
#417: Submitted by James Dyke [SFJan97]
#418: [PEMar94]

#419: Submitted by Michael W. Malone [PEAug96]
#420: Submitted by Dick Underdahl-Peirce [PENov89]
#421: [PEJul02]
#422: [PEApr01]
#423: [PEApr82]
#424: Randall Mundt [PEJul01]
#425: [PEAug86]
#426: [PEJul01]
#427: Babs Eggleston [PEApr02]
#428: An actual account, submitted by Dan and Barb Stephens [PEJan99]
#429: James Hewett [PEJun82]
#430: [PEMar97]
#431: Submitted by Randal Pollard [SFFeb87]
#432: Submitted by C. Richard Stone [PEJul91]
#433: Adapted from a submission by Micheal Kelley [PESep97]
#434: [PEJan02]
#435: Submitted by Teresa Yates [SFJan97]
#436: [PEMar82]
#437: Submitted by James Champ [PEJul83]
#438: [PEAug83]
#439: [PEMar00]
#440: [SFSep88]
#441: Submitted by Dicky Love [PESep96]
#442: [PEMay01]
#443: Submitted by Doris S. Bray [SFSep96]
#444: Mark Twain [PEFeb99]
#445: [PENov82]
#446: Submitted by Loren Seibold [PEJul90]
#447: Alexander Pope, submitted by Michael W. Malone [PESep96]
#448: [PEFeb94]
#449: Robert Power, submitted by Gene Sikkink [PESep95]
#450: [PEFeb01]
#451: [SFApr92]
#452: [PEMar02]
#453: [PEMay95]
#454: Adapted from a submission by Byron Neufeld [PEDec97]

#455: [PEMar01]
#456: Submitted by Gary Crandall [SFMar97]
#457: Submitted by Jim Petty [PEMar00]
#458: [PEJun91]
#459: Bruce Rowlison [PEDec89]
#460: Leighton Ford [PEJul88]
#461: [PEMar83]
#462: Submitted by Lester Weeks [PEJun89]
#463: [PEOct00]
#464: Submitted by Jim Petty [PEJun99]
#465: Geoff Tunnicliffe [PENov91]
#466: [SFAug89]
#467: [PEMar01]
#468: [PESep93]
#469: [PEMar83]
#470: [SFJun87]
#471: Submitted by Dicky Love [PESep96]
#472: Submitted by Babs Eggleston [PEAug00]
#473: Source unknown, submitted by Doug Sabin [PEJun96]
#474: [PEApr01]
#475: [SFSep97]
#476: Submitted by James Dyke [SFNov97]
#477: [SFMay97]
#478: Cordell Hull [PEAug83]
#479: [PEJun01]
#480: Submitted by Jim Petty [PENov99]
#481: [PEMar98]
#482: Submitted by Doyal Van Gelder [PENov84]
#483: Submitted by Deb Somer [PEFeb02]
#484: [PEMar97]
#485: [PEOct02]
#486: [PEOct97]
#487: Submitted by John Oliver [PEMay86]
#488: [PEJun98]
#489: Submitted by Calvin Habig [PEJul95]
#490: A true incident reported by Lee Moberg [PEJan86]

#491: Submitted by Christine Oscar [PEJul90]
#492: Submitted by Jim Petty [PEFeb99]
#493: Submitted by Babs Eggleston [PEMay99]
#494: Adapted [PESep94]
#495: Submitted by Samuel M. Silver [PEJan91]
#496: Adapted from a submission by Eugene Barron [PEJan95]
#497: [PEMay99]
#498: Adapted from a submission by John McHaffie [PEAug00]
#499: Submitted by Gene Sikkink [PEOct91]
#500: Rich Thomson [PEDec96]
#501: [PESep97]
#502: [PEAug81]
#503: Source unknown [PEFeb83]
#504: Adapted from a submission by Richard Burgie [PEDec97]
#505: [PEMar83]
#506: Submitted by Brett Kays [PEAug99]
#507: Submitted by Jim Petty [PEJul99]
#508: Submitted by Kenneth Langley [PEJun96]
#509: Submitted by David Parsons [PEDec95]
#510: Submitted by Edwin Evans [SFJun87]
#511: [PEFeb01]
#512: Submitted by Milton Weisshaar [PEMar99]
#513: [PEApr01]
#514: [PEApr01]
#515: [PEJun91]
#516: Submitted by Calvin Habig [PEJun94]
#517: Submitted by Steve Morrison [PEJan96]
#518: [PEJul97]
#519: Submitted by Kent Anderson [PEOct98]
#520: [PENov97]
#521: Submitted by Stephan McCutchan [PESep82]
#522: [PEJun97]
#523: [PEMar81]

#524: [PEApr02]
#525: Submitted by James T. Hickman [SFJul92]
#526: William H. Mauldin [PEFeb98]
#527: Submitted by Billy D. Strayhorn [PEJan96]
#528: From an actual account, submitted by H. D. Mitchell [PEDec86]
#529: [PEMar02]
#530: [SFJul97]
#531: Submitted by Keith Knauf [PEJan90]
#532: [SFApr97]
#533: [PEJan98]
#534: From a Spanish proverb, submitted by Kenneth Langley [PEDec97]
#535: [PEJan98]
#536: [PEApr86]
#537: [SFApr97]
#538: [PEAug97]
#539: [PEMar02]
#540: Michael E. Hodgin [PESep93]
#541: Adapted from a submission by Robert J. Strand [PEMar96]
#542: Jack Benny, submitted by C. Richard Stone [PESep96]
#543: Submitted by Steve Morrison [PEMay98]
#544: Source unknown, submitted by Martin R. Bartel [PEApr98]
#545: Submitted by Brett Kays [PEOct99]
#546: Submitted by John Lefever [PEApr02]
#547: Submitted by Don and Barb Julian [PEApr98]
#548: [PEAug97]
#549: [PEAug97]
#550: [PEApr97]
#551: [PEMar01]
#552: Anonymous [PEOct95]
#553: [PEJul87]
#554: Submitted by Blair Taber [PEMar88]
#555: [SFAug94]
#556: Submitted by Roger Clemens [PEOct82]
#557: [PEOct83]
#558: [PEApr97]

#559: [PEMay01]
#560: [PEFeb99]
#561: [SFAug94]
#562: [PEAug98]
#563: [SFMay95]
#564: Submitted by Craig Burkholder [PEMar97]
#565: [PEFeb01]
#566: Submitted by Penny Wilson [SFJul86]
#567: [PEFeb98]
#568: Oliver Wendell Holmes [PEOct82]
#569: Submitted by C. David Zollars [PEApr90]
#570: [PEAug98]
#571: Submitted by Dicky Love [PESep96]
#572: Submitted by Charles F. Krieg [SFJul87]
#573: Danish proverb [SFJul87]
#574: Submitted by Nick Boeke [PESep92]
#575: [PESep00]
#576: [PEJun97]
#577: Submitted by David Rushton [SFOct96]
#578: [PEJan94]
#579: [PEMar97]
#580: [PEJun82]
#581: [PEAug83]
#582: [PEMay01]
#583: [PEApr85]
#584: [PESep98]
#585: [PEFeb02]
#586: [PEApr92]
#587: [PEJun01]
#588: [PEApr02]
#589: [PEJan98]
#590: Submitted by Kenneth Dodge [PEAug84]
#591: Adapted from a submission by Mary Spitzer [PEFeb94]
#592: Submitted by Jim Petty [PEAug99]
#593: Submitted by G. Patrick White [PEApr84]
#594: Guy Bellamy [PEDec88]
#595: [PESep97]
#596: [PEDec99]
#597: [PEMay01]

#598: [PEMay93]
#599: Harry J. Kantas, submitted by Steve Morrison [PESep98]
#600: [PEFeb02]
#601: Adapted from a submission by Martin R. Bartel [PENov99]
#602: [SFJan94]
#603: Edited and adapted by Michael Hodgin [SFSep95]
#604: Submitted by Ryan Hodgin [PEMay02]
#605: Theodore Roosevelt [PEMay82]
#606: [PEMay83]
#607: [PESep99]
#608: Submitted by Dicky Love [PEAug98]
#609: Submitted by Doug Sabin [PEJan02]
#610: Submitted by Lawrence Guzowski [PEMay84]
#611: [PEJun81]
#612: [SFNov96]
#613: [SFOct86]
#614: Submitted by Phil Hines [PEMay83]
#615: Robert Orben, submitted by Dicky Love [PEOct96]
#616: Michael Hodgin [PEJul97]
#617: [PEMar01]
#618: Adapted [SFMay93]
#619: [SFApr92]
#620: [PEOct02]
#621: Submitted by Jan Hartlove [PEMar98]
#622: [PEJan99]
#623: [PEMar94]
#624: Submitted by Micheal Kelley [PESep97]
#625: [PEJun01]
#626: [PEJan87]
#627: [PEDec97]
#628: [PEAug00]
#629: Submitted by James Ankerberg [PESep92]
#630: Adapted from an actual account, submitted by Billy D. Strayhorn [PEApr01]
#631: [PENov00]
#632: [PESep01]

#633: Submitted by Ryan Hodgin [PEApr00]
#634: Submitted by Charles F. Krieg [SFOct97]
#635: [SFJan94]
#636: [SFJan94]
#637: Submitted by Dicky Love [SFSep96]
#638: [PEJan01]
#639: [PEJun85]
#640: Submitted by Robert J. Strand [PEMay96]
#641: [SFJun87]
#642: [SFJun87]
#643: [PEOct83]
#644: [SFMay85]
#645: Adapted from a submission by Rich Thornton [PEOct92]
#646: Submitted by Robert Jarboe [PENov92]
#647: Submitted by Bruce Rowlison [PESep92]
#648: Submitted by Babs Eggleston [PEAug02]
#649: Submitted by Jim Petty [PEMar98]
#650: [PEJul00]
#651: [PESep93]
#652: [PEAug83]
#653: Ralph C. Erickson, submitted by Roger Inouye [SFMar85]
#654: Randall Mundt [PEJul01]
#655: Martin Mull [PEAug88]
#656: Submitted by Roger Imhoff [SFMar85]
#657: Ken Adair, submitted by Billy D. Strayhorn [SFSep96]
#658: Submitted by Robert Slater [PEMar84]
#659: [PEJul84]
#660: Submitted by Creed, Lifeline Ministries, Seattle [SFMar89]
#661: Paul Eldridge [PEJul81]
#662: Submitted by Jim Petty [PEJun00]
#663: Earl Wilson [PEJan85]
#664: John Lefever [PEAug98]
#665: Gene Sikkink [PEJun01]
#666: Charles H. Spurgeon [SFNov87]

#667: Submitted by James Swanson [SFNov87]
#668: Woody Allen [PEMar85]
#669: Submitted by Don E. McKenzie [PESep86]
#670: Submitted by Emmett O'Neill [PEJul91]
#671: Submitted by Jeff Taylor [PEDec94]
#672: Submitted by Bruce Rowlison [PEJul86]
#673: Submitted by C. Richard Stone [SFJul91]
#674: [PEJun01]
#675: Chinese proverb, submitted by Robert J. Strand [SFMar86]
#676: [PEMar02]
#677: [SFApr92]
#678: [PENov97]
#679: [PEJun01]
#680: Submitted by Gene Sikkink [SFJun91]
#681: Submitted by Jim Petty [PEJan00]
#682: [SFApr92]
#683: Japanese proverb, submitted by Dicky Love [PESep96]
#684: Groucho Marx [PEApr97]
#685: Adapted from an observation by Frances Duffy, submitted by Dicky Love [PESep96]
#686: [PEApr83]
#687: Will Rogers, submitted by C. Richard Stone [SFApr97]
#688: Adlai Stevenson, submitted by Chris Newport [PENov95]
#689: Groucho Marx [PENov98]
#690: L. Kiston, submitted by Martha Lynn-Johnson [PEAug98]
#691: Henry Kissinger [PENov97]
#692: [SFJan88]
#693: Wernher Von Braun, submitted by Gene Sikkink [PEJul90]
#694: [PESep93]
#695: Adapted [PEFeb99]
#696: Adapted from a submission by Don E. McKenzie [PESep93]
#697: Submitted by Ryan Hodgin [PEApr00]

#698: Submitted by Jim Petty [PEJun01]
#699: Submitted by Jim Petty [PEDec99]
#700: Submitted by Dick Underdahl-Peirce [PEJan87]
#701: J. R. R. Tolkien [PEMar81]
#702: Submitted by Gene Sikkink [PESep91]
#703: Billy Sunday [PENov94]
#704: Submitted by Don E. McKenzie [PENov81]
#705: Submitted by Mark Sirnic [SFJun86]
#706: Dave Baldridge [PESep91]
#707: Submitted by Lew Button [PEFeb93]
#708: [PEMar94]
#709: Submitted by Robert J. Strand [PEApr96]
#710: Submitted by Don Julian [PEFeb99]
#711: Submitted by Samuel M. Silver [PEJul00]
#712: [PEApr02]
#713: [PEJun01]
#714: Submitted by Jules Glanzer [SFNov91]
#715: Robert Louis Stevenson, submitted by C. Richard Stone [PEMar98]
#716: [PEMar98]
#717: Submitted by Emmett O'Neill [PEAug85]
#718: Submitted by C. Richard Stone [SFMay91]
#719: [PEOct84]
#720: [PEDec97]
#721: [PEFeb98]
#722: [PENov00]
#723: [PEMar01]
#724: [PEMar01]
#725: [PEMay00]
#726: [PEMar99]
#727: [PEMay86]
#728: Adapted from an old Vaudeville joke [SFJan89]
#729: Submitted by Don Maddox [PEMar00]
#730: [PEJun02]

#731: Adapted from *Integrity* by Ted Engstrom, submitted by John Fitts [SFMar97]
#732: [PEAug02]
#733: [PESep02]
#734: Ben Merold, submitted by Bret G. Nealis [SFFeb85]
#735: [PESep00]
#736: English proverb, submitted by Don Middlemiss [PEDec96]
#737: Submitted by Doug Sabin [PEJan02]
#738: Submitted by Dicky Love [PEOct95]
#739: Submitted by Philip Hines [PEApr85]
#740: Submitted by Don Cheadle [PEJan89]
#741: [PEFeb98]
#742: Submitted by C. Richard Stone [PEJul00]
#743: [PEJan98]
#744: Richard Barnes, submitted by Robert J. Strand [PEJun96]
#745: [PEMay98]
#746: [PEFeb01]
#747: Submitted by Kenneth Dodge [PENov97]
#748: [PEJun02]
#749: [PESep00]
#750: Submitted by Robert J. Strand [PEMay97]
#751: Submitted by Norm Wilson [PEJul98]
#752: Jack Scott, submitted by Steve Hodgin [PEAug94]
#753: [PEFeb97]
#754: Richard Moore [PEMar82]
#755: Submitted by Billy D. Strayhorn [PESep93]
#756: Submitted by Kenneth Dodge [PENov97]
#757: [PEJun97]
#758: [PEOct86]
#759: [PEApr97]
#760: [PEAug97]
#761: [PESep01]
#762: [PEJan97]
#763: [PEJul91]
#764: Submitted by Kenneth Dodge [PENov97]

#765: Adapted from a submission by Bob Kabat [SFJun88]
#766: Adapted from a submission by Jim Petty [PEDec98]
#767: Submitted by Doyal Van Gelder [PENov85]
#768: Submitted by Wayne Allman [PESep93]
#769: Submitted by Paul Wakefield [PEMar95]
#770: Charles Ashman, submitted by Don Julian [PEDec99]
#771: Submitted by Norman Howard [SFMay85]
#772: [PEJan83]
#773: Submitted by Calvin Habig [PEJan96]
#774: Submitted by Micheal Kelley [PEJun97]
#775: Submitted by Stephen Crane [PEJan83]
#776: Submitted by Dick Underdahl-Peirce [SFFeb85]
#777: Submitted by Bernard Brunsting [PEMay88]
#778: Submitted by Jay Martin [PEAug94]
#779: [PENov96]
#780: [SFMay85]
#781: Submitted by Paul A. Noxon [PEJan93]
#782: [PEMay00]
#783: Submitted by Micheal Kelley [PEJan02]
#784: [PESep89]
#785: George H. W. Bush [PEMay01]
#786: [SFFeb85]
#787: [PEDec01]
#788: [PEAug02]
#789: Fred Hintz [PEJun83]
#790: Submitted by Kenneth Langley [PESep91]
#791: Anonymous [PEMar81]
#792: [PEAug94]
#793: Submitted by Dick Ford [PEJul00]
#794: [PEFeb01]
#795: Submitted by Martin R. Bartel [PEJun96]
#796: Submitted by Paul Wharton [PEMay83]

#797: Submitted by J. D. Brown [SFJan96]

#798: Submitted by Rich Thomson [PEDec96]

#799: [PESep00]

#800: [PEJun91]

#801: Damon Runyon [PESep81]

#802: Submitted by Michael Hodgin [PESep00]

#803: Neil Simon, submitted by Michael W. Malone [PESep96]

#804: Marlene Dietrich, submitted by John Fitts [PESep92]

#805: Submitted by Barry Lind [PEOct98]

#806: Adapted from a submission by Wayne Rouse [SFAug94]

#807: [PESep97]

#808: Submitted by Jim Petty [PEAug99]

#809: [PEMay82]

#810: Adapted from an illustration by J. Vernon McGee, submitted by Richard Price [SFApr93]

#811: Thomas Lane Butts [PEJul81]

#812: [PENov00]

#813: Submitted by Dick Ford [PEJul00]

#814: [PEFeb02]

#815: Rich Thomson, with a nod to *Hamlet*, Ac. III, Sc. 1 [PEDec96]

#816: [PEApr83]

#817: George Bernard Shaw [PEJun02]

#818: [PEJun91]

#819: Submitted by Billy D. Strayhorn [PENov91]

#820: Rich Thomson [PEFeb99]

#821: Submitted by J. Danny Doss [PEJun98]

#822: [PEJul00]

#823: [PESep00]

#824: Submitted by Micheal Kelley [PEJul02]

#825: Submitted by John Martin [PEJun85]

#826: [PEAug98]

#827: Submitted by Richard Moore [PEMar82]

#828: Submitted by Micheal Kelley [PESep96]

#829: C. Richard Stone [PEAug93]

#830: Submitted by Larry and Ann Menschel [PEAug91]

#831: [PEApr97]

#832: [PEAug82]

#833: Adapted from a submission by Samuel M. Silver [PEJun99]

#834: Submitted by Steve Morrison [PEMar00]

#835: Submitted by John Lefever [PEJun99]

#836: [SFMay97]

#837: [PEFeb01]

#838: [PEFeb01]

#839: Adapted from a submission by Calvin Habig [PEOct99]

#840: Submitted by Martin R. Bartel [PEApr98]

#841: Submitted by John Bray [PEFeb97]

#842: Michael Hodgin [PENov97]

#843: Submitted by Dicky Love [PEAug97]

#844: [PEMay98]

#845: Submitted by John Gosswein [PEMay85]

#846: Submitted by Robert S. Jarboe [PEJan94]

#847: [SFMay85]

#848: [PEMay91]

#849: [PEApr97]

#850: [PEJul97]

#851: James Hewett [PEMay86]

#852: [PEOct02]

#853: Leo J. Burke, submitted by Dick Underdahl-Peirce [PEJan85]

#854: [PEApr02]

#855: James Dyke [PESep97]

#856: Submitted by Samuel M. Silver [PEJul00]

#857: From a sermon by Mark Trotter [PEJul86]

#858: Bruce Rowlison, adapted [PEMay97]

#859: Fred Hintz [PEJun83]

#860: Submitted by Rich Thomson [PEDec97]

#861: Submitted by Jan Bengtson [PEJul89]
#862: [PEMar01]
#863: From *King Lear* by Shakespeare [PEAug00]
#864: [PEOct02]
#865: Submitted by James R. Oliver [PEJun94]
#866: [PEAug00]
#867: Told by John Turpin [PEJul85]
#868: Submitted by Robert J. Strand [PEFeb86]
#869: Submitted by James Dyke [PEJun97]
#870: Adapted from a submission by David Rushton [PEApr97]
#871: [SFApr92]
#872: [SFApr92]
#873: [SFApr92]
#874: Submitted by Wayne W. Eisbrenner [PEOct98]
#875: Submitted by Samuel M. Silver [PEMay99]
#876: Pamela Parsons [PEJun01]
#877: [PEFeb98]
#878: Submitted by Jay Martin [PEJan94]
#879: Submitted by David C. Newhart [SFFeb85]
#880: [PEJan98]
#881: Submitted by Larry Kineman [SFNov84]
#882: Submitted by Ronald Stewart [SFNov84]
#883: [PESep93]
#884: Adapted from a submission by Jim Petty [PEAug01]
#885: [SFOct86]
#886: [PEMay93]
#887: Submitted by Don Maddox [PESep91]
#888: [PESep93]
#889: Adapted by James Hewett [PEJun85]
#890: Adapted [PEJul95]
#891: [PEApr94]
#892: [PEMay88]
#893: [PEMar97]
#894: [PEMar99]
#895: [PEMay98]
#896: [PEAug01]

#897: Submitted by Stephen Grunlan [PEAug02]
#898: Steve Hodgin [PEJul00]
#899: [PEOct96]
#900: [PEAug97]
#901: Submitted by Calvin Habig [PESep97]
#902: [PEJul84]
#903: [SFMar85]
#904: [SFOct86]
#905: Submitted by Micheal Kelley [PEOct96]
#906: [PEJan02]
#907: [PEMay02]
#908: [PENov91]
#909: Larry Betrozoff [PENov91]
#910: [PEMar01]
#911: Jeff Taylor [PEOct94]
#912: [PEMay01]
#913: [PEAug83]
#914: Submitted by Bill Flanders [PESep93]
#915: [PEOct02]
#916: Submitted by C. Richard Stone [PENov99]
#917: [PEJan98]
#918: Submitted by John Lefever [PEJun99]
#919: [PEJan98]
#920: Steve Hodgin [SFNov97]
#921: Michael Hodgin [SFNov96]
#922: Submitted by Charles F. Krieg [SFNov91]
#923: Submitted by Nick Boeke [SFNov91]
#924: Submitted by Robert J. Strand [SFNov85]
#925: Submitted by Bruce Wilander [SFNov85]
#926: [PEDec97]
#927: Submitted by Billy D. Strayhorn [SFNov91]
#928: [SFApr97]
#929: [PEJun01]
#930: John Wayne [PEJul90]
#931: [PEJan97]
#932: Casey Stenge [PEFeb94]
#933: Ian Pitt-Watson [PEJun81]
#934: [SFJan03]
#935: [PEFeb02]
#936: Paul Valery [PEApr97]

#937: Adapted [PEJul84]
#938: Submitted by Micheal Kelley [PEJan02]
#939: [PENov00]
#940: [PEJun02]
#941: Adapted, submitted by Wayne Rouse [PESep94]
#942: Submitted by Dr. M. L. Adams [PEDec82]
#943: [PEJun83]
#944: [PESep88]
#945: Chris Albritton, submitted by Bruce Rowlison [PEAug92]
#946: Bernard R. Brunsting [PEAug92]
#947: Submitted by Don E. McKenzie [PESep92]
#948: Adapted from a submission by Mary Spitzer [PEJul95]
#949: [PENov97]
#950: Submitted by Steve Morrison [PESep93]
#951: Adapted from a submission by Micheal Kelley [SFMay97]
#952: [PESep91]
#953: Mark Twain [SFJul85]
#954: [PEJun91]
#955: [PEAug00]
#956: Adapted from an actual account submitted by Dennis Niezwaag [PEJul85]
#957: Submitted by Charles F. Krieg, adapted from a fable by Aesop [PEAug91]
#958: Submitted by David Rushton [PEJul01]
#959: Submitted by Steve Schoepf [PEFeb86]
#960: Submitted by Robert J. Strand [PEJan01]
#961: [PEFeb01]
#962: Submitted by Samuel M. Silver [PESep02]
#963: [SFFeb88]
#964: [PESep88]
#965: [PEMar01]
#966: [PENov00]
#967: Submitted by Babs Eggleston [PEOct01]
#968: Submitted by Micheal Kelley [PEApr98]

#969: [PESep97]
#970: [PEMay99]
#971: Doyal Van Gelder [SFApr88]
#972: From an Irish toast [PEDec88]
#973: Adapted [PEJun84]
#974: John Van Tine [PEJul89]
#975: [PEJun82]
#976: [PENov96]
#977: [PEJul82]
#978: Submitted by Micheal Kelley [PESep96]
#979: Submitted by Samuel M. Silver [PEJul00]
#980: Submitted by Micheal Kelley [PEOct96]
#981: Submitted by Don Maddox [PEAug99]
#982: Submitted by Fred Lowery [SFJun94]
#983: [PEMar98]
#984: Submitted by Billy D. Strayhorn [PESep96]
#985: Thomas Jefferson [PENov95]
#986: Submitted by C. Richard Stone [PEMay98]
#987: Adapted, submitted by Doug Sabin [PEJan99]
#988: [PENov95]
#989: Adapted from a submission by Keith Kendell [PEJun83]
#990: Submitted by Carl Ericson [PEMay91]
#991: Franklin P. Jones [PEApr92]
#992: [PEJan93]
#993: Submitted by Frank King [PEJul97]
#994: [PEMar01]
#995: [PENov96]
#996: Adapted from a submission by Charles F. Krieg [PENov97]
#997: [PEApr94]
#998: Submitted by Jay Martin [PEApr94]
#999: Submitted by Rich Thomson [PEMar84]
1000: James M. Barrie, submitted by C. Richard Stone [PEMay96]
1001: Submitted by John H. Hampsch [PEJun92]
1002: [PEMar02]

1001 Humorous Illustrations for Public Speaking

Michael Hodgin

Drawn from a broad array of sources, topics in this compilation range from "Ability and Acceptance" to "Words, Work, and Worship."

You have something important to say. Are you sure your audience is listening? Clocks start ticking in the minds of your listeners the minute you begin your presentation. These clocks measure the amount of time you have to interest them before their attention wanders elsewhere. Could be three minutes. Could be thirty seconds. But make your audience laugh and they forget about their clocks. They are too busy listening. Make them laugh and they will listen. Humor is one of your most powerful tools as a speaker, and *1001 Humorous Illustrations for Public Speaking* lets you wield it with power. Michael Hodgin has compiled hundreds of humorous anecdotes on dozens of topics and brought them together in one book. Hodgin's illustrations are arranged according to topic and indexed to help you quickly find the perfect anecdote. The book also provides space to record the times and places you use each illustration, so no one will hear you tell the same joke twice. Ideal for preachers, teachers, executives, and anyone else who speaks publicly, *1001 Humorous Illustrations for Public Speaking* will keep your audience laughing—and listening to every word you say.

Softcover: 0-310-47691-8

GRAND RAPIDS, MICHIGAN 49530 USA

WWW.ZONDERVAN.COM

1001 More Illustrations for Public Speaking

Michael Hodgin

1001 More Humorous Illustrations for Public Speaking, much like its rib-tickling predecessor, is a gold mine of one-liners, jokes, and humorous anecdotes for almost any topic.

Experienced speakers know the value of humor for adding punch to their point and muscle to their message. That's why *1001 More Humorous Illustrations for Public Speaking* belongs in every pastor's and speaker's library—including yours! Pick your topic: Attitudes, Evangelism, Romance, Weddings . . . you'll find what you're looking for, conveniently alphabetized, numbered, and indexed for instant referencing. There's even a space for you to record the times and places you use each illustration, so no one will hear you tell the same joke twice. Most of these humorous gems have already been tested by preachers and other speakers. And the huge variety ensures you'll find something to tickle any congregation's funny bone—and grab its attention.

Softcover: 0-310-21713-X

Pick up a copy today at your favorite bookstore!

ZONDERVAN™

GRAND RAPIDS, MICHIGAN 49530 USA

WWW.ZONDERVAN.COM

We want to hear from you. Please send your comments about this book to us in care of zreview@zondervan.com. Thank you.

GRAND RAPIDS, MICHIGAN 49530 USA

WWW.ZONDERVAN.COM